AF560675

MOVING TOWARDS TOURISM

MOVING TOWARDS TOURISM

By

Neil Thompson

DISCOVERY PUBLISHING HOUSE PVT. LTD.
NEW DELHI-110 002

Published by:

Tilak Wasan

DISCOVERY PUBLISHING HOUSE PVT. LTD.

4831/24, Prahlad Street, Ansari Road
Darya Ganj, New Delhi-110002 (India)
Phone : +91-11-23279245, 43764432
Fax : +91-11-23253475
E-mail : parul.wasan@gmail.com
discoverypublishinghouse@gmail.com
info@discoverypublishinggroup.com
web : www.discoverypublishinggroup.com

First Edition: **2011**
ISBN: 978-81-8356-941-5

Moving Towards Tourism

© 2011, Author

All rights reserved. No part of this publication should be reproduced, stored in a retrieval system, or transmitted in any form or by any means: electronic, mechanical, photocopying, recording or otherwise, without the prior written permission of the author and the publisher.

This book has been published in good faith that the material provided by authors is original. Every effort is made to ensure accuracy of material, but the publisher and printer will not be held responsible for any inadvertent error(s). In case of any dispute, all legal matters are to be settled under Delhi jurisdiction only.

Printed at:
Mehra Offset Press
Delhi

PREFACE

It has been suggested there is a strong correlation between tourism expenditure per capita and the degree to which countries play in the global context. Not only as a result of the important economic contribution of the tourism industry, but also as an indicator of the degree of confidence with which global citizens leverage the resources of the globe for the benefit of their local economies. This is why any projections of growth in tourism may serve as an indication of the relative influence that each country will exercise in the future.

It is a matter of debate whether there exists what we often call the 'travel industry' in the sense of a distinct group of enterprises like steel, textile or automobile industry. The problem arises because travel industry (a) is not a manufacturing industry and, (b) is not one industry but is a collection of businesses, all selling travel-related services. The general public may be more familiar with its various components like Airlines Industry, Hotel Industry, Restaurants and Transport Companies.

Accommodation may in itself be an important tourist attraction. In fact, a large number of tourists visit a particular destination or town simply because there is a first class luxury hotel or resort which provides excellent services and facilities. Some countries like Switzerland, Holland, France, Austria and Belgium have gained a reputation for providing excellent accommodation with good cuisine. Any form of tourism that showcases the rural life, art, culture and heritage at rural locations, thereby benefiting the local community economically and socially as well as enabling interaction between the tourists and the locals for a more enriching tourism experience can be termed as rural tourism. Rural tourism is essentially an activity which takes place in the countryside.

While compiling research material for this book, we surf many websites, visit many libraries for ensuring the authenticity of the matter and current updates. We are sincerely grateful to all these resources as without this the publication of this book wouldn't have been possible. Our main aim is to spread the light of knowledge to the readers, so that the darkness of ignorance dispels away.

—Author

CONTENTS

1

INTRODUCTION

Tourism is travel for recreational, leisure or business purposes. The World Tourism Organization defines tourists as people who "travel to and stay in places outside their usual environment for more than twenty-four (24) hours and not more than one consecutive year for leisure, business and other purposes not related to the exercise of an activity remunerated from within the place visited." Although tourism is a phenomenon not easy to define, several attempts have been made to define it. Some of these are fairly comprehensive. All these definitions explain tourism in the context of movement. It is precisely the significance of the word 'tour' which forms the root of the word 'tourism'.

The International Dictionary of Tourism, published in 1953 by the International Academy of Tourism at Monte Carlo, points out that tour in English and in French means a journey, a circulative trip. The nineteenth century dictionary defines tourist as "people who travel for pleasure of travelling, out of curiosity; and because they have nothing better to do," and even "for the joy of boasting about it afterwards."

The International Union of Official Travel Organisation (IUOTO), now called World Tourism Organisation (WTO), has defined tourist as a temporary visitor staying for at least twenty-four hours in a country visited when the purpose of the journey can be classified under one of the following headings: (a) leisure-recreation, holiday, health, study, religion and sports; or (b) business, family, mission meetings. Travellers staying less than twenty-four hours according to WTO are 'excursionists'.

The United Nations accepted the above definition of a tourist provided by IUOTO in their Conference on International Travel and Tourism in 1963.

Conceptually, tourism arises from the movement of people to, and their stay in, different destinations. The 'journey' is the dynamic element in it and the 'stay', static. The 'journey' and 'stay' are to, and in, destinations outside the normal place of residence and work. Destinations are visited for purposes not connected with paid work or regular employment. Again, this movement is of a temporary and short duration-a few days, weeks or months.

The following definition of tourism by Swiss Professors, Hunziker and Krapt, and adopted by the International Association of Scientific Experts on Tourism (IASET) aptly describes the concept of tourism: "Tourism is the sum of phenomena and relationships arising from the travel and stay of non-residents, in so far as they do not lead to permanent residence and are not connected with any earning activity."

The World Tourism Organisation (WTO) acknowledges the problem relating to precise definition. "There very often exists some confusion with regard to the term 'tourist'. In many cases, the term is applied only to persons who travel for holiday reasons.... (In reality) the word 'tourist' embraces many categories of travellers over and above the holiday makers."

The following diagram (page 6) developed by WTO on who should be counted as 'tourist' and who need not be makes it easier for us to understand the distinction.

Another broad definition was formulated by IASET and the Tourism Society of Cardiff in 1981, "Tourism may be defined in terms of particular activities selected by choice and undertaken outside the home environment. Tourism may or may not involve overnight stay away from home."

Within the parameters of the above definitions, tourists would mean those travelling for pleasure, domestic reasons, health, business purposes, conferences, meetings, diplomatic and religious purposes plus arrivals on cruise, even though they do not involve overnight stay. Persons not to be considered 'tourists' are the individuals transiting through a country, those coming to take up a residence, those who live in one country but cross over to another to work, i.e., workers from Spain who cross to Gibraltar for work, or Hongkong workers going to Macau for work, etc; students attending universities of one country from another country and persons arriving with or without work permit at another country for work are not included.

World Tourism Statistics and Rankings

Most Visited Countries by International Tourist Arrivals

In 2008, there were over 922 million international tourist arrivals, with a growth of 1.9% as compared to 2007. In 2009, international tourists arrivals fell to 880 million, representing a worldwide decline of 4% as compared to 2008. The region most affected was Europe with a 6% decline.

The World Tourism Organization reports the following ten countries as the most visited from 2006 to 2009 by the number of international travellers. When compared to 2006, Ukraine entered the top ten list, surpassing Russia, Austria and Mexico, and in 2008, surpassed Germany. In 2008, the United States displaced Spain from the second place. Most of the top visited countries continue to be on the European continent, followed by a growing number of Asian countries.

In 2009, Malaysia made it into the top 10 most visited countries' list. Malaysia secured the ninth position, just below Turkey and Germany. In 2008, Malaysia was in 11th position. Both Turkey and Germany climbed one rank in arrivals, occupying seventh and eighth positions respectively, while France continued to lead the ranks in terms of tourist arrivals.

Country	UNWTO Regional Market	International tourist arrivals (2009)	International tourist arrivals (2008)	International tourist arrivals (2007)
France	Europe	74.2 million	79.2 million	80.9 million
United States	North America	54.9 million	57.9 million	56.0 million
Spain	Europe	52.2 million	57.2 million	58.7 million
China	Asia	50.9 million	53.0 million	54.7 million
Italy	Europe	43.2 million	42.7 million	43.7 million
United Kingdom	Europe	28.0 million	30.1 million	30.9 million
Turkey	Europe	25.5 million	25.0 million	22.2 million
Germany	Europe	24.2 million	24.9 million	24.4 million
Malaysia	Asia	23.6 million	22.1 million	21.0 million
Mexico	North America	21.5 million	22.6 million	21.4 million

International Tourism Receipts

International tourism receipts grew to US$944 billion (€642 billion) in 2008, corresponding to an increase in real terms of 1.8% from 2007. When the export value of international passenger transport receipts is accounted for, total receipts in 2008 reached a record of US$1.1 trillion, or over US$3 billion a day.

The World Tourism Organization reports the following countries as the top ten tourism earners for the year 2009. It is noticeable that most of them are on the European continent, but the United States continues to be the top earner.

Country	UNWTO Regional Market	International tourist arrivals (2009)	International tourist arrivals (2008)	International tourist arrivals (2007)
United States	North America	$93.9 billion	$110.0 billion	$97.1 billion
Spain	Europe	$53.2 billion	$61.6 billion	$57.6 billion

France	Europe	$49.4 billion	$55.6 billion	$54.3 billion
Italy	Europe	$40.2 billion	$45.7 billion	$42.7 billion
China	Asia	$39.7 billion	$40.8 billion	$37.2 billion
Germany	Europe	$34.7 billion	$40.0 billion	$36.0 billion
United Kingdom	Europe	$30.0 billion	$36.0 billion	$38.6 billion
Australia	Oceania	$25.6 billion	$24.8 billion	$22.3 billion
Turkey	Europe	$21.3 billion	$22.0 billion	$18.5 billion
Austria	Europe	$19.4 billion	$21.6 billion	$18.9 billion

International Tourism Expenditures

The World Tourism Organization reports the following countries as the top ten biggest spenders on international tourism for the year 2009. For the fifth year in a row, German tourists continue as the top spenders.

Country	UNWTO Regional Market	International tourist arrivals (2009)	International tourist arrivals (2008)	International tourist arrivals (2007)
Germany	Europe	$81.2 billion	$91.0 billion	$83.1 billion
United States	North America	$73.2 billion	$79.7 billion	$76.4 billion
United Kingdom	Europe	$50.3 billion	$68.5 billion	$71.4 billion
China	Asia	$43.7 billion	$36.2 billion	$29.8 billion
France	Europe	$38.5 billion	$41.4 billion	$36.7 billion
Italy	Europe	$27.9 billion	$30.8 billion	$27.3 billion
Japan	Asia	$25.1 billion	$27.9 billion	$26.5 billion
Canada	North America	$24.2 billion	$27.2 billion	$24.7 billion
Russia	Europe	$20.8 billion	$23.8 billion	$21.2 billion
Netherland	Europe	$20.7 billion	$21.7 billion	$19.1 billion

Most Visited Cities by International Tourist Arrivals

Top 10 most visited cities by estimated number of international visitors by selected year

City	Country	International visitors (millions)	Year/Notes 2009 (Excluding extra-muros visitors)
Paris	France	14.8	
London	United Kingdom	14.1	2009
Singapore	Singapore	11.6	2010
Antalya	Turkey	9.25	2010
Kuala Lumpur	Malaysia	9.11	2009
Hong Kong	China	8.95	2009
New York City	United States	8.7	2009
Bangkok	Thailand	8.45	2009
Istanbul	Turkey	7.51	2009
Dubai	United Arab Emirates	6.81	2009

Tourism Re-defined

On 4 March 1993, the United Nations Statistical Commission adopted WTO's recommendations on tourism statistics. This endorsement represents a milestone for the tourism industry. Standard definitions and classifications provide decision makers with a common basis for accurately measuring the economic impact of tourism.

Essentially, WTO has taken the concept of 'tourism' beyond a stereotype image of 'holiday making'. The officially accepted definition in the report is:

'Tourism comprises the activities of persons travelling to and staying in places outside their usual environment for not more than one consecutive year for leisure, business and other purposes."

The report distinguishes the following types of tourism:

(a) Domestic tourism involving residents of a country visiting their own country.

(b) Inbound tourism involving non-residents visiting a country other than their own.

(c) Outbound tourism involving residents of a country visiting other countries.

These three basic forms of tourism can in turn be combined to derive the following categories of tourism:

(a) Internal tourism which comprises domestic tourism and inbound tourism,

(b) National tourism which comprises domestic tourism and outbound tourism, and

(c) International tourism which comprises inbound and outbound tourism.

Underlying the above conceptualisation of tourism is the overall concept of 'Traveller' defined as "any person on a trip between two or more countries or between two or more localities within his/her country of usual residence."

All types of travellers engaged in tourism are described as 'visitors'-a term that constitutes the basic concept for the whole system of tourism statistics.

A 'Visitor' is defined as a person who travels to a country other than that in which he has his usual residence but outside his usual environment for a period not exceeding twelve months and whose main purpose of visit is other than the exercise of an activity remunerated from within the place visited.

'Visitors' are sub-divided into two categories:

(i) Same-day visitors: Visitors who do not spend the night in a collective or private accommodation in the country visited.

(ii) Tourists: Visitors who stay for at least one night in a collective or private accommodation in the country visited.

Relationship Between 'Leisure', 'Recreation', and 'Tourism'

The words 'Leisure, 'Recreation' and Tourism' are often used to express similar meanings.

What exactly is the relationship between these words?

Leisure is a measure of time left over after work, rest, sleep and household chores. Leisure is the time when an individual can do what he likes to refresh his/her spirits.

Recreation means a variety of activities which a person could choose to refresh his/her spirit. It may include activities as diverse as a game of golf, watching television or travelling abroad.

Tourism, therefore, is simply one of these activities which a person could undertake to refresh his/her spirit. It places tourism firmly as part of recreation activities spectrum of a person.

Motivations For Travel

In the course of history, motivation for most travel has been fairly obvious-religion, economic gain, war, escape, migration. What is left is travel for pleasure, which is the most common form of travel in the modern world. The following may be listed as motivations to travel:

Education and Culture

(a) To see how people in other countries live, work and play.

(b) To enjoy scenic beauty and cultural sights.

(c) To gain a better understanding of what goes on elsewhere.

(d) To attend special events/festivals/cultural functions.

Relaxation and Pleasure

(a) To get away from the routine of life.

(b) To have a good time away from home.

(c) To have a romantic or exotic experience.

Ethnic

(a) To go to places from where one's family came from.

(b) To visit places where one's family or friends lived in the past. Indians settled abroad and holding foreign passports keep on coming to India again and again, swelling the number of tourist arrivals in India.

Classification

Tourism can be classified into six distinct categories according to the purpose of travel.

1. Recreational: Recreational or leisure tourism takes a person away from the humdrum of everyday life. In this case, people spend their leisure time at the hills, sea beaches, etc.
2. Cultural: Cultural tourism satisfies the cultural and intellectual curiosity and involves visits to ancient monuments, places of historical or religious importance, etc.
3. Sports/ Adventure: Trips taken by people with a view to playing golf, skiing in the mountains or hiking, fall within this category.
4. Health: Under this category, people travel for medical treatment or visit places where there are curative possibilities, for example, hot springs, spas, yoga, etc.
5. Convention Tourism: It is becoming an increasingly important component of travel. People travel within a country or overseas to attend conventions relating to their business, profession or interest.
6. Incentive Tourism: Holiday trips are offered as incentives by major companies to dealers and salesmen who achieve high targets in sales. This is a new and expanding phenomenon in tourism. These are in lieu of cash incentives or gifts. Today, incentive tourism is a 3 billion dollar business in the USA alone.

Barriers To Travel

In spite of numerous factors listed above favouring the development of tourism, there are some that act as barriers to travel. These fall into the following categories:

1. Cost: People are subjected to monetary restraints and cannot afford the expense of travel. According to a study on the subject, in the Unites States alone, over fifty per cent of the people cannot undertake holiday travel due to high costs. In India, it is 90%.

2. Time: This is characteristic of those who are not in a position to leave their business or profession to take time off from work.
3. Health: Many persons, especially old people, cannot travel due to poor health and physical limitations.
4. Family: Parents of small children are not in a position to travel due to the family responsibilities and inconveniences of travel.
5. Lack of interest: Ignorance and lack of information about other places and other people can be a major barrier to travel.

History

Wealthy people have always traveled to distant parts of the world, to see great buildings, works of art, learn new languages, experience new cultures and to taste different cuisines. Long ago, at the time of the Roman Republic, places such as Baiae were popular coastal resorts for the rich. The word tourism was used by 1811 and tourist by 1840. In 1936, the League of Nations defined foreign tourist as "someone traveling abroad for at least twenty-four hours". Its successor, the United Nations, amended this definition in 1945, by including a maximum stay of six months.

Leisure Travel

Leisure travel was associated with the Industrial Revolution in the United Kingdom - the first European country to promote leisure time to the increasing industrial population. Initially, this applied to the owners of the machinery of production, the economic oligarchy, the factory owners and the traders. These comprised the new middle class. Cox & Kings was the first official travel company to be formed in 1758.

The British origin of this new industry is reflected in many place names. In Nice, France, one of the first and best-established holiday resorts on the French Riviera, the long esplanade along the seafront is known to this day as the

Promenade des Anglais; in many other historic resorts in continental Europe, old, well-established palace hotels have names like the Hotel Bristol, the Hotel Carlton or the Hotel Majestic - reflecting the dominance of English customers.

Many leisure-oriented tourists travel to the tropics, both in the summer and winter. Places of such nature often visited are: Bali in Indonesia, Brazil, Cuba, the Dominican Republic, Malaysia, Mexico the various Polynesian tropical islands, Queensland in Australia, Thailand, Saint-Tropez and Cannes in France, Florida, Hawaii and Puerto Rico in the United States, Barbados, Sint Maarten, Saint Kitts and Nevis, The Bahamas, Anguilla, Antigua, Aruba, Turks and Caicos Islands and Bermuda.

Winter Tourism

Although it is acknowledged that the Swiss were not the inventors of skiing it is well documented that St. Moritz, Graubünden, became the cradle of the developing winter tourism: Since that year of 1865 in St. Moritz, many daring hotel managers choose to risk opening their hotels in winter but it was only in the seventies of the 20th century when winter tourism took over the lead from summer tourism in many of the Swiss ski resorts. Even in Winter, portions of up to one third of all guests (depending on the location) consist of non-skiers.

Major ski resorts are located mostly in the various European countries (e.g. Andorra, Austria, Bulgaria, Czech Republic, France, Germany, Iceland, Italy, Norway, Poland, Serbia, Sweden, Slovenia, Spain, Switzerland), Canada, the United States (e.g. Colorado, California, Utah, New York, New Jersey, Michigan, Montana, Vermont, New England) New Zealand, Japan, South Korea, Chile, Argentina, Kenya and Tanzania.

Mass Tourism

Mass tourism could only have developed with the improvements in technology, allowing the transport of large numbers of people in a short space of time to places of leisure interest, so that greater numbers of people could begin to enjoy the benefits of leisure time. In the United States, the first seaside resorts in the European style were at Atlantic City, New Jersey and Long Island, New York.

In Continental Europe, early resorts included: Ostend, popularised by the people of Brussels; Boulogne-sur-Mer (Pas-de-Calais) and Deauville (Calvados) for the Parisians; and Heiligendamm, founded in 1793, as the first seaside resort on the Baltic Sea.

Adjectival Tourism

Adjectival tourism refers to the numerous niche or specialty travel forms of tourism that have emerged over the years, each with its own adjective. Many of these have come into common use by the tourism industry and academics. Others are emerging concepts that may or may not gain popular usage. Examples of the more common niche tourism markets include:

- Agritourism
- Culinary tourism
- Cultural tourism
- Ecotourism
- Extreme tourism
- Geotourism
- Heritage tourism
- LGBT tourism
- Medical tourism
- Nautical tourism
- Pop-culture tourism
- Religious tourism
- Slum tourism
- Space tourism
- War tourism

- Wildlife tourism

Recent Developments

There has been an upmarket trend in the tourism over the last few decades, especially in Europe, where international travel for short breaks is common. Tourists have high levels of disposable income, considerable leisure time, are well educated, and have sophisticated tastes. There is now a demand for a better quality products, which has resulted in a fragmenting of the mass market for beach vacations; people want more specialised versions, quieter resorts, family-oriented holidays or niche market-targeted destination hotels.

The developments in technology and transport infrastructure, such as jumbo jets, low-cost airlines and more accessible airports have made many types of tourism more affordable. WHO estimates that up to 500,000 people are on planes at any time. There have also been changes in lifestyle, such as retiree-age people who sustain year round tourism. This is facilitated by internet sales of tourism products. Some sites have now started to offer dynamic packaging, in which an inclusive price is quoted for a tailor-made package requested by the customer upon impulse.

There have been a few setbacks in tourism, such as the September 11 attacks and terrorist threats to tourist destinations, such as in Bali and several European cities. Also, on December 26, 2004, a tsunami, caused by the 2004 Indian Ocean earthquake, hit the Asian countries on the Indian Ocean, including the Maldives. Thousands of lives were lost and many tourists died. This, together with the vast clean-up operation in place, has stopped or severely hampered tourism to the area.

The terms tourism and travel are sometimes used interchangeably. In this context, travel has a similar definition to tourism, but implies a more purposeful journey. The terms tourism and tourist are sometimes used pejoratively, to imply a shallow interest in the cultures or locations visited by tourists.

Sustainable Tourism

"Sustainable tourism is envisaged as leading to management of all resources in such a way that economic, social and aesthetic needs can be fulfilled while maintaining cultural integrity, essential ecological processes, biological diversity and life support systems."

Sustainable development implies "meeting the needs of the present without compromising the ability of future generations to meet their own needs".

Sustainable tourism can be seen as having regard to ecological and socio-cultural carrying capacities and includes involving the community of the destination in tourism development planning. It also involves integrating tourism to match current economic and growth policies so as to mitigate some of the negative economic and social impacts of 'mass tourism'. Murphy (1985) advocates the use of an 'ecological approach', to consider both 'plants' and 'people' when implementing the sustainable tourism development process. This is in contrast to the 'boosterism' and 'economic' approaches to tourism planning, neither of which consider the detrimental ecological or sociological impacts of tourism development to a destination.

However, Butler (2006) questions the exposition of the term 'sustainable' in the context of tourism, citing its ambiguity and stating that "the emerging sustainable development philosophy of the 1990s can be viewed as an extension of the broader realization that a preoccupation with economic growth without regard to it social and environmental consequences is self-defeating in the long term." Thus 'sustainable tourism development' is seldom considered as an autonomous function of economic regeneration as separate from general economic growth.

Ecotourism

Ecotourism, also known as ecological tourism, is responsible travel to fragile, pristine, and usually protected areas that strives to be low impact and (often) small scale. It helps educate the traveler; provides funds for conservation; directly benefits the economic development and political empowerment of local communities; and fosters respect for different cultures and for human rights.

Pro-poor Tourism

The pro poor tourism has to help the very poorest in developing countries has been receiving increasing attention by those involved in development and the issue has been addressed either through small scale projects in local communities and by Ministries of Tourism attempting to attract huge numbers of tourists. Research by the Overseas Development Institute suggests that neither is the best way to encourage tourists' money to reach the poorest as only 25% or less (far less in some cases) ever reaches the poor; successful examples of money reaching the poor include mountain climbing in Tanzania or cultural tourism in Luang Prabang, Laos.

Recession Tourism

Recession tourism is a travel trend, which evolved by way of the world economic crisis. Identified by American entrepreneur Matt Landau (2007), recession tourism is defined by low-cost, high-value experiences taking place of once-popular generic retreats. Various recession tourism hotspots have seen business boom during the recession thanks to comparatively low costs of living and a slow world job market suggesting travelers are elongating trips where their money travels further.

Medical Tourism

When there is a significant price difference between countries for a given medical procedure, particularly in Southeast Asia, India, Eastern Europe and where there are different regulatory regimes, in relation to particular medical procedures (e.g. dentistry), traveling to take advantage of the price or regulatory differences is often referred to as "medical tourism".

Educational Tourism

Educational tourism developed, because of the growing popularity of teaching and learning of knowledge and the enhancing of technical competency outside of the classroom environment. In educational tourism, the main focus of the tour or leisure activity includes visiting another country to learn about the culture, such as in Student Exchange Programs and Study Tours, or to work and apply skills learned inside the classroom in a different environment, such as in the International Practicum Training Program.

Creative Tourism

Creative tourism has existed as a form of cultural tourism, since the early beginnings of tourism itself. Its European roots date back to the time of the Grand Tour, which saw the sons of aristocratic families traveling for the purpose of mostly interactive, educational experiences. More recently, creative tourism has been given its own name by Crispin Raymond and Greg Richards, who as members of the Association for Tourism and Leisure Education (ATLAS), have directed a number of projects for the European Commission, including cultural and crafts tourism, known as sustainable tourism. They have defined "creative tourism" as tourism related to the active participation of travellers in the culture of the host community, through interactive workshops and informal learning experiences.

Meanwhile, the concept of creative tourism has been picked up by high-profile organizations such as UNESCO, who through the Creative Cities Network, have endorsed creative tourism as an engaged, authentic experience that promotes an active understanding of the specific cultural features of a place.

More recently, creative tourism has gained popularity as a form of cultural tourism, drawing on active participation by travelers in the culture of the host communities they visit.

Several countries offer examples of this type of tourism development, including the United Kingdom, the Bahamas, Jamaica, Spain, Italy and New Zealand.

Dark Tourism

One emerging area of special interest has been identified by Lennon and Foley (2000) as "dark" tourism. This type of tourism involves visits to "dark" sites, such as battlegrounds, scenes of horrific crimes or acts of genocide, for example: concentration camps. Dark tourism remains a small niche market, driven by varied motivations, such as mourning, remembrance, education, macabre curiosity or even entertainment. Its early origins are rooted in fairgrounds and medieval fairs.

Doom Tourism

Also known as "Tourism of Doom," or "Last Chance Tourism" this emerging trend involves traveling to places that are environmentally or otherwise threatened (the ice caps of Mount Kilimanjaro, the melting glaciers of Patagonia, The coral of the Great Barrier Reef) before it is too late. Identified by travel trade magazine TravelAge West editor-in-chief Kenneth Shapiro in 2007 and later explored in The New York Times, this type of tourism is believed to be on the rise. Some see the trend as related to sustainable tourism or ecotourism due to the fact that a number of these tourist destinations are considered threatened by environmental factors such as global warming, over population or climate change. Others worry that travel to many of these threatened locations increases an individual's carbon footprint and only hastens problems threatened locations are already facing.

Growth

The World Tourism Organization (UNWTO) forecasts that international tourism will continue growing at the average annual rate of 4 %. With the advent of e-commerce, tourism products have become one of the most traded items on the internet. Tourism products and services have been made available through intermediaries, although tourism providers (hotels, airlines, etc.) can sell their services directly. This has put pressure on intermediaries from both on-line and traditional shops.

It has been suggested there is a strong correlation between tourism expenditure per capita and the degree to which countries play in the global context. Not only as a result of the important economic contribution of the tourism industry, but also as an indicator of the degree of confidence with which global citizens leverage the resources of the globe for the benefit of their local economies. This is why any projections of growth in tourism may serve as an indication of the relative influence that each country will exercise in the future.

Space tourism is expected to "take off" in the first quarter of the 21st century, although compared with traditional destinations the number of tourists in orbit will remain low until technologies such as a space elevator make space travel cheap.

Technological improvement is likely to make possible airship hotels, based either on solar-powered airplanes or large dirigibles. Underwater hotels, such as Hydropolis, expected to open in Dubai in 2009, will be built. On the ocean, tourists will be welcomed by ever larger cruise ships and perhaps floating cities.

Sports Tourism

Since the late 1970s, sports tourism has become increasingly popular. Events such as rugby, Olympics, Commonwealth games, Asian Games and football World Cups have enabled specialist travel companies to gain official ticket allocation and then sell them in packages that include flights, hotels and excursions.

Latest Trends

As a result of the late-2000s recession, international arrivals suffered a strong slowdown beginning in June 2008. Growth from 2007 to 2008 was only 3.7% during the first eight months of 2008. The Asian and Pacific markets were affected and Europe stagnated during the boreal summer months, while the Americas performed better, reducing their expansion rate but keeping a 6% growth from January to August 2008. Only the Middle East continued its rapid growth during the same period, reaching a 17% growth as compared to the same period in 2007. This slowdown on international tourism demand was also reflected in the air transport industry, with a negative growth in September 2008 and a 3.3% growth in passenger traffic through September. The hotel industry also reports a slowdown, as room occupancy continues to decline. As the global economic situation deteriorated dramatically during September and October as a result of the global financial crisis, growth of international tourism is expected to slow even further for the remaining of 2008, and this slowdown in demand growth is forecasted to continue into 2009 as recession has already hit most of the top spender countries, with long-haul travel expected to be the most affected by the economic crisis. This negative trend intensified as international tourist arrivals fell by 8% during the first four months of 2009, and the decline was exacerbated in some regions due to the outbreak of the influenza AH1N1 virus.

Forms of Tourism

Tourism can be divided into different forms on the basis of length of stay, type of transport used, price paid or the number of people in a group. From a geographical point of view, important distinctions are international and domestic tourism and long haul and short haul tourism.

Domestic tourism includes those travelling within their own country. Domestic tourism does not involve use of foreign currency nor causes any balance of payment problem.

When people travel to a country other than their own with different economic and political system, the movement becomes international tourism. It involves preparation of several documents-passport, visa, etc., - to cross the national boundaries of a foreign country. It also involves conversion of one's own currency to the currency of the country where one is travelling. It is also likely that the visitor may face the problems of a foreign language.

The size of a country determines the extent of international tourism. USA, for instance, is a very large country and has many domestic tourist attractions. Therefore, the extent of the international tourism is only 10 per cent of the total tourism in the country.

The Netherlands, on the other hand, is a small country and international boundaries are not far from any city in the country. Therefore, the size of international tourism is over half of the total tourism of the Netherlands. So is that of Switzerland, Austria and Belgium.

Increasingly, distinctions between these two forms of tourism are diminishing as barriers to tourism are crumbling in several parts of the world. No passports and visas are needed between the members of the European Economic Community (EEC). Americans do not need a passport or a visa to travel to Canada and vice versa. The Japanese and citizens of some European countries do not need a visa to enter USA.

Long haul tourism comprises journeys exceeding 5,000 kilometres-below that is termed short haul tourism. The distinction is relevant from the point of view of aircraft operations and marketing. Long haul tourism is very important for India because the majority of India's tourists come from Europe, USA or Japan-long travel journeys. Potential tourist markets of India are long haul. India's neighbouring countries are not rich enough to take holidays on a large scale.

A further basic distinction in tourism relates to the purpose of visit-specially from the marketing point of view. Holiday Tourism is what most countries try to promote. Other forms of tourism do not need much promotion.

Holiday tourism can be further subdivided into 'sun, sand and sea' type of tourism where beach-related open air activities and good weather are important factors. The mountain tourism, like the Himalayan tourism, also comes under this category. The other is 'culture' and 'sightseeing' where the focus is on culture, history, art and architecture of a country. This tourism has a significant role in India's pattern of inbound tourism. Cultural Tourism is a major tourism resource of the country.

Special Interest Tourism comprises those who visit a country for a common purpose, i.e., visiting friends and relatives, health, education, etc. Those visiting a country for meeting friends and relatives do not make heavy demands on the facilities and infrastructure of the country as they often stay with their relatives and friends.

Under this category, it may be necessary to define individual and group travel. In the former case, the tourist moves individually, and in the latter, he travels as a member of the group. It is further subdivided into (a) Independent Travel and (b) Inclusive Tours. In the case of independent tours, transport, accommodation and other elements of travel are arranged separately, either by the tourist himself or by his travel agent. The independent traveller mentioned above is described as FIT- Free and Independent Traveller-in travel lingo. As a member of an inclusive tour group, an individual buys a trip where he is unable to find out the prepaid cost of his fare, accommodation, sightseeing, meals and other elements of travel. Inclusive Tours are also called Package Tours enabling people to travel economically. The tour operators who package these tours, get specially discounted wholesale prices for transportation and accommodation. They share a part of the discounts received from the suppliers with their customers.

Another term-Mass Tourism-refers to the participation of a large number of people in tourism, i.e., millions of tourists visiting Spain, Italy or France, often out-numbering the residents. This is a phenomenon as yet limited to developed countries. Travel for holiday is a part of the lifestyle of Western societies not yet applicable to India where disposable income is low and draw for holiday confined to affluent people.

Finally, we have the category of the people who visit a country for business. Included among them are businessmen or professionals attending trade fairs, conventions and conferences, participants in the incentive travel offered by their companies and people coming to negotiate business deals and contracts.

Clearly, business is no leisure activity. Since the business visitors use the same facilities as the holiday makers do, they are included in the category of 'tourists' or 'visitors'. Everyday is not a business day and they often take time off to do some sightseeing or take an excursion to a nearby tourist centre. For instance, most conventioneers attending business conventions in New Delhi do take a day trip to Agra - the city of the Taj. Like all pleasure travellers, businessmen come for a short stay in the host country and do not take up employment. Although a distinct category, the business travellers are included in the definition of 'Tourists'. It is desirable to identify and quantify such visitors for the purpose of planning and marketing. Airlines love business travellers because they more often pay the full fare and patronise business and first class.

Travel Industry Network

It is a matter of debate whether there exists what we often call the 'travel industry' in the sense of a distinct group of enterprises like steel, textile or automobile industry.

The problem arises because travel industry (a) is not a manufacturing industry and, (b) is not one industry but is a collection of businesses, all selling travel-related services. The general public may be more familiar with its various components like Airlines Industry, Hotel Industry, Restaurants and Transport Companies.

Sometimes, different segments of travel industry do not act as an integrated group and often have conflicting views and interests, especially hoteliers and travel agents. A definition of travel industry has been provided by Likorish and Kershaw. "Travel industry is that part of national economy which caters to the traveller who is visiting places outside the locality where he/ she resides or works."

In the early years of this century, travel, apparently, was not looked upon as an industry as such but as a collection of businesses whose common link was to provide services to travellers.

With increasing links among travel-related businesses established through easy and fast communications, travel has undoubtedly become an industry to be studied in its totality.

There have been some new developments. Initially, the travel industry was essentially a private sector affair. But the industry, today, involves both the private and public or government sectors. In some countries, governments not only put up the infrastructure but also develop tourist product. The role of India Tourism Development Corporation (ITDC) in the early years of tourism development and promotion in India is a case in point. Now, the State Tourism Development Corporations are providing similar services at state level-even selling package tours. In China today, the state is the only provider of tourist services. In Russia, both private and public sectors co-exist.

The role of Government in the regulation of tourism and aviation has increased in many other countries. The role of a state is very important and we will discuss it in a separate chapter.

"Travel industry is, therefore, a composite of organisations, both public and private, that are involved in the development, production and marketing of products and services to serve the demands of the travellers.'

The next question is-which agencies, organisations or businesses are to be included in the travel industry, and how should they be categorised?

Broadly, we can categorise them in three ways:

1. Direct Providers of Services. Examples: airlines, hotel, ground transportation, travel agents, restaurants and retail shops.
2. The second category is of support services to direct suppliers. Examples: specialised services such as tour

organisers, hotel management firms, travel research organisations and travel trade publications. There may be other services too, such as food service contractors, laundry services, etc.

3. The third category consists of developmental organisations that include planners, government organisations, financial institutions, vocational training institutes, etc. They do not cater to day-to-day needs of travellers. Their plans may take years to fructify, such as the development of a resort, shopping complex for tourists or training of the staff for tourism-related enterprises.

Human Right

On the 15th of April 2010 a headline in the British newspaper, The Sunday Times, proclaimed that European Commissioner Antonio Tajani had unveiled a plan declaring tourism a human right. According to the article itself: Tajani's view is that pensioners, youths and those too poor to afford it should have their travel subsidised by the taxpayer. Tajani's program will be piloted until 2013 and then put into full operation. In introducing his plan, Tajani stated, "Travelling for tourism today is a right. The way we spend our holidays is a formidable indicator of our quality of life." His spokesman added, "Why should someone from the Mediterranean not be able to travel to Edinburgh in summer for a breath of cool, fresh air; why should someone from Edinburgh not be able to travel to Greece in winter?" The characterization of Tajani's position as advocating an expansion of human rights was repeated by other media such as the conservative Canadian newspaper National Post and Wikipedia. According to Euractive it proved impossible for the commissioner's office to correct the misleading impression created by the Sunday Times headline in the Wikipedia articles on tourism and Antonio Tajani as the Sunday Times is a "reliable published source" while the actual text of the Commissioner's speech is only a "primary source".

EurActiv, an independent media portal, criticized the article by The Sunday Times as an example of misleading information about the EU which appears in the British press and then picked up by other Anglo-Saxon media and blogs, and Wikipedia. EurActiv notes that "the article on The Sunday Times never quotes the Commissioner as having made such a statement. Nevertheless, it pursues the argument under the headline "Brussels decrees holidays as a human right," underlining the alleged "hundreds of millions of pounds" that pursuing the idea would cost taxpayers." EurActiv criticized Wikipedia on the grounds that it proved impossible for Commissioner Tajani's team to correct the wrong information in the encyclopedia, and echoed European Commission spokesperson Pia Ahrenkilde Hansen's statement that "ethics in digital communications is definitely a subject which deserves to be addressed."

Attractions

The principal resource of a destination is its attraction or aggregate of attractions a country offers. There is no easy way to catalogue or analyse attractions specially when one recognises that what may appeal to one may be of no interest to others. Broadly speaking, Germans love beaches with a lot of sun. The French have more interest in art and culture. But, this does not apply to all Germans and all French-individual tastes differ.

Attraction can be broadly divided into two parts-Site Attractions and Event Attractions.

A site attraction may be a country, a geographical region like the Himalayas in India, the Alps in Europe or the Sahara Desert. Examples of event attractions are Edinburgh festival, an international exhibition like an Expo or a sports event like the International Olympics, Asian Games or the annual Pushkar Fair in India.

There is a difference between natural and man-made attraction. Natural attraction is a Himalayan valley like Kashmir, Niagara Falls or the Grand Canyon in the USA.

Man-made attractions are historical buildings like Taj Mahal, or Disneyland in Los Angeles, Miami or Tokyo.

The success of tourist destinations depends on the combination of unique natural beauty of a country as well as its man-made wonders.

If a country has many natural and man-made attractions, it does not mean it will necessarily draw the maximum number of tourists. It depends on the image of the country in the minds of the people in the generating markets. India is a good example. It has the Himalayas as well as great architectural wonders. But, it does not attract the number of tourists which a small country like Singapore does. Though people know about the richness of India in tourism assets, it is offset by the hazy image of its poverty, lack of hygiene, etc. There are other geographical factors, i.e., distance from major tourist markets.

Facilities/Amenities

Facilities at a tourist destination include tourist infrastructure- good roads, surface and air transportation, food, accommodation and entertainment. If any of these factors is missing, the destination will not be able to draw many tourists to its shores.

Again, taking the example of India, tourism has been hurt in the country over the years due to inadequate facilities. Facilities in India, as Mr. Inder Sharma, past President of the Pacific Asia Travel Association (PATA) points out, are "uneven". Major cities have good amenities but many other tourist sites in the country lack facilities limiting growth.

Accessibility

Accessibility from tourist markets is a key factor. Tourists generally love comfort and are willing to pay for it. An intrepid explorer may be willing to put himself to a lot of inconveniences to see a beautiful region-normal tourists do not. They love comfort.

Accessibility means existence of regular scheduled air services from the countries of origin to the host country-the destination. It means existence of convenient forms of transport in terms of time, distance, good railways, airports, coach services, taxis and guide services.

Statistical Measurement of Tourism

How many international tourists come to India in a year and how much money do they spend within the country while they are here? Does their visit help the country in increasing employment? These are some of the questions to which decision-makers in the Government would like to find answers. They want to know the answers because they are also required to take decisions regarding the need for new roads and other facilities in areas where the tourists go. Tourism has become a big business and the Governments cannot avoid taking interest in it.

Qualitative and Quantitative Approach

Tourism research is required to give them well-documented answers to these questions. The research in international tourism is needed, specially relating to basic questions like the quantum of international tourism, duration of visitors' stay, the time when they come in large numbers and the period when they do not come in large numbers and other related questions. The answers to these questions are relatively easy to find.

It is easier because almost all countries of the world have immigration checks for foreigners coming to their country. While in the plane, passengers are given a form to fill in-it is called the Disembarkation Form, or Card. The landing passengers are asked to give answers to several questions besides giving their name, address, passport number, nationality, etc. They may be asked how long they wish to stay, where they plan to stay-in hotels or with friends and relatives and the purpose of visit, etc. Disembarkation cards of some countries like Singapore have additional questions, to know the profile of the visitor- Is it your first visit? If not, is it second, third or fourth? Are you coming for holiday, business, conference? Disembarkation cards of countries like India do not contain such questions-perhaps, not to offend the visitors. But, such questions have become norms in most countries because this is the most economical way of getting information from the visitors on their profile. This research methodology is called quantitative approach.

Although the beginning of modern tourism can be dated from the second half of the nineteenth century, no one thought of compiling information on travel volume as in the twentieth century. Tourism was either insignificant or did not materially affect the life of the people. Countries did not have any passport system. A few years before the First World War, tourism became economically significant in Europe. Italy, France, Austria and Switzerland emerged as great tourist destinations. Before the First World War, Switzerland was known to receive half a million visitors annually though it was only an estimate. After the First World War, we are told that in 1929, foreign visitors to Austria were about 1 to 2 million, Italy 1.5 million and Switzerland 1.25 million. Statistical measurement of foreign visitors had started in a modest way.

But it may be recalled that before World War I no country had formal immigration control as we have today. Strict immigration controls are a post-World War II phenomenon.

It was only in the thirties that tourism began to be examined against the background of economic problems of European countries. A couple of books appeared at that time in England-The Tourist Movement-An Economic Study by F.W. Ogilvie and The Tourist Industry, A National and International Survey, by A.J. Norval.

During the years following World War II, economies of European countries was in shambles and tourism was considered an answer to the economic problems of Europe. Economies of some European countries did revive through American tourism during the fifties and later. In the sixties, some of the European countries too were in a position to let their own people travel abroad for a holiday. England and France relaxed foreign exchange restrictions on foreign travel, and Germany soon followed.

In the sixties, the United Nations focussed its attention on developing countries. Again, researchers found tourism as a solution for foreign exchange requirement of the developing countries. It was at that time that need arose for primary data on tourism to measure the flow of expenditure through foreign visitors and to relate information to provide infrastructure for increasing number of visitors who were now looking beyond Europe and North America.

Among the developing countries, India was one of the first to start a Department of Tourism as early as 1958 and set up a marketing section for collection of tourist statistics. The statistics were compiled from Disembarkation cards of tourists. The cards were borrowed from the immigration authorities under the Home Ministry and analysed in the Department of Tourism from the point of view of tourism research. Since then, India's Department of Tourism has been publishing its statistical reports annually. It is true of most other countries of the world. England and the European countries started doing it much earlier while developing countries in Asia followed India's lead in this respect.

2

FRAMEWORK

The term "tourist", meaning "an individual who travels for the pleasure of travelling, out of curiosity" made its first appearance around 1800, and the word "tourism" was cited for the first time in the Oxford English Dictionary in 1811. But the origins of this activity go back considerably further. Humankind has always had the desire to travel, to visit exotic places and to encounter different cultures. Even in the time of the ancient Greeks, travellers such as Herodotus (c.484-425 BC) visited countries and places other than their own and reported their experiences. Similarly, wealthy Romans travelled to Egypt and Greece, to visit sanctuaries, bathe in thermal baths, and generally relax.

Much later, during the Middle Ages, people travelled mainly for religious purposes. Many pilgrimages to holy shrines in Rome, Santiago de Compostela and Canterbury were made, usually on foot, in large groups, and sometimes necessitating the crossing of whole continents. Aimeri de Picaud, a French monk, is generally credited as the author of the first tourist guide: written in 1130 for pilgrims making their way to the Spanish shrine of Santiago de Compostela.

But it was not until after the Renaissance that people began to travel in greater numbers for pleasure, education and knowledge. In the 18th and 19th Centuries, the "Grand Tour" became extremely fashionable among European aristocrats. English gentlemen often travelled on the Continent for as long as three years at once. However, tourism did not become more accessible to the population in general until the time of the Industrial Revolution. During this era, the first paid annual holidays, combined with the opportunities for cheap travel provided by the railways, began to generate a mass exodus to newly-created seaside resorts in, for example, France, England and New York State. Moreover, widespread social and technological developments helped to create a new middle class that could afford to travel for pleasure. (Wood and House, 1991)

By 1856 Thomas Cook was advertizing railway excursions, including a "grand circular tour of the Continent", aboard his "wagons-lits". Englishmen "discovered" Switzerland around 1850, and the Germans followed soon after. During this time a considerable amount of travel for pleasure was essentially a quest for spectacular scenery. This period also witnessed the first serious environmental impacts attributable to tourism.

For those living in the industrializing countries, tourism was also stimulated as a result of the increased awareness of a world beyond Europe. Soldiers travelling to distant lands had seen opportunities for securing a better way of life and wanted to return in peacetime. And the colonial era brought India, Africa, Australia and many other parts of the world into closer focus. In addition, the advent of photography enabled the mass production of visual and enticing evidence of "exotic" marvels, and began to attract the interest of the more adventurous, who wished to see such sights for themselves.

Early this century - by which time summer holidays were taken regularly by Europeans and Americans - the motorcar provided far greater mobility, thereby stimulating yet further tourism activity. Commercial flights also played a decisive role, especially after the end of World War II. Soon Western tourists were travelling to previously remote destinations. But it was not until the 1950s and 1960s, when air travel became widespread and commercially and economically feasible, that tourism really "took off".

However, by about this time, tourism started to earn itself a very bad name due to thoughtless development, and disruption of local cultures, values and economies. During the birth of mass international travel, beginning in the late 1940s, and continuing through most of the 1960s, tourism was often regarded as a panacea for developing countries, that is, as a "smokeless" industry that could raise foreign exchange earnings, GNP and tax revenue, and also increase employment. But growth in public concern (albeit mainly in the industrialized countries) about the environment, and the negative impacts of mass tourism, ultimately led to reexamination of this notion. Purported economic benefits from tourism came under harsh scrutiny and recognition of the problems involved in measuring the economic benefits of tourism led to increased analysis of its costs (Lawrence, 1992). At the same time, conservation organizations were formed to lobby governments to set aside land not just for the enjoyment of tourists, or for the sake of showy animals, but to preserve the natural integrity of whole ecosystems.

Basic Principles

The force behind this very complex activity encompassing a wide range of relationships in tourism is a phenomenon of modern times. Understanding the meaning and the nature of this phenomenon and its various components is very essential. In order to understand tourism systematically, it is necessary to know the various components which together make tourism happen. Three of these are considered to be basic:

(a) Transport;

(b) Attractions / Locale;

(c) Accommodation

Transport : There can be no travel if there were no transport. Travel involves movement of people and this is possible only if there is some mode of transport. Connectivity is very vital for tourism development. This could be possible only if adequate transportation infrastructure and access to destination is efficient, comfortable and inexpensive. A tourist, in order to get to his destination therefore, needs some mode of transport. This mode of transport may be a motor car, a coach, an aeroplane, a ship or a train which enables a traveller to reach his predetermined destination.

Locale : The locale may include the holiday destination and what it offers to the tourist. The holiday destination may offer natural attractions like sunshine, scenic beauty or sporting facilities, etc. The locale, with its attractions and amenities, is the most important as these are very basic to tourism. Unless these are there, the tourists will not be motivated to go to a particular place. However, since interests and tastes of tourists vary widely, they might choose from a wide range of attractions available at various destinations all over the world. Tourist demands are also very much susceptible to changes in fashion. Fashion is an important factor in the demand for various tourist attractions and amenities. The tourists who visit a particular place for its natural beauty may decide to visit some other attractions due to a change in fashion. Peter has drawn up an inventory of the various attractions which are of significance in tourism.

According to Robinson, the attractions of tourism are, to a very large extent, geographical in character. Location and accessibility (whether a place has a coastal or inland position, and the ease with which a given place can be reached) are important. Physical space may be thought of as a component for there are those who seek the wilderness and solitude. Scenery or landscape is a compound of landforms, water and the vegetation and has an aesthetic and recreative value. Climatic conditions, especially in relation to the amount of sunshine, temperature and precipitation (snow as well as rain), are of special significance. Animal life may be an important attraction, firstly, in relation, to bird watching or viewing game in their natural habitat and, secondly, for sporting purposes, e.g., fishing and hunting. Man's impact on the natural landscape in the form of his settlements, historical monuments and archaeological remains is also a major attraction. Finally, a variety of cultural features - ways of life, folklore, artistic expressions, etc. provide valuable attractions to many.

Accommodation : Accommodation plays a central role and is very basic to tourist destinations. World Tourism Organisation in its definition of a tourist has stated that the tourist must spend at least one night in the destination visited to be qualified as a tourist. This presupposes availability of some kind of accommodation. The demand for accommodation away from one's home is met by a variety of facilities. The range and type of accommodation is quite varied and has undergone considerable changes since last half a century. There has been a decline in the use of boarding houses and small private hotels. Larger hotels are increasing their share of holiday trade, especially in big metropolitan areas and popular tourist spots. In more traditional holiday and seaside resorts in Europe and elsewhere, big hotels are keeping their share of holiday resorts. In recent years some changes have been reflected in the type of accommodation. There has been a increasing demand for more non-traditional and informal type of accommodation. The latest trends in accommodation are holiday villages. In recent years there has been an increase in the popularity of such accommodation.

Accommodation may in itself be an important tourist attraction. In fact, a large number of tourists visit a particular destination or town simply because there is a first class luxury hotel or resort which provides excellent services and facilities. Some countries like Switzerland, Holland, France, Austria and Belgium have gained a reputation for providing excellent accommodation with good cuisine. Many hotel establishments elsewhere in various countries, especially the resort hotels, have gained a reputation for their excellent cuisine, services and facilities. The French Government for instance, paved the way for tourist development of Corsica by launching a big hotel development programme.

In addition to the three basic components, there are certain elements or ingredients which are also crucial to tourism. These include:

(a) Pleasing weather

(b) Scenic attractions

(c) Historical and cultural factors

(d) Accessibility

(e) Amenities

Pleasing Weather : One of the most important and crucial attractions of any tourist place is fine weather with warm sunshine. For holidaying, good weather is a particularly important ingredient, since it plays an important role in making a holiday a pleasant or an unpleasant experience. Millions of tourists from countries with extreme climates visit beaches in search of fine weather and sunshine. Sunshine and clear sea breeze at the beaches have attracted many since a very long time. In fact, development of spas and resorts along the sea coasts in many countries, were a result of the travellers' urge to enjoy good weather and sunshine. In Europe, countries like France, Italy, Spain and Greece have developed beautiful beach resorts. North Europeans visit Mediterranean coasts searching for older resorts like Monte Carlo, Nice and Cannes on the Riviera and new resorts in Italy and Spain. Italy has built beautiful resorts in its southern parts of Calabria, Sicily and Sardinia along the Adriatic and Mediterranean coasts taking advantage of brilliant sunshine. Many of the Mexican resorts, of the Pacific and California, Florida, and Hawaiian Islands in the United States are yet other examples where weather has played a prominent part in attracting tourists. Beautiful beaches of India, Sri Lanka, Thailand, Indonesia, Australia and some other new destinations are yet more examples of what good weather can do. All these areas, in fact, capitalising on good weather, have become important tourist spots. Destinations with attractive winter climates, winter warmth and sunshine are also important centres of tourist attraction. Many areas have become important winter holiday resorts attracting a large number of tourists. Around these winter resorts, a variety of winter sport facilities have been installed to cater to the increasing needs of tourists. In countries with tropical climates, many upland cool areas have been developed as 'hill station resorts'. Climate then, is of particular significance to tourism and, there are many areas which, because of their beautiful, bracing climates, can be potential tourist areas.

Scenic Attractions : Scenic attractions, like good weather, are very important factors in tourism. Scenery or the landscape consisting of mountains, lakes, waterfalls, glaciers, forests, deserts, etc., are strong forces attracting people to visit them. Breath-taking mountain scenery and the coastal stretches exert a strong fascination for the tourist. The magnificent mountain ranges provide an atmosphere of peace and tranquillity. Tourists visiting the northern slopes of the Alps in Switzerland and Austria and the southern slopes in Italy and also the Himalayan mountain slopes of India and Nepal for the first time, cannot but be charmed by their physical magnificence. Great natural wonders such as the Grand Canyon in the United States, the Giants Causeway of Northern Ireland, the Niagara Falls, the Geysers of Iceland, the glaciers of the Alps, the forests of Africa, the mighty rivers, the lakes and the deserts are a source of great interest to many tourists and have become the basis of an expanding tourist industry.

Historical and Cultural interest characteristics exert a powerful attraction for many. Since many centuries these have had a profound influence on the traveller. A large number of tourists are attracted every year by the great drawing power of Stratford-on Avon in England because of its association with Shakespeare, or the city of Agra in India with its famous Taj Mahal or Pisa in Italy for its famous Leaning Tower. Thousands of Americans and Canadians visit Europe because of its long historical heritage; besides, many view Europe as their original homeland and have a sentimental attachment to it. Any foreign visitor to England must visit London not because it is the largest city in the country and the capital, but because of its historical associations and traditions and its many cultural attractions. In a similar way the visitor in France includes Paris in his itinerary as he does Rome and Moscow in a visit to Italy and the Russia respectively. Many countries which are developing tourist industries are using the legacy of their historical past as their major tourist attractions. In India, the world-famous caves of Ajanta and Ellora are an example. These caves are India's oldest and most beautiful testimony of religious architecture and painting, and are man-made caves hewn out of rocky mountains, conceived and executed some 2000 years ago.

Accessibility : Accessibility is a very crucial factor as it is a means by which a tourist can reach the area where attractions are located. Tourist attractions of whatever type would be of little importance if their locations are inaccessible by the normal means of transport. If the tourist attractions are located at places where no transport can reach or where there are inadequate transport facilities, these become of little value. The tourist attractions which are located near to the tourist generating markets and are linked by a network of efficient roads and can be easily reached by air receive the maximum number of tourists. The distance factor also plays an important role in determining a tourist's choice of a destination. Longer distances cost much in the way of expenses on travel as compared to short distances. An example can be that of India. About two million and a half tourist arrivals for a country of the size of India may look rather unimpressive. However, if one looks at certain factors like the country's distance from the affluent tourist market of the world such as the United States, Europe, Canada, Japan and Australia, one may conclude that the long distance is rather one of the factors responsible for low arrivals. It costs a visitor from these countries quite a substantial amount to visit India for a holiday. It has been stated earlier that Europe and North America continue to be the main generating and receiving areas for international tourism, accounting for as much as 70 per cent and 20 per cent, respectively, of international tourist arrivals. The intra-regional tourism (tourism between countries of the same region) has an appreciable influence on the distribution of world arrivals. Of the total international tourist movements within Europe and North America, at least 75 per cent are intra-regional. In the Americas the United States and Canada alone account for nearly 50 per cent of all international tourist traffic in the regions, where intra-regional international tourist movements are also predominant. In Europe; intra-regional tourism accounts for over 70 per cent of international tourist movements. Easy accessibility thus is a key factor for the growth and development of tourist movements.

Amenities : Facilities are a necessary aid to the tourist centre. For a seaside resort, facilities like swimming, boating, yachting, surf-riding and other facilities like dancing, recreation and amusements are important for every tourist centre. Amenities can be of two types: natural, e.g., beaches, sea-bathing, possibilities of fishing, opportunities for climbing, trekking, viewing, etc. and man-made, e.g., various types of entertainments and facilities which cater to the special needs of the tourists. Excellent sandy beaches, sheltered in sunshine with palm and coconut trees and offering good bathing conditions form very good tourist attractions. Certain other natural amenities such as spacious waters for the purpose of sailing, or the opportunities for fishing and shooting are also very important.

Geographical Components : Robinson has brought out a list of components of tourism which have been termed as geographical components of tourism. These are brought out in the following table :

Geographical Components

1. Accessibility and location
2. Space
3. Scenery:
   (a) land forms, e.g., mountains, canyons, coral reefs, cliffs, etc.
   (b) water, e.g., rivers, lakes, waterfalls, geysers, glaciers, the sea.
   (c) Vegetation, e.g., forests, grasslands, moors, deserts, etc.
4. Climate Sunshine, clouds, temperature conditions, rain and snow.
5. Animal life :
   (a) wildlife, e.g., birds, game reservations, zoos.
   (b) hunting and fishing.

6. Settlement features
   (a) Towns, cities, villages
   (b) Historical remains and monuments
   (c) Archaeological remains
7. Culture : ways of life, traditions, folklore, arts and crafts etc.

Tourism Geography

Tourism Geography is the study of travel and tourism, as an industry and as a social and cultural activity. Tourism geography covers a wide range of interests including the environmental impact of tourism, the geographies of tourism and leisure economies, answering tourism industry and management concerns and the sociology of tourism and locations of tourism. Tourism geography is that branch of science which deals with the study of travel and its impact on places.

Geography is fundamental to the study of tourism, because tourism is geographical in nature. Tourism occurs in places, it involves movement and activities between places and it is an activity in which both place characteristics and personal self-identities are formed, through the relationships that are created among places, landscapes and people. Physical geography provides the essential background, against which tourism places are created and environmental impacts and concerns are major issues, that must be considered in managing the development of tourism places.

The approaches to study will differ according to the varying concerns. Much tourism management literature remains quantitative in methodology and considers tourism as consisting of the places of tourist origin (or tourist generating areas), tourist destinations (or places of tourism supply) and the relationship (connections) between origin and destination places, which includes transportation routes, business relationships and traveler motivations. Recent developments in Human geography have resulted in approaches such as those from cultural geography, which take more theoretically diverse approaches to tourism, including a sociology of tourism, which extends beyond tourism as an isolated, exceptional activity and considering how travel fits into the everyday lives and how tourism is not only a consumptive of places, but also produces the sense of place at a destination.

Main Regions : Geographically four main regions have been identified that function as tourist attractions, the way in which transport networks evolve to link tourist generating regions with potential destinations and their regional expression. These regions are :

Europe : The world's focus of international tourism generation and the world's primary destination region.

North America : An equally significant world tourist region in terms of volume of tourist movement, whose general patterns of tourist development show striking similarities with those of Europe.

The Pacific and Australia : The world's most rapidly growing tourist region

South Asia, Subsaharan Africa, The Middle East and Central and South America : These regions are peripheral in terms of their economic relationships with the developed world and in terms of their tourist linkages with the major western tourist generating regions.

Travel geography is about the geographical distribution of tourism throughout the world. It seeks to describe and explain the spatial patterns of tourist activity and development on regional, national, international and world scales. It is about the location of tourist resources and the factors (e.g. economic and political etc.) that influence when, how and where they are used for tourism. It is about the people who are tourists, where and why they travel and the effect they have on the places they visit. The tourist travels away from home for a variety of reasons (other than work). The essence of tourism is therefore; that it involves travel to a location, that is not the tourist's home.

The simplest spatial model of the tourist system consists of three spatial elements :

(i) The tourist's home area (the tourist generating region)

(ii) The places people travel to (the destination regions)

(iii) The routes people follow between the generating and destination regions.

Travel geography is concerned with the study of all three elements of the system, at all spatial scales (from the study of domestic tourism with a city or region, through to the world of international travel).

Geographical Features Which Attract Travellers

Following are the main geographical features which attract travellers to them.

Climatic Resources for Tourism

(i) Rainfall

(ii) Cloud cover

(iii) Sunshine

(iv) Hot climates

(v) Tropical climates

(vi) Mediterranean climates

(vii) Cool temperate climates

(viii) The cold climates

(ix) Mountain climates

Coastal Resources and the Sea

(i) The sea

(ii) The beach

(iii) The waves

(iv) The tides

Landscape and Wildlife Resources

(i) Natural landscapes

(ii) Tropical forests

(iii) National parks

(iv) Wildlife sanctuaries

(v) Hot deserts

Historic Resources for Tourism

(i) Early civilization

(ii) The classical world

(iii) The age of migrations

(iv) Medieval times

(v) 17th century to the present

Cultural, Entertainment and Man-made Resources for Tourism

(i) Theme parks

(ii) Entertainment

(iii) Leisure shopping

(iv) Sporting events

(v) NIGHT-LIFE

General Patterns

Where do international tourists come from; i.e. which countries and regions of the world generate international tourism, and is there any clear spatial pattern of tourist generation in the world ? Why do these countries and regions generate tourism, i.e. what combination of social, economic and political circumstances leads to the development of international (and also domestic) tourism in a country ? Has the level of world tourism generation changed over time, i.e. has the performance of world economy affected the generation of tourism on a world scale? The tourist generation is particularly closely related to economic circumstances, and that tourist generation on a world scale is heavily concentrated in Europe, North America and to some extent, in the Pacific region. There is a relationship between the performance of the world's economy and the generation of international tourist travel.

This relationship also holds good at the level of the individual country. A country's ability to generate tourism is related to its social, political and economic character. Each country goes through a clearly defined sequence of phases of tourist generation from phase 1 when only a tiny elite travel abroad, through phase 2 and 3 when first mass domestic and then mass outbound (international) tourism develops, and through to phase 4 when, finally, the proportion of the population travelling abroad is greater than that holidaying at home. These phases occur in parallel with economic and political change taking place in the country. Different countries of the world are at different stages of economic development and tourist generation. The countries of the affluent economic core (mainly the continents of Northern Hemisphere) currently generate the vast majority of the world's international and domestic tourists. Thus tourist generation on a world scale in heavily concentrated in Europe, North America and to a lesser extent, in the Pacific region. The countries on the economic periphery (essentially the countries of South and South East Asia, Africa and Central and South America) play a relatively small part in generating world international or domestic tourist traffic.

Transport Systems

Interest in ITS comes from the problems caused by traffic congestion and a synergy of new information technology for simulation, real-time control, and communications networks. Traffic congestion has been increasing worldwide as a result of increased motorization, urbanization, population growth, and changes in population density. Congestion reduces efficiency of transportation infrastructure and increases travel time, air pollution, and fuel consumption.

The United States, for example, saw large increases in both motorization and urbanization starting in the 1920s that led to migration of the population from the sparsely populated rural areas and the densely packed urban areas into suburbs. The industrial economy replaced the agricultural economy, leading the population to move from rural locations into urban centers.

At the same time, motorization was causing cities to expand because motorized transportation could not support the population density that the existing mass transit systems could. Suburbs provided a reasonable compromise between population density and access to a wide variety of employment, goods, and services that were available in the more densely populated urban centers. Further, suburban infrastructure could be built quickly, supporting a rapid transition from a rural/agricultural economy to an industrial/urban economy.

Recent governmental activity in the area of ITS - specifically in the United States - is further motivated by the perceived need for homeland security. Many of the proposed ITS systems also involve surveillance of the roadways, which is a priority of homeland security. Funding of many systems comes either directly through homeland security organizations or with their approval. Further, ITS can play a role in the rapid mass evacuation of people in urban centers after large casualty events such as a result of a natural disaster or threat. Much of the infrastructure and planning involved with ITS parallels the need for homeland security systems.

In the developing world, the migration of people from rural to urbanized habitats has progressed differently. Many areas of the developing world have urbanized without significant motorization and the formation of suburbs. In areas like Santiago, Chile, a high population density is supported by a multimodal system of walking, bicycle transportation, motorcycles, buses, and trains. A small portion of the population can afford automobiles, but the automobiles greatly increase the congestion in these multimodal transportation systems. They also produce a considerable amount of air pollution, pose a significant safety risk, and exacerbate feelings of inequities in the society.

Other parts of the developing world, such as China, remain largely rural but are rapidly urbanizing and industrializing. In these areas a motorized infrastructure is being developed alongside motorization of the population. Great disparity of wealth means that only a fraction of the population can motorize, and therefore the highly dense multimodal transportation system for the poor is cross-cut by the highly motorized transportation system for the rich. The urban infrastructure is being rapidly developed, providing an opportunity to build new systems that incorporate ITS at early stages.

Europe

(a) The Iberian peninsula : Spain and Portugal

(b) The Balkan region : Albania, Greece and former Yugoslavia

(c) Turkey : Cyprus and Malta

(d) The Alps : Austria and Switzerland

(e) Central Europe : France, Italy, Benelux and Germany

(f) Eastern Europe and the CIS

(g) UK and Ireland

(h) Northwest Europe : Scandinavia

North Africa and Middle East, Subsaharan Africa

The Americas

(i) North America

(ii) Mexico and Carribean

(iii) Central and South America

Asia and the Pacific Region

(i) Australia and New Zealand

(ii) The Pacific Islands

(iii) East Asia

(iv) South East Asia

(v) South Asia : The Indian Subcontinent

Travel geography plays a crucial role in understanding clearly the distribution of tourism throughout the world and is a key element in planning and marketing a destination. While seeking to describe and explain the spatial patterns of the tourist activity, it gives direction to planners and developers of tourism to utilize scarce resources in the best possible manner.

Customer Care

According to Turban et al. (2002), "Customer service is a series of activities designed to enhance the level of customer satisfaction - that is, the feeling that a product or service has met the customer expectation."

Its importance varies by product, industry and customer; defective or broken merchandise can be exchanged, often only with a receipt and within a specified time frame. Retail stores will often have a desk or counter devoted to dealing with returns, exchanges and complaints, or will perform related functions at the point of sale.

Customer service may be provided by a person (e.g., sales and service representative), or by automated means called self-service. Examples of self service are Internet sites. However, in the Internet era, a challenge has been to maintain and/or enhance the personal experience while making use of the efficiencies of online commerce. Writing in Fast Company, entrepreneur and customer systems innovator Micah Solomon has made the point that "Online customers are literally invisible to you (and you to them), so it's easy to shortchange them emotionally. But this lack of visual and tactile presence makes it even more crucial to create a sense of personal, human-to-human connection in the online arena."

Customer service is normally an integral part of a company's customer value proposition. In their book Rules to Break and Laws to Follow, Don Peppers and Martha Rogers, Ph.D. write that "customers have memories. They will remember you, whether you remember them or not." Further, "customer trust can be destroyed at once by a major service problem, or it can be undermined one day at a time, with a thousand small demonstrations of incompetence."

From the point of view of an overall sales process engineering effort, customer service plays an important role in an organization's ability to generate income and revenue.

From that perspective, customer service should be included as part of an overall approach to systematic improvement. A customer service experience can change the entire perception a customer has of the organization.

Some have argued that the quality and level of customer service has decreased in recent years, and that this can be attributed to a lack of support or understanding at the executive and middle management levels of a corporation and/or a customer service policy. To address this argument, many organizations have employed a variety of methods to improve their customer satisfaction levels, and other KPIs

A choice of a tourist destination, however, depends on a variety of other factors in addition to the ones discussed above Hospitality is one such factor. A friendly and appreciative attitude on the part of the nationals of the host country will make the visitor feel at home and help him enjoy his stay better. A satisfied tourist is an asset and helps promote a destination in a much more effective way than any tourist promotional campaign or publicity. The French government, for instance, regularly mounts a campaign to explain to their citizens the advantage to be gained from a flourishing tourist trade and the value of being courteous and helpful to the visiting tourist. At each of the innumerable tourist places, one encounters friendly guides who answer any questions a tourist might have. Clear directions at roads, metro stations, shopping areas theatres and a host of other places make a visit of a tourist very comfortable and memorable. Many other countries including India have also launched similar campaigns for their citizens.

Establishment of Information Bureaus is another important step in the direction of welcoming a visitor. It is very necessary to have information bureaus where the foreign visitor who, unfamiliar with the country or a resort in a country, and who perhaps is not familiar with the language of the country, can readily acquire information about places of interest and the various facilities available there. Trained and competent guides familiar with the tourist's language are also essential and are a great help to the tourist. The various formalities to be completed by the tourist should be reduced to the minimum. The United Nations Conference on Tourism held in Rome in the year 1963 had recommended the gradual elimination of all barriers, restrictions and formalities to facilitate international travel. In fact, some countries have already gone a long way towards abolishing certain formalities for visiting tourists resulting in increased facilitation. Many countries in Western Europe have abolished the system of visas between themselves and have done away with entry permits for nationals of all countries on a unilateral basis. Apart from certain essential formalities such as health, customs and currency restrictions, it is desirable that formalities should be reduced to the minimum.

Modern tourism has had spectacular growth especially since World War II. From 25.3 million international tourist arrivals in the year 1950 the figure went up to over 380 million in the year 1988. According to the most recent estimates produced by the Secretariat General, World Tourism Organisation, international tourist arrivals in 2000 are expected to total 715 million.

While economic and political conditions may continue to fluctuate throughout the world, there is every reason to believe that more and more people throughout the world will continue to travel. Tourism has become an irreversible fact in most parts of the world, and the expected upturn in overall economic growth, together with success in stabilising prices is likely to promote further increases in international tourism demand. With the expanding right to paid holidays and the irreversible increase in travel for cultural purposes, the number of persons taking to travel is bound to increase. As a result of labour legislation in various countries introducing paid holidays, over 750 millions workers and their families have acquired a right to travel. However, not all of them are able to exercise the right because of non-availability of sufficient facilities and increasing prices. However, a vast potential exists which needs to be exploited by those responsible for tourism development and growth.

Social Purpose Tourism

The demand for tourism in any country is influenced by a number of factors including the very society and the sociopolitical system in which the potential tourists live. In many countries especially in East Europe and CIS, the state plays leading role in promoting tourism for their citizens. In these countries, the government provides relief to their citizens by way of giving them a holiday as a reward. In fact, in some countries of Eastern Europe there are government policies whereby the State provides a holiday to everyone. In Russia the worker knows in advance when and what type of holidays he is entitled to. In fact, social tourism can be said to be a form of tourism whereby the State renders facilities to its citizens to engage in tourism.

Definition : Although there is as yet no agreed definition of social tourism, there has been a considerable study on the subject. Dr. W. Hunziker at the second Congress of Social Tourism held at Vienna and Salzburg in Austria in May 1959, proposed the following definition. "Social tourism is a type of tourism practised by low income groups, and which is rendered possible and facilitated by entirely separate and therefore easily recognizable services". Another recent definition, propounded by M. Andre Poplimont, is as follows: "Social tourism is the type of tourism practised by those who would not be able to meet the cost without social intervention, i.e., without the assistance of an association to which the individual belongs." From these definitions of social tourism it is clear that it has certain elements. The first is the idea of limited means. Manual workers are thus included in the scope of social tourism. In addition to manual workers there are also others who cannot save enough to pay for travel and accommodation because their incomes are too low or their commitments too great. On the whole, however, the majority of such tourists are manual workers. Secondly, social tourism is subsidised. The subsidies may be provided by the states, local authorities, trade unions, employers, clubs or other associations to which the worker belongs. Thirdly, it involves travel outside the normal place of residence, preferably to a different environment.

Paid Holiday : The element of limited means is most important. Social tourism as we have seen, is concerned specifically with the participation in tourism of people with limited means and with the measures to encourage this participation and to make it possible. In fact, it may be correct to state that the establishment of annual paid holidays in the west heralded the birth of social tourism. Social tourism as we understand it today, in fact, owes its origin to annual paid holidays. The concept of annual paid holidays was established during the inter-war years as a reality for a considerable part of the working population. By the year 1939, in UK alone, some eleven million people were covered by the Holidays with Pay Act (1938). The paid holidays provided both the leisure time and the financial means to profit from it by travel and relaxation. Since paid holidays were introduced, thousands of millions have benefited from them. Paid holidays now have universal recognition and are established all over the world, and in most countries a minimum duration (one, two or three weeks) is specified either by law or by collective agreements. Today it is recognised that in Western Europe the fifth week, even from the standpoint of output may also be regarded as a productive investment. Sweden recently enacted legislation introducing this additional week of paid holidays.

Internal Tourism

While discussing the tourism phenomenon, the emphasis was only on international tourism, its meaning, components, elements and significance. However, one of the important elements of tourism is the subject of domestic tourism. A distinction is drawn between domestic or internal and foreign or international tourism. In domestic tourism, people travel outside their normal domicile to certain other areas within the country as contrasted with travelling outside the boundaries of the country as in international tourism. The basic difference between domestic and international tourism is that of jurisdiction of travel. The tourist activity of residents of a country within their own country, which does not cross the boundaries of the country, is thus described as internal or domestic tourism. Because the travel takes place within the limits of the boundaries of a country, the various travel formalities which are necessary in international tourism are not observed in domestic tourism. Travel thus is an easy affair. The barriers of currency exchange, language, passport, visa, health documents, etc., are not to be faced by a domestic tourist. A tourist's own language serves as a medium of communication. The currency which they use in their everyday transactions continues to be the medium of exchange.

Presently there exists no generally accepted definition of the term 'domestic tourist'. The domestic tourist is generally regarded as a person travelling for a purpose other than exercising a gainful activity or settling at the place visited. The XXIII General Assembly of IUOTO held in Caracas, Venezuela in October, 1973 recommended that a study should be carried out at the international level with a view to arriving at a standardised definition of domestic tourism. The following definition was put forward by IUOTO in 1974-75. This however was not adopted as an official definition, but merely as a basis for discussion.

For statistical purposes, the term 'domestic tourist' designates any person who travels within the country where he resides to a place other than his usual place of residence for at least twenty four hours or one night, for a purpose other than exercising a gainful activity and which may be classified under one of the following headings:

(i) Leisure (recreation, holiday, health, study, religion and sport).

(ii) Business, family, mission, meeting.

There is not yet any internationally accepted definition of domestic tourism. However, three elements are common to the definition normally in use. These elements are:

(i) Place of residence;

(ii) Geographical setting of travel; and

(iii) Duration of travel. With regard to place of residence most countries regard domestic tourism as travel by a country's residents within that country. The geographical setting is the national territory. Duration of travel is an important element in a number of definitions. The unit most often mentioned is the night spent at an accommodation establishment. By analogy with the accepted definition of 'international tourist', the domestic tourist is one who spends not less than twenty four hours or makes an overnight stay away from his usual residence.

Two further elements are common to most definitions of domestic tourism. These are as follows:

(i) Distance travelled; and

(ii) Travel motivation. With regard to distance travelled, some countries specify a minimum distance in their definitions. The distance may vary between 25 and 100 miles (between 40 and 160 kilometres) approximately. The concept of the travel motivation is considered important by most countries. The domestic tourist is generally considered as a person travelling for a purpose other than exercising a gainful activity at the place visited. Sometimes, domestic tourism is considered as including holiday or leisure travel only.

Developing Manpower

Human Resource Management consist of those activities designed to provide for and coordinate human resource. Their functions include determining the organisation's human resource needs-like recruiting, selecting, developing counselling and rewarding employees. The quality of service delivered depends to a great extent on how effectively human resource is managed and contained. The following matter brings forward the functions which relate HRD to right quality of service to the customers and the organisation and an introduction to 'Total Quality Management' which provides a new look to Resource Management.

The Administration

In The Hospitality Industry : Quality is the one of the most important issues involving hospitality. For it is the quality of the services offered that distinguishes one competitor from the other. Quality, here is more a function of attitude than that of technology. It is the outcome of the resources and activities expanded to deliver a service, which the customer expects from that particular service.

Quality in hospitality can be broken down to technical quality (what is received in service) and functional quality (how the customer receives the service). Technical improvements are possible through altering the machines, installation of computers, automation and imparting technical skills to the employees. The functional quality can be improved by focussing on behaviour areas such as attitudes, service-mindedness, accessibility, interpersonal relations, appearance, commitment etc.

Hence, there is prime importance of Quality Management in the Hospitality industry.

Principal Versus Total in TQM : General perceptions about TQM take two forms. First it is a philosophy of management or a guiding set of principles that allows one to function better. Second, TQM may be believed to be an assortment of sophisticated statistical and measurement tools. Both points of view are partially correct. There are two distinct elements of TQM (1) the principles of TQM and (2) the tools.

The philosophy of TQM allows one to breach the traditional barriers that restrain executives and managers from utilizing the tremendous potential stored in each and everyone of their people.

Following the examples of those who have implemented TQM and succeeded, one can better understand how it is possible. The essence of TQM allows one to set expectations higher than have been done in the past to recognize and remove barriers, to change and to enable high-level managers to solicit the opinion and ideas to their associates and do something with those good ideas. They allow one to measure improved quality along the way towards continuous improvement and recognize them when one achieves the goals of improved productivity, performance efficiency work-life and eventually, improved quality.

Applying these tools to service and administrative processes in hotels allows one to improve the majority of the work process around, every day. One recognizes quality in this new environment, reduced customer complaints. The TQM goals being :

"Get it Right the First Time" : The Albuquerque Marrit a 410 room hotels, earned recognition as the top hotel for guest satisfaction in 1988 and 1989. Nevertheless in 1989 the hotel started a TQM program, shortly after attending a "Quality Fair". A kitchen supervisor Anna Casau, observed that the customary breakfast garnish, a small cherry cobbler with whipped cream, frequently returned to the kitchen untouched.

Anna approached the executive chief, who asked her to track the garnish for one month to determine the cost. Anna did so using TQM tools. The following month, Anna changed the garnish to strawberries with whipped cream and again measured the returns to the kitchen. The amount of uneaten breakfast garnish dropped dramatically-from 70 percent to less than 10 percent. Because of the price of strawberries, the process improvement didn't result in cost savings. But it did reduce waste and increased customer satisfaction-two supremely important factors in the hospitality industry.

Human Resource Management (HRM) consists of those activities designed to provide for and coordinate the human resource of an organisation. Today the role of human resource managers has changed dramatically. Their functions include determining the organisation's human resource needs, recruiting, selecting, developing, counselling and rewarding employees, acting as a liaison with unions and government organisation, and handling other matters of employee well-being. Human resource managers now are taking on a strategic role in their organisations. They are also being required to consider and plan for the development of the organisations corporate culture, as well as day-to day operations involved with maintenance of HRM systems.

An example of the strategic use of HRM can be seen at the Park Royal Hotel, New Delhi. It has identified five critical factors that must be consistently implemented well in order to widen its lead over competitors. One of these is superior service to its customers. The ability to consistently deliver value-added service requires superior performance in the areas :

1. People, recruitment and selection
2. Training
3. Creative use of information technologies
4. Continuing education
5. Accessibility to customers
6. Performance measuring and monitoring
7. Recognition for superior performance
8. Customer satisfaction monitoring

Five of these eight areas for superior performance involve HRM issues. All the right areas are also related to quality issues of excellence in selection and recruitment, internal performance, customer service and continuous improvement.

A Framework of Hrm : Two perspectives of human resource management are-HUMAN RELATIONS AND SYSTEMS.

Human relations includes, individual group behaviour, and organisation development approaches.

Systems include, labour relations which relies on labour laws, public policies,

the economics of wages and costs, demographics and manpower management,

collective administration and grievances to explain management-worker interaction; and personnel management which includes activities involved in managing large numbers of people in the aggregate, including recruiting, selecting, training, compensating and development.

Human Resource Management in a TQM Environment : The Total Quality Management focus is changing the rule of Human Resource Management by changing the perspectives of employees, HRM professionals and line and staff managers from an adversial, control-oriented relationship to a cooperative position based on mutual organisational and individual goods, trust and respect. Human Resource Manager tend to reflect the culture within which they are working, as well as influence it. Thus, values can and do play a key role in determining how HRM function is carried out. Two typical philosophical position that seem to capture the managerial and HRM assumption that affect the development of TQM within organizations can be seen in the figure on the following page.

Characteristics of Philosophical Positions

	TQM/HRM Approach	*Traditional HRM*
Philosophy	Shared responsibility Commitment, rewards	Fair day's work for a fair day's pay.
Business Objectives profitability,	Increased quality, productivity, customer	Increased productivity,
	satisfaction and loyalty	quality in secondary, focus on labours.
Quality Objectives	TQM and continuous improvement at and across every level	Adequate-quality to remain in business; staff-driven approaches to quality improvement.
Business on Information job Sharing	Open books Share board information on perfects, productivity quality costs, capital spending plans.	Limited to information an as-needed basis for performance.
Major Constituencies Employee Involvement	Customers, all employees, stock holders Extensive, within and between levels and functions way of life. usually no formal system.	Managers, stockholders, customers, employees Programs, suggestions plans, individual employee awards,
Education and Training	Quality and economic education, multiple skill and group process	On the job-training. Feedback training, problem-solving
Reward Structure	Designed and adjusted by management-employee committee, formal, early union involvement	Management designed and administered.
Job Formal Commitment, Security	A key consideration in all decisions	Labour as a variable cost, lay off common.

Current Status of Tourism

The tourism industry is currently highly fragmented, with many different participants, ranging from one-person operations selling home-made souvenirs or offering guided tours, to large multi-billion dollar airlines. Thus although establishing an airline requires substantial capital, entering the tourism business can be as easy as renting out a spare room to travellers or guiding visitors around for a small fee. The low barriers to entry, and its labour intensity make this industry attractive to governments and development agencies alike.

Several trends in tourism can be discerned, as outlined below.

" Continued growth of tourism. It is estimated that throughout the 1990s the average annual arrivals growth rate will be around 7% (when compared with that of the 1950-1989 period) (WTO, 1990). Total international tourist arrivals of 515 and 637 million are forecast for 1995 and 2000, respectively. Global receipts from international tourism are expected to rise by almost 9% a year, and to exceed US$527 billion in the year 2000. Domestic tourism will also rise dramatically. It is anticipated that it will account for US$2,195 billion by 1997 (WTO 1991).

This growth in both domestic and international tourism is determined by market forces and exogenous variables (that is, factors not directly related to tourism but which influence the extent and form of tourist activity). Exogenous variables that influence tourism growth include:

- demographic and social change (aging of the population, increase in the number of working women and dual-income households, growing proportion of single adults, trend towards later marriage)
- relaxation of immigration restrictions
- increased paid leave and more flexible working time
- earlier retirement
- improved educational levels and increased awareness of travel possibilities
- economic and financial developments (growth of GNP, travel cost increases remaining consistently below inflation)

- political, legislative and regulatory changes (political changes in Eastern Europe, liberalization of air travel, reduced visa requirements)
- technological developments (in aeronautical engineering, electronic data systems for booking)
- enlarged transport infrastructure
- improved travel safety
- political instability
- international currency fluctuations.
- Higher-than-average growth in numbers of international arrivals in Asia/Oceania, the Americas and Africa. This growth will be at the expense of Europe, whose share is expected to fall from 62% of international arrivals in 1989, to 53% by the year 2000. Asia/Oceania will probably receive more international arrivals than any other region. Their share of international tourist arrivals is expected to rise from 14.7% in 1989 to 21.9% in 2000. (Their increase in receipts will probably be even more marked - from 19.5% to 30.5%). But for the African region, although the share of arrivals is expected to increase from 3.8% to 5%, it is predicted that its share of global tourist receipts will fall from 3.2% to 2.7% (WTO, 1990).
- Diversification of tourism. Tourists will become increasingly specialized, as is indicated by the Specialty Travel Index. This directory of special interest travel published periodically by the American Society of Travel Agents, Inc. (ASTA), listed a total of 236 activity categories in its September 1992 issue, illustrating the exceedingly broad range of activities undertaken by tourists.
- Increased interest in travelling to more natural settings and less disturbed areas as a result of increased interest worldwide in environmental matters and nature. For this reason, Europe - with its predominantly post-industrial landscape - is becoming proportionately less significant as a tourist destination. Conversely, areas such as Southeast Asia and tropical America that still contain large tracts of

virgin land and wilderness, are becoming more popular. Visits (both domestic and foreign) to national parks are generally on the increase around the world. Hopefully, this enthusiasm for the preservation of the environment will alsc nourish improved tourist behaviour in natural areas. At any rate, protected areas managers will have to prepare themselves to receive growing numbers of visitors.

- Increased interest in "activity" holidays. The beach holiday shows no sign of losing popularity, but the old-style passive beach holiday appears to be going out of fashion. The beach is no longer merely a place to lie in the sun, but it and the surrounding sea are seen rather as a kind of outdoor gymnasium for surfing, windsurfing, canoeing, paragliding, sailing, snorkelling, scuba diving, and so on. Mountaineering, backpacking, bike travel, birdwatching, white-water raftings and so on, are also attracting more and more participants.
- Increased interest in developed countries in "exotic" cultures and locations as a result of TV documentaries, books and magazines. This trend is also being stimulated by the growing interest in learning foreign languages.

3

Moving Towards Sustainable Tourism

Sustainable tourism is an industry committed to making a low impact on the environment and local culture, while helping to generate future employment for local people. The aim of sustainable tourism is to ensure that development brings a positive experience for the local people, tourism companies and the tourists themselves, but sustainable tourism is not the same as ecotourism. Sustainable tourism is tourism development that avoids damage to the environment, economy and cultures of the locations where it takes place. The aim of sustainable tourism is to ensure that development is a positive experience for local people; tourism companies; and tourists themselves. Under sustainable tourism, it may be unlikely to experience the kind of 'boom and bust' that led to the rapid growth, and then despoliation of locations such as the east coast of Spain in the 1970s.

But despite this optimistic objective, sustainable tourism is still not widely understood. For a start, 'sustainable tourism' is not necessarily 'ecotourism'. Ecotourism became popular in the 1980s as a form of tourism that focused exclusively on wildlife, nature, or exotic cultures. Recent research, however, has indicated that such tourism may not actually be good for environment, or for the people who experience this attention. Safaris in Kenya, for example, are undoubtedly 'ecotourism'.

But Kenya is full of cases where lions have been forced into erratic behaviour because of excessive tourists, or where the local Masai people have failed to benefit from this kind of development. More importantly, 'ecotourism' does not involve more mainstream beach-or city-based tourism, where impacts are much greater than any nature-based tourism. Sustainable tourism, therefore, is an attempt to improve the impacts of all types of tourism, and this implies seeking ways to build partnerships between tourism companies and local governments or managers of resorts.

But how can sustainable tourism be achieved? Evidence suggests that it requires co-operation between concerned companies and the managers of destinations. It does not, however, require a marked interest from consumers. Some companies have suggested that they will only take steps to achieve sustainable tourism if they recognize a clear 'market demand' for holidays that are overtly 'green' or 'environmentally friendly'. Research, however, has indicated that few tourists want holidays that are 'green' within the mass tourism market; and that holidays that are 'green' may repeat the pitfalls of ecotourism. It may not be profitable or sustainable to encourage market demand for 'green' tourism as this demand may not occur, and also may not lead to sustainable tourism.

Instead, evidence has suggested that sustainable tourism does not have to be advertised as environmentally or culturally sensitive in order to succeed. Research has indicated that profits may be increased simply by adopting some general environmental principles, such as recycling waste, planning for long-term sustainability, and seeking local partnerships for resort management. If these actions result in cleaner, less crowded, holiday resorts, then they are in effect sustainable tourism without being labelled so.

But how can companies and resort managers achieve this kind of success? This question is more controversial. One proposal has been to increase the vertical integration of tourism companies, so that individual companies have greater control over the marketing of holidays, transportation of tourists, and then management of resorts. Such integration may help avoid the disappointment and despoliation of resorts that occurs when tourists interested in conventional mass tourism are sent to sites perhaps better suited to bird watchers or hill walkers, as has occurred in Corfu. But this suggestion, however, is occasionally opposed as it may imply that smaller tourism companies cannot enter the market. Furthermore, reducing competition from smaller companies may result in reducing the pressure for lower prices of holidays. Since the 1980s, the British tourism industry has experienced rapid cuts in prices as a result of deep competition between major companies such as Airtours, First Choice, and Thompson. But it is generally the presence of competition from smaller, less regulated, companies that leads to the rapid over-development of resorts, or the reluctance of large companies to increase their costs by attending to the long-term sustainability of locations.

The achievement of sustainable tourism, therefore depends in part on providing the right incentives for companies and resort managers to reduce the negative impacts of tourism, and then a variety of local practical steps (such as limiting numbers, or zoning land use) to reduce these impacts. But in the long term, the ultimate achievement of sustainable tourism also requires tourists and companies to think more about how tourism may impact on other people's homes and livelihoods. Marcel Proust once wrote that most tourists seem to want to travel through one hundred countries with one pair of eyes, whereas the best journey would be to travel through one country with a hundred pair of eyes. By seeking more diversity and depth in holiday destinations, tourists may help avoid the impacts of tourism on destinations, and also achieve a more satisfying experience.

Sustainable tourism is a kind of approach to tourism meant to make the development of tourism ecologically supportable in the long term. The very importance of sustainable tourism lies in its motives to conserve the resources and increase the value of local culture and tradition. Sustainable tourism is a responsible tourism intending to generate employment and income along with alleviating any deeper impact on environment and local culture.

Characteristics of Sustainable Tourism

- Sustainable Tourism tries its utmost to maintain the importance of local culture and tradition.
- Sustainable Tourism is informatory, as it doesn't only let tourist know about the destinations but also it helps locals knowing about the culture and civilisation of tourists.
- This kind of tourism is aimed to conserve the resources of destinations where one is visiting to.
- Sustainable Tourism seeks deeper involvement of locals, which provide local people an opportunity and make their living. Above all, Sustainable Tourism stresses pointedly upon integrity of the tourist places.

Principles of Sustainable Tourism

With the increased footfalls of tourists, the deep need today is that tourism like other sector be planned and managed suitably. Sustainable development of tourism is possible only if its follows some of its guidelines and principles.

- Tourism ought to be initiated at any location with the help of local community. The involvement of local community helps maintaining the appropriate tourism development.
- The local community has to meet the direct benefit of flourishing tourism in their area. Link between local business and tourism enable local people gain economically as well.
- To cause large growth in sustainable development, there is need that codes, ethics and some fair guidelines be appointed.
- In order to heighten the importance of heritage and natural resources, and manage them better, training and education programme should be instituted.

Relationship Between Ecotourism and Sustainable Tourism

Ecotourism basically deals with nature based tourism, and is aimed "to conserve the environment and improves the well-being of local people". On the other hand, sustainable tourism includes all segments of tourism, and has same function to perform as of ecotourism - to conserve the resources and increase the local cultural and traditional value. Though the goals of ecotourism and sustainable tourism is much similar, but the latter is broader and conceals within itself very many aspects and categories of tourism.

Responsible Tourism

Responsible Tourism can be regarded as a behaviour. It is more than a form of tourism as it represents an approach to engaging with tourism, be that as a tourist, a business, locals at a destination or any other tourism stakeholder. It emphasises that all stakeholders are responsible for the kind of tourism they develop or engage in. Whilst different groups will see responsibility in different ways, the shared understanding is that responsible tourism should entail an improvement in tourism. Tourism should become 'better' as a result of the responsible tourism approach.

Within the notion of betterment resides the acknowledgement that conflicting interests need to be balanced. However, the objective is to create better places for people to live in and to visit. Importantly, there is no blueprint for responsible tourism: what is deemed responsible may differ depending on places and cultures. Responsible Tourism is an aspiration that can be realised in different ways in different originating markets and in the diverse destinations of the world (Goodwin, 2002).

Focusing in particular on businesses, according to the Cape Town Declaration on Responsible Tourism, it will have the following characteristics:

- minimises negative economic, environmental, and social impacts
- generates greater economic benefits for local people and enhances the well-being of host communities, improves working conditions and access to the industry

- involves local people in decisions that affect their lives and life chances
- makes positive contributions to the conservation of natural and cultural heritage, to the maintenance of the world's diversity
- provides more enjoyable experiences for tourists through more meaningful connections with local people, and a greater understanding of local cultural, social and environmental issues
- provides access for physically challenged people and
- is culturally sensitive, engenders respect between tourists and hosts, and builds local pride and confidence.

Sustainable tourism is where tourists can enjoy their holiday and at the same time respect the culture of people and also respect the environment. It also means that local people (such as the Masaai) get a fair say about tourism and also receive some money from the profit which the game reserve make. The environment is being damaged quite a lot by tourists and part of Sustainable tourism is to make sure that the damaging does not carry on.

There are many private companies who are working into embracing the principles and aspects of Responsible Tourism, some for the purpose of Corporate Social Responsibility activities, and others such WorldHotel-Link, which was originally a project of the International Finance Corporation, have built their entire business model around responsible tourism, local capacity building and increasing market access for small and medium tourism enterprises.

Responsible Hospitality

As with the view of Responsible Tourism, Responsible Hospitality is essentially about creating better places for people to live in, and better places for people to visit. This does not mean all forms of hospitality are also forms of tourism although hospitality is the largest sector of the tourism industry. As such we should not be surprised at overlaps between Responsible

Hospitality and Responsible Tourism. In the instance where place of permanent residence is also the place where the hospitality service is consumed, if for example a meal is consumed in a local restaurant, this does not obviate the requirement to improve the place of residence. As such, the essence of Responsible Hospitality is not contingent upon touristic forms of hospitality.

While Friedman (1962) famously argued that, admittedly within legal parameters, the sole responsibility of business was to generate profit for shareholders the idea that businesses' responsibility extends beyond this has existed for decades and is most frequently encountered in the concept of corporate social responsibility (Carroll, 1999). There are numerous ways businesses can and do engage in activities that are not intended to benefit shareholders and management, at least not in the short term. However, often acts of corporate social responsibility are undertaken because of the perceived benefit to business. Usually in hospitality this relates to the cost reductions associated with improved energy efficiency (Pizam, 2009) but may also relate to, for example, the rise in ethical consumerism and the view that being seen to be a responsible business is beneficial to revenue growth.

As per the Cape Town Declaration on Responsible Tourism (see www.icrtourism.org), Responsible Hospitality is culturally sensitive. Instead of then calling for the unachievable, Responsible Hospitality simply makes the case for more responsible forms of hospitality, hospitality that benefits locals first, and visitors second. Certainly, all forms of hospitality can be improved and managed so that negative impacts are minimised whilst striving for a maximisation of positive impacts.

Carroll, A. (1999). Corporate Social Responsibility. Business & Society, 38(3), 268-295.

Friedman, M. (1962). Capitalism and Freedom. Chicago: University of Chicago Press.

Pizam, A. (2009). Editorial: Green hotels: A fad, ploy or fact of life? International Journal of Hospitality Management, 28(1), 1.

Coastal Tourism

Many coastal areas are experiencing particular pressure from growth in lifestyles and growing numbers of tourists. Coastal environments are limited in extent consisting of only a narrow strip along the edge of the ocean. Coastal areas are often the first environments to experience the detrimental impacts of tourism. A detailed study of the impact on coastal areas, with reference to western India can be an example.

The inevitable change is on the horizon as holiday destinations put more effort into sustainable tourism. Planning and management controls can reduce the impact on coastal environments and ensure that investment into tourism products supports sustainable coastal tourism.

Some Conceptual Models in Coastal Tourism

Some of the recent studies have led to some interesting conceptual models applicable for coastal tourism. The 'inverted funnel model' and the 'embedded model' can be good metaphors for understanding the interplay of different stake-holders like government, local community, tourists and business community in developing tourist destinations.

Community-based Management

There has been the promotion of sustainable tourism practices surrounding the management of tourist locations by locals or more concisely, the community.

This form of tourism is based on the premise that the people living next to a resource are the ones best suited to protecting it. This means that the tourism activities and businesses are developed and operated by local community members, and certainly with their consent and support.

Sustainable tourism typically involves the conservation of resources that are capitalized upon for tourism purposes, such as coral reefs and pristine forests. Locals run the businesses and are responsible for promoting the conservation messages to protect their environment.

Community-based sustainable tourism (CBST) associates the success of the sustainability of the ecotourism location to the management practices of the communities who are directly or indirectly dependent on the location for their livelihoods.

A salient feature of CBST is that local knowledge is usually utilised alongside wide general frameworks of ecotourism business models. This allows the participation of locals at the management level and typically allows a more intimate understanding of the environment. The use of local knowledge also means an easier entry level into a tourism industry for locals whose jobs or livelihoods are affected by the use of their environment as tourism locations. The involvement of locals restores the ownership of the environment to the local community and allows an alternative sustainable form of development for communities and their environments that are typically unable to support other forms of development.. However, recent research has found that economic linkages generated by CBST may only be sporadic, and that the linkages with agriculture are negatively affected by seasonality and by the small scale of the cultivated areas. This means that CBST may only have small-scale positive effects for these communities .

Stakeholders

Stakeholders of sustainable tourism play a role in continuing this form of tourism. This can include organizations as well as individuals.

Non-governmental Organizations

Non-governmental organizations are one of the stakeholders in advocating sustainable tourism. Their roles can range from spearheading sustainable tourism practices to simply doing research. University research teams and scientists can be tapped to aid in the process of planning. Such solicitation of research can be observed in the planning of Cat Ba National Park in Vietnam.

Dive resort operators in Bunaken National Park, Indonesia, play a crucial role but developing exclusive zones for diving and fishing respectively, such that both tourists and locals can benefit from the venture

Large conventions, meetings and other major organized events drive the travel, tourism and hospitality industry. Cities and convention centers compete to attract such commerce, commerce which has heavy impacts on resource use and the environment. Major sporting events, such as the Olympic Games, present special problems regarding environmental burdens and degradation. But burdens imposed by the regular convention industry can be vastly more significant.

Green conventions and events are a new but growing sector and marketing point within the convention and hospitality industry. More environmentally aware organizations, corporations and government agencies are now seeking more sustainable event practices, greener hotels, restaurants and convention venues, and more energy efficient or climate neutral travel and ground transportation.

Additionally, some convention centers have begun to take direct action in reducing the impact of the conventions they host. One example is the Moscone Center in San Francisco, California, which has a very aggressive recycling program, a large solar power system, and other programs aimed at reducing impact and increasing efficiency.

Tourists

With the advent of the internet, some traditional conventions are being replaced with virtual conventions, where the attendees remain in their home physical location and "attend" the convention by use of a web-based interface programmed for the task. This sort of "virtual" meeting eliminates all of the impacts associated with travel, accommodation, food wastage, and other necessary impacts of traditional, physical conventions.

Travel over long distances requires a large amount of time and/or energy. Generally this involves burning fossil fuels, a largely unsustainable practice and one that contributes to climate change, via CO2 emissions.

Air travel is perhaps the worst offender in this regard, contributing to between 2 and 3% of global carbon emissions . Given a business-as-usual approach, this could be expected to rise to 5% by 2015 and 10% by 2050. Car travel is the next worst offender.

Mass transport is the most climate friendly method of travel, and generally the rule is "the bigger the better" - compared to cars, buses are relatively more sustainable, and trains and ships are even more so. Human energy and renewable energy are the most efficient, and hence, sustainable. Travel by bicycle, solar powered car, or sailing boat produces no carbon emissions (although the embodied energy in these vehicles generally comes at the expense of carbon emission).

HUMANE TOURISM

Humane tourism is part of the movement of responsible tourism. The idea is to empower local communities through travel related businesses around the world, first and foremost in developing countries. The idea of humane travel or humane tourism is to connect travelers from Europe, North America, Australia and New Zealand seeking new adventures and authentic experiences directly, to local businesses in the specific locations they wish to visit - thus, giving economic advantages to local businesses and giving travelers authentic and truly unique travel experiences. Humane travel or humane tourism focuses on the people, the local community. The idea is to enable travelers to experience the world through the eyes of its local people while contributing directly to those people, ensuring that tourist dollars benefit the local community directly.

Humane tourism is about giving opportunity to the local people, empower them, enable them to enjoy the fruits of tourism directly. The Internet is changing tourism. More and more travelers are planning their travels and vacations via the net. The Internet enables people to cut off commissions. The traveler can search for new destinations to visit, talk or read about other people experience, and buy the services directly. The Internet platform can encourage local people to start new businesses and that already existing small businesses will begin to promote themselves through the net and receive the economic advantages of this directly in their communities. The world is now in a new tourism age, with globalization and the Internet playing a key role.

The new travelers have traveled the world, they have seen the classic sites. Staying at a Western hotel is not attractive enough, and they are excited by the prospect of experiencing the authentic local way of life: to go fishing with a local fisherman, to eat the fish with his family, to sleep in a typical village house. These tourists or travellers, are happy to know that while doing so they promote the economic wellbeing of those same people they spend time with.

Humane tourism is part of Responsible tourism. The concept of Responsible Tourism originated in the work of Jost Krippendorf in The Holiday Makers (1987) called for "rebellious tourists and rebellious locals" to create new forms of tourism. His vision was "to develop and promote new forms of tourism, which will bring the greatest possible benefit to all the participants - travellers, the host population and the tourist business, without causing intolerable ecological and social damage." As one can see he already talked, back in the 80s about benefits for the host population and used the term human tourism. Humane travel focuses on that host local population.

The South African national tourism policy (1996) used the term "responsible tourism" and mentioned the wellbeing of the local community as a main factor.

The Cape Town Declaration on Responsible Tourism in Destinations, agreed in 2002, that Responsible Tourism is about "making better places for people to live in and better places for people to visit." The decleration focused on "places" but did nention the local population.

From the Rio summit or earth summit on 1992 until the UN Commission on Sustainable Development in 1999, the main focus of the tourism industry was the earth, the planet, the places, "green" or "eco" tourism. Now there is a trend to include the local population. This trend or branch of responsible tourism is called humane tourism or humane travel.

SUSTAINABLE TOURISM CRC

Sustainable Tourism Cooperative Research Centre (STCRC), headquartered in Gold Coast, Queensland, was an Australian Cooperative Research Centre established by the Australian Government's Cooperative Research Centres Program to establish a competitive and dynamic sustainable tourism industry in Australia. It ceased to operate on 30 June 2010. STCRC is a not-for-profit company owned by its industry, government and university partners. STCRC stands as the world's largest travel and tourism research centre.

History

STCRC was established under the Australian Government's Cooperative Research Centres Program to underpin the development of a dynamic, internationally competitive, and sustainable tourism industry. Since its inception the STCRC has supported over 170 PhD scholars through a suite of scholarships and the provision of a Career Development Program. STCRC currently supports over 90 postgraduate students. All are of exceptional academic standard. Most hold a first class honours degree and many have also received university awards for excellence. All supplementary scholarship holders also hold an APA or university-equivalent scholarship.

Organisational Aims

STCRC's aims are the development and management of intellectual property (IP) to deliver innovation to business, community, and government enhancing environmental, economic and social sustainability of tourism - one of the world's largest, fastest growing industries.

In doing so, STCRC aims to develop Australia's long-term tourism research capactities through a vigorous postgraduate research education programme. Presently this programme has produced a number of PhD students and the program is supported by scholarships for students in industry-designed projects, and by developing and distributing education and training products.

Commercialisation Unit

The Commercialisation of STCRC research, sustainability oriented technologies and certification programs is done through EC3 Global which is wholly owned by the STCRC. EC3 Global provides an array of programs and services for companies, communities and other interest groups to set and achieve sustainability targets. With origins leading back to 1987, EC3's research encompasses 250 tourism and environmental sustainability leaders in 16 universities . EC3's influence has grown to encompass hundreds of projects, creating a strong market presence in over 50 countries.

Presently EC3 Global commercialises four main products, Decipher, Earthcheck, IPAT and Green Globe.

University Partners

There are currently 16 Australian universities who are partners with the STCRC, these are listed below.

Charles Darwin University

Charles Darwin University was formed in 2003, with over 50 years history delivering tertiary education to the Northern Territory. Charles Darwin's Main Campus is located in Darwin, Australia and is named after Charles Darwin, the English Naturalist

Formed in 2003 through a merger between the Northern Territory University, Alice Springs-based Centralian College, NT Rural College in Katherine and the Menzies School of Health Research. Charles Darwin University is the largest university in the Northern Territory.

Curtin University of Technology

Curtin University of Technology formed in 1986 is Western Australia's Largest University with over 40,000 students presently. Curtin University has a strong emphasis on innovation and technology, which are the main themes of the university.

Curtin University has an important Research & Development history , with an annual income from research of around $12 Million Australian Dollars annually.

Edith Cowan University

Edith Cowan University is the second largest university in Western Australia and has approximately 23,000 students of which over 3,000 originate from countries outside Australia. It was established in 1991, and is the only Australian university named after a woman, Edith Dircksey Cowan.

The university specialises in the service professions, and the teaching of education remains a key focus. Joint research and study with other universities and international consultancies remains an important area for the university.

Griffith University

Griffith University is an Australian public university with five campuses in Queensland between Brisbane and the Gold Coast. As of 2008, there were more than 37,000 enrolled students and 3,500 staff. As such, Griffith stands as one of Queensland's largest universitis and holds Queensland's oldest academy.

Griffith has diverse multidisciplinary teaching and research fields, and has students and academic staff from over 120 countries throughout the world.

James Cook University

James Cook University is a public university based in Townsville, Queensland, Australia and was proclaimed on 20 April 1970 in Townsville. James Cook University is the second oldest university in Queensland. James Cook University is listed as one of the best universities in Queensland and is one of only 17 in Australia that was listed in the ARWU top 500 academic world universities in 2007..

The main fields of research include marine sciences, biodiversity, sustainable management of tropical ecosystems, tropical health care and tourism. James Cook University receives over $23 Million dollars in research funding annually, highlighting the importance of its ongoing research projects .

La Trobe University

La Trobe University is a multi-campus university in Victoria, Australia. La Trobe is generally considered to be ranked amongst the top ten universities in Australia and in 2005 was ranked in the top 100 universities in the world.

Presently La Trobe university has over 28,000 enrolled students and has become a well established centre for teaching, training, scholarship and research.

Monash University

Monash University is a public university with campuses located in Australia, Malaysia and South Africa. It is Australia's largest university with about 55,000 students. Monash consistently ranks amongst the top universities in Australia and the world..

The University has a total of eight campuses, and also a centre in Prato, Italy. This makes it by far Australia's most internationalised university. Indeed, it is arguable that Monash has the greatest international presence of any research-intensive university in the world.. It was recently ranked by The Times Higher Education Supplement (THES) at number 43 in its annual ranking of the world's top 200 universities for 2007.

Murdoch University

Murdoch University is located in Perth, Western Australia and has three campuses at Murdoch, Rockingham and Peel. It currently has a student population of over 15,000 students including 3,000 international students. Murdoch is a modern

Australian university with a national reputation for excellence in teaching and research.

Southern Cross University

Southern Cross University (SCU)' is a university based on the Mid North and North coast of New South Wales, Australia. It is a regional University with more than 14,000 students. The University is the country's seventh largest provider of distance education. It also has international students from more than 50 countries. More than 700 students are enrolled on-campus and with on-shore partners in Australia, with a further 1300 enrolled in overseas programs.

The University is renowned for its tourism studies, especially in the local Northern Rivers area.

University of New South Wales

University of New South Wales (UNSW) is one of Australia's largest and most prestigious research institutions, the UNSW has over 40,000 students including 8,800 international students from 90 different countries.

It is a member of Australia's "Group of Eight" lobby group, and is also a founding member of Universitas 21, an international network of leading research-intensive universities. UNSW ranks third for both total funds allocated and the number of grants from the Australian Research Council among Australian universities following University of Sydney and Australian National University, by securing more than $26 million in Discovery Project grants. The University also gains the highest number of Linkage Project grants of any university.

University of Canberra

The University of Canberra is an Australian university, located in Canberra, the capital of Australia. It is the second largest university in Canberra. The University was one of nine Australian universities recognised by the Australian government in 2006 for high achievement in learning and teaching.. In a 2005 ranking of the international standing of

Australian universities, University of Canberra received 44% and ranked approximately two-thirds down the list of Australian universities. Presently it has over 10,000 students, from over 80 different countries and more than 1,000 staff.

University of Queensland

The University of Queensland is Queensland's first university, being founded in 1909. Presently it has over 37,000 enrolled students . The University of Queensland also prides itself on being one of Australia's foremest research institutions, the University is a founding member of the Group of Eight, an alliance of research-strong "sandstone" universities in Australia.

UQ remains the most successful Australian university in winning and being shortlisted for Australian Awards for University Teaching since they were established in 1997. On a variety of measures it is one of the top three or four research universities in the country.

University of South Australia

The University of South Australia is a public university in the Australian state of South Australia. It was formed in 1991 with the merger of the South Australian Institute of Technology and Colleges of Advanced Education. The university is a leading expert in technical education and applied research, as well being a founding member of the Australian Technology Network.

University of South Australia is ranked as the 291st university in the 2007 Times Higher Education Supplement Top 400 Universities list. The University has nearly 32,000 enrolled students as of 2008.

University of Tasmania

The University of Tasmania is an Australian university, with three campuses in Tasmania. A 'sandstone university', it is the fourth-oldest university in Australia, and was established over a century ago. It was founded on 1 January 1890, and is a member of the international Association of Commonwealth

Universities. The university works with overseas universities to offer students an international experience, with exchange arrangements in place with over 40 institutions throughout Europe, Asia and North America.

The university has a particularly notable and long-standing reputation in examining the practical and theoretical challenges involved in addressing social and environmental concerns.

University of Technology, Sydney

The University of Technology, Sydney (UTS) is part of the Australian Technology Network of universities, and is the third largest university in Sydney in terms of enrolment. Founded in its current form in 1988, it is also the only university with its main campuses within the Sydney CBD. UTS has been ranked in the World's Top 100 universities by the Times Higher Education Supplement and was given A1 ratings across all major disciplines in 2007 by the Federal Government Education department.

Victoria University

The Victoria University is a University in Melbourne, Victoria. The University offers both Higher Education and Technical and Further Education (TAFE) courses. Presently there are over 45,000 enrolled students, including over 8,500 international students. Founded in 1916, it is one of Australia's older universities, with a rich history and many successful students.

4

Moving Towards The Wildlife Tourism

Wildlife tourism can be an eco and animal friendly tourism, usually showing animals in their natural habitat. Wildlife tourism, in its simplest sense, is watching wild animals in their natural habitat. Wildlife tourism is an important part of the tourism industries in many countries including many African and South American countries, Australia, India, Canada, Indonesia, Malaysia and Maldives among many. It has experienced a dramatic and rapid growth in recent years world wide and is closely aligned to eco-tourism and sustainable-tourism. Wildlife tourism is also a multi-million dollar industry offering customized tour packages and safaris.

Negative Impacts of Wildlife Tourism

Wildlife tourism can cause significant disturbances to animals in their natural habitats. The growing interest in traveling to developing countries has created a boom in resort and hotel construction, particularly on rain forest and mangrove forest lands. Wildlife viewing can scare away animals, disrupt their feeding and nesting sites, or acclimate them to the presence of people. In Kenya, for example, wildlife-observer disruption drives cheetahs off their reserves, increasing the risk of inbreeding and further endangering the species.

Direct Impacts

The effect that wildlife tourism will have on wildlife depend on the scale of tourist development and the behavior and resilience of wildlife to the presence of humans. When tourists activities occur during sensitive times of the life cycle, and when they involve close approaches to wildlife for the purpose of identification or photography, the potential for disturbance is high. Not all species appear to be disturbed by tourists even within heavily visited areas.

Disturbing Breeding Patterns

The pressures of tourists searching out wildlife to photograph or hunt can adversely affect hunting and feeding patterns, and the breeding success of some species. Some may even have long-term implications for behavioral and ecological relationships. For example, an increase in boat traffic has disturbed the feeding of giant otters in Manu National Park, Peru. Further disturbance to wildlife occurs when tourist guides dig up turtle nests and chase swimming jaguars, tapirs and otters to give clients better viewing opportunities. On the shores of Lake Kariba in Zimbabwe, the number of tourist boats and the noise generated as disrupted the feeding and drinking patterns of elephants and the black rhinoceros - it is feared that further increases in boat traffic will affect their reproductive success.

Disturbing Feeding Patterns

Feeding of wildlife by tourists can have severe consequences for social behavior patterns. Artificial feeding by tourists caused a breakdown of the territorial breeding system of land iguanas on the South Plaza in the Galapogos Islands. Territories were abandoned in favor of sites where food could be begged from tourists, and this has had a negative effect on the breeding success of iguanas. Artificial feeding can also result in a complete loss of normal feeding behaviors. In the Galapagos Islands, overfeeding by tourists was so extreme that, when stopped, some animals were unable to locate their natural food sources. Similarly, until the early 1970s, the diet of some Grizzly bears in Yellow Stone National Park (USA) consisted, to a large extent, of food wastes left by visitors at park refuse sites. When these sites were closed, the beats showed significant decreases in body size, reproductive rate and litter size.

Disruption of Parent-offspring Bonds

Wildlife tourism can also cause disruption to intra-specific relationships. Attendance by female harp seals to their pups declined when tourists were present in Canada's Gulf of St Lawrence, and those females remaining with their pups spent significantly less time nursing and more time watching the tourists. There is also a risk of the young not being recognized, and being more exposed to predator attacks. A similar concern has been expressed over whale watching, whale calves normally maintain constant body contact with their mothers but, when separated, can transfer their attachment to the side of the boat.

Increased Vulnerability to Predators and Competitors

The viewing of certain species by wildlife tourists can make that species more vulnerable to predators. Evidence of this phenomenon has been recorded in birds, reptiles and mammals. Problems have occurred in breeding colonies of brown pelicans visited by tourists in Mexico. Breeding success decreased by 52-100% in visited sites compared to unvisited sites.

Safari into the Wild Life World and Tourism

Aboard this jeep for a sneak peek safari, courtesy the binoculars of Wild Life World 360 that takes you to jungles far and wide. This portal, just as it sounds, provides you a 360 degree view into the life of the wild world which is gradually facing the disruptions caused by human intrusion.

Read up further to ride on a quick round of wildlife tourism and also get faced with the importance of, what your bit is towards the conservation and protection of the wild life world. The depletion of natural resources interfering with the habitat of animals certainly is a topic needing much attention.

Sensibility with Sensitivity is our mantra! And you're truly gonna be up for it after a tete-a-tete with the animal kingdom! So, what are you still waiting for? Camouflage with Wild Life World 360 on an adventure spree into the unbeated woods before to mark on a round wildlife tourism!

Jaguarundi Facts

Also known as jaguar, Jaguarundi is an American mammal, which is the regarded as the largest feline cat in this continent. We all have heard about the jaguars while exploring the Mayan ruins indicating that this animal was once worshipped as god. Even today, this belief is somewhat indicated by the fact that Jaguarundi is the symbol of strength, power, and splendor. In fact, the name 'Jaguar' is derived from a term of Native American language, which stands for 'the killer that holds the victim in just one jump' directly revealing much about its power and strength.

- Scientifically known as the Panther Onca, this feline animal belongs to the Panthera genus. If you are looking at it for the first time, you will feel as if it is a leopard. However, for a clear cut distinction, look for the rosette shaped prints that are completely different from those seen on a leopard. Are you interested in knowing more about the Jaguarundi? I am sure that you will be as this is the mammal of historic, religious, and cultural importance since times immemorial.

Argali Facts

Considered as the largest of the wild sheep, Argali is the mammal of the Central Asia highlands. Its look is somewhat similar to the zodiac sun sign of Aries. The term 'Argali' is derived from the Mongolian name that means 'ram'. Coming to its physical description, Argali is a multi-color sheep whose shades range from buff to grey-brown including the in-between white seen especially in the older sheep. These sheep are extensively hunted for their highly priced horns as well as meat both of which play a role in making the traditional Chinese medicine. However, the horns are also used in producing trophies. This is one of the responsible Argali facts that have posed a serious threat to these sheep irrespective of their range. In fact, a few of their subspecies are totally on the verge of extinction making the situation worse for them. Perhaps one more reason behind their extinction is the fact of bringing more and more land under cultivation along with extensive loss of their habitats. Listed below are some more Argali facts.

Siberian Tiger Facts

Also known as Amur, a Siberian tiger refers to the giant carnivores that mostly tend to survive in the coldest regions of our planet. It is certainly the largest cat in the world, but is sadly today among the endangered animals. Currently, these superb tigers are seen typically in southeastern Russia, especially in Siberia; which says much about their origins. Although they were seen in plenty in Korea, Mongolia, as well as China; illegal poaching has reduced their numbers here. Across the world, it is now accepted that some 350 to 400 tigers only survive in the forests and other 500 in the zoos. In order to save them, efforts have been made due to which now they are heavily safeguarded in wild, but a majority of them are now in zoos. These were some vital Siberian Tiger facts regarding their current situation. Now, I will disclose a few interesting facts of these mammoth tigers!

Mountain Lion Facts

Also called cougars, the Mountain Lions are American wild cats seen extensively in the Western hemisphere and called by separate names in different areas. With its 40 names, one of the most interesting Mountain Lion facts is that this cat's name is recorded in the Guinness World Record as the only mammal having maximum different names. Some of these include - puma, panther, silver lion, deer cat, Mexican lion, king cat, mountain devil, red tiger, and so on.

Despite the fact that 'big cats' are referred to the large looking wild cats such as leopard and jaguar; mountain lions, just due to their size, still belong to this category. After lion, tiger, and jaguar; mountain lions rank fourth along with leopard in the list of heaviest wild cat on this planet. However, only in the context of America, such lions rank second after jaguar.

Sagarmatha National Park, Nepal

Regarded as the world's highest national park, the Sagarmatha National Park is the home of the highest point on Earth called Mount Everest that itself is known as 'Sagarmatha = Sky for Sagar and head for Matha'. Therefore, it is obvious that this park is perched as high as on 3000 meters whose most of the landscape is a rocky deep terrain as well as steep gorges of the high Himalayas. Because of the rising height, the Sagarmatha National Park boasts four different climatic zones: a forested lower zone, the upper alpine zone, a zone of alpine scrub, and the Arctic zone without any foliage. Depending on the altitude, you get to see the different and diverse mammals and birds. The park flanks some of the tallest peaks in the world making it one of the must to visit places for the adventurers and backpackers. Lastly, the park holds much religious as well as cultural significance as it is full of several sacred sites like Thyangboche besides being the homeland of the Sherpas.

The park is not only the home of the impressive hill scenes and the diverse flora as well as fauna, but it is also the land of a few monasteries and gompas. The Visitor Center of the park is at Mendalphu that means the Headquarters. It is atop the hill in Namche Bazaar where you can also visit the museum of natural history and cultural heritage. In the area, also look for Thame Gomba - a vital religious center where in May, the famous Mani Rimdu festival is held. If you are coming in June, be a part of the Dumje festival in Khumjung Gomba as well as at the Namche and Pangboche monasteries. And yes, do also visit the Tengboche Gomba that offers magnificent vistas of Mt. Everest and the peaks.

Within the Sagarmatha National Park, there are many majestic mountains, deep valleys, and glaciers all of which are ruled by the highest peak of Mount Everest soaring up to 8,848

m. For the wildlife lovers, several rare species are easily seen, such as the lesser panda and the snow leopard. And finally, you just cannot go without meeting one of the Sherpas who live uniquely as compared to the other altitude dwellers. I recommend talking with them for some time to explore their interestingly unique culture.

Iguazu National Park, Argentina

Nestled in the Iguazu province of Argentina, the World Heritage Site of Iguazu National Park not only protects the vigorous subtropical jungle, but also ensures endless natural surprises to its tourists. Edging the globally famous Iguazu Falls and housing the myriad of animal as well as plant species, the park is among the hot spots for the nature as well as botany lovers. So, you can expect spotting not only the wonderful falls, but also the some great natural scenery along with the rare as well as endangered species in the Iguazu National Park. In fact, the word 'Iguazu' stands for 'Great Waters' whose charm is reserved by the Iguazu falls made by the river of the same name. While cascading, the water's vapor ascends upwards each minute and by coming in contact with the sun, a set of rainbows is created, which itself is the best background for photography. So, no you know why this park is named as the 'Great Waters' or 'Iguazu'. As compared to the Niagara, the falls here are four times wider and scatter on both the Brazilian as well as the Argentinean sides. And one more great wonder is that the falls are separated into several islands that themselves are the biggest attractions.

If you come here from the Brazilian side, do not leave without enjoying the thrill of the Devil's Throat - the sight where 14 plunges down the rugged terrain featuring a thundering force that results in a permanent 100 foot plume overhead. And yes, that rainbow scene is possible here also. You can come at this point just by a small train in 10 minutes, which is exciting for kids. If you want to have a close-up look, stroll through the subtropical forest and reach the base of the Salto Floriano where a lift awaits you to take you on the falls' top or stroll over the Salto Union's drop.

Are you coming from the Argentine side? Okay, then take up an exciting way to reach via the series of catwalks that meander over the water and finally intersect the Devil's Gorge. Get a bit adventurous as your protection is ensured by the rain suits. Some of the areas on this side are also suitable for swimming. You will also come across the footpaths, bridges, and trails on this side for more thundering experience of the falls as well as the great flora and fauna. This is the preferred side for adventurous people! Look for two circuits here: Lower Circuit as the foot of the waterfalls and 'arriba' called the Upper Circuit. Take a tour of these relatively short loops from the Visitor's Center from where a green trail or train can be your option.

I suggest that from the Lower Circuit you take a boat for exploring the San Martin Island - a must see sight. However, never ever forget to seek for the instructions from the locals. And yes, be ready to face the cuticle parasites.

While hiking, spot some of the rare species such as tapir, titicas, jaguar, ocelote, anteater, jungle eagle, yacaré overo and pavas de monte along with the others such as Tucan, butterflies, Capuchin monkeys, Nasua, and lude Tropidurus as small lizards. While you are in the park, a ride on the Rainforest Ecological Train or Waterfalls Train is a must for a better tour!

Ocelot Facts - The Exotic Cat That Is Now Endangered

The ocelot is ideally twice the size of the average house cat. It is a sleek animal and the most identifiable characteristic has to be its dappled coat, which is best described as 'gorgeous'. These nocturnal cats are known to use their keen hearing capabilities and sight so as to hunt down their prey. They ideally hunt on rodents, rabbits, iguanas, frogs and fish. They also generally take to the trees; and this is what adds the stalking of birds and monkeys to their list. Unlike most cats who will avoid water, one of the most interesting and distinguishing of the ocelot facts is that they are indeed good swimmers.

Javan Rhino - Rhinoceros Sondaicus

The Javan rhinoceros is the name of a herbivorous creature that belongs to the order of Perissodactyla and is said to be one of the three species of rhinos that are native to the Asian continent. This lesser one-horned rhino is perhaps the rarest of the large mammal species in the world. What we mean by 'rare' here is that it is almost on the brink of extinction. Lesser than 60 of these mammals are said to survive in the wild today; and none of these are in captivity. The Javan rhino is said to exist in two protected areas - Ujung Kulon National Park (Indonesia) and Cat Tien National Park (Vietnam). However, owing to the pressures of human population and the ever-increasing threat of poaching, things do not look too bright. he WWF is active in both areas of Cat Tien and Ujung Kolon; but there is a long way to go before this battle for the survival of the Javan rhino is won. The Javan rhino is dusky-grey in color and has a single horn. The skin is said to have a number of loose folds which give the rhino an appearance of having donned armor plating. This species of the rhino is extremely similar to the Indian rhino; but it is slightly smaller in size. The head is definitely smaller and the folds of the skin are less apparent than they would be in the Indian rhino. As per recent evidence, the horn might be completely absent or negligibly small in the case of the females. The upper lip is slightly pointed; and this is used to pull the food towards the mouth.

Howler Monkey - Loudest Species In The Animal Kingdom

Howlers are found in the regions of tropical Central and South America. They are New World Monkeys and are aptly named for their cries that can be described as being cacophonous. When a number of them begin letting their lungs loose in concert, the cacophony can be heard till a distance of about three miles away. The male howler monkey is said to be blessed with a specialized vocal chamber which is shell-like. This will help them to turn up their volume so that you can hear this distinctive call. The noise will help to send out a clear message to all of the other monkeys in the region; thus telling them that this territory has already been taken over by a troop.

These vocal primates can boast of being the biggest of all the New World monkeys. What differentiate them from the Old World monkeys are the wide, side-opening nostrils and the prehensile tail. The tail can almost be used as an extra arm so that they can grip branches or even hang from them. This extra-arm-like tail is an added advantage in the case of the howler monkey, because this creature doesn't like descending to the ground too much. They will generally prefer staying aloft and munching on the tender leaves that grow higher on the trees.

Clouded Leopard of Borneo

The first ever person to describe the clouded leopard was Sir Stamford Raffles. However, Griffith was the first person to give this creature a scientific name. The elusive animal is rarely seen. If you speak to anyone who has seen the animal, they'd describe it as having the skull and definition of the big cats, but having the body of a smaller cat. The adult clouded leopard will be the size of a small leopard; and will have a longer body and tail, when compared to the short legs. The coat is generally said to be rich yellowish in color or could be an earthy brown. The name of this animal comes from the blotchy cloudlike marks that cover its body.

Their long tails help as counterbalances when these animals have to climb trees. Although these leopards look similar to the marbled cat, their skulls are narrower and longer. The flexible vocal cords present indicate that, like the smaller cats, these animals also possess the ability to purr.

The ankle joints on this animal are said to exhibit a lot of flexibility. This is said to be essential for these cats that are known as tree cats by the Malaysians.

The eyes of these leopards are distinctive, given the fact that the pupils are, in reality, vertically oblong; and they aren't round like other cats.

Blackpool Zoo Has Aged Beautifully

The Blackpool zoo is one zoo that I know has definitely come of age. It was set up in the year 1972, by the Blackpool Council. In today's age and date, it is owned by Parques Reunidos. Located just a couple of miles off the sea-front of Blackpool; this zoological garden boasts of about 1500 exotic animals. This is far cry from the original herd of about 12 animals that the officials began with. The zoo sits close to the Stanley Park and is said to boast of an extremely esteemed collection of reptiles, animals and even exotic birds.

Big 5 Animals, Africa

If you have recently begun researching on the African safari, or you plan on doing one soon, you must have surely come across the term of the Big 5 animals. Do you know what this means? The Big Five was a term that was coined to refer to 5 African animals - leopard, lion, rhino, elephant and the Cape buffalo.

But then again, this will make you wonder why the gorilla, giraffe and hippo do not make it to this list. Aren't those big animals as well? Yes, they are. But the name Big 5 animals were given to these animals by the big game hunters (and not by the safari tour operators, as you may have believed). This term was coined to refer to the difficulty that they had when they tried to bag these large animals (hunting on foot), and this difficulty owed to the ferocity of these animals when they were cornered and shot at.

African Elephant:

The African elephant is said to be the largest mammal in the world. It is remarkably adaptable for an animal that huge. These elephants are quite peaceful if they're left alone. But you wouldn't want to stand in the way, if they feel threatened. These elephants are known to measure up to a cool 14 feet in height and around 30 feet in width. They are known to gobble up 30 gallons of water in a single day and are strict vegetarians.

African Rhino:

The black rhinos and the white rhinos - there are two categories that can be seen in Africa. The black rhinos have been known to suffer a lot of reduction in numbers during the last one decade. There are said to be only about 4000 of them left around the globe. There have been conservation efforts to save those numbers. Black rhinos are said to be more solitary, while the white rhinos are known to be more social, living in groups. The easiest way to distinguish between a black rhino and a white one (they're all actually grey in color) is the fact that the black rhinos will have a prehensile lip which is helpful when it comes to stripping leaves off the bushes (they are known to live in the shrubby, tropical bush areas). The lips on white rhinos are flat, and these are suited to grazing. Another interesting piece of information about these creatures is that an adult rhino could weigh about 6000 pounds.

African Leopard:

The African leopard is said to have larger numbers than its rhino counterparts when it comes to being in the league of the Big 5 animals. The spots of the leopard are what offer for excellent chances of it camouflaging itself into its surroundings. These animals are shy and are best described as nocturnal. These leopards will rarely stay in the same place, and are known to have quite a wide range among which they try to move. The males will have ranges that are wider than the females, and they will mark it by urinating and leaving marks created by their claws. An adult male leopard will be smaller than the adult lion, but can still weigh a whopping 200 lbs.

African Lion:

This is the king of the sub-Saharan savanna, which is known to be admired for its beauty and strength. This is said to be one of the most exciting animals that you can view when on a safari. These large cats are known for their hunting skills; but you might end up seeing them sleeping rather than hunting.

These lions are highly social by nature. They are known to live in prides, with several females, the young ones, and a couple of males. They will cooperate and coordinate when it comes to hunting a more difficult prey like the buffalo, but when it comes to an antelope, they'd rather hunt alone. Female lions are known to synchronize the births of their cubs, so that could raise them together.

Cape Buffalo:

The Cape buffalo is a common sighting when you're in one of the protected wildlife areas of Africa. If there is a lot of water available, chances are that you'll see the Cape buffalo close by. There have been four subtypes documented of the African buffalo - West African Savanna Buffalo, Central African Savanna Buffalo, Forest Buffalo and Southern Savanna Buffalo.

Cape buffalos are large and each adult could stand at around 5 - 6 feet high. The males would weigh somewhere around 1500 pounds. Even the supreme most predators, the African lion, wouldn't dare take a chance at a Cape buffalo, unless he has other members from the pride along with him. These animals are known to live in herds as large as 1000 buffaloes. Surprisingly, they have very few scuffles between them. This is perhaps because the buffaloes known that their strong horns could cause for some serious injuries. This doesn't mean that battles do not happen; but when they do happen, they're brief.

The Volcano at Mount Longonot National Park Seems Active

There is a sight that is a must-see when you come to Nairobi. This is seen when you approach the cliffs of the Great African Rift Valley. The mount of Mount Longonot rises up from the floor of the valley that surrounds the region.

A lot of years back, there was a national park that was created in the region surrounding the mountain. This effort was made to ensure that more tourists visited the region. This volcano had, anyway, been a dormant volcano for a very long time now.

However, if you take into consideration the stories published on the blogs of volcanologists', then the story is altogether different. The stories are much more sinister than the official story put together by the park officials and tourist attractions.

The pictures that were taken over the past one decade have shown that there has been an elevation in the mountain by a couple of inches. This growth is a sign of the fact that there has been a significant increase in the volcanic activity that is happening at a deeper level; and the elevation is a subsequent effect of the rising magma.

Although there haven't been any other visible signs in the present times, there was a recent report, as per people taking flights over the region, who saw that there was smoke and steam emanating from the region. Another possibility, however, claim park officials is that the smoke and steam is produced by the geothermal power station which is located close to the mountain. This power station is known to tap into the deeper crusts of the Earth in order to produce electricity.

As per the park officials and officials at the geothermal power station, KENGEN (Kenya's National Power Generating Company) would have to keep a close eye on any sort of tremors being felt at Mount Longonot. It is absolutely essential for them to stay on top of any sort of potential developments.

The Great African Rift Valley is one that has stemmed from seismic activity; and there exist geysers and hot springs along the floor of the valley. These are ever present reminders of the fact that there is all that heat stirring endlessly and uneasily below the region.

Texas Wildlife

Texas is known to be a state that is comprised of a number of diverse natural resources. Luckily, it is said that Texas is also said to be an extremely strong state of park systems. It is known to have a high number of federal lands as well. Whether you prefer woods, sandy beaches or mountains, you will have your pick of National Wildlife Refuges from which you could view nature.

Newer Bird Species Might Exist In Philippines

Philippines may have been known to boast of a number of interesting bird species in the past, but as per the new studies, there has been some light shed on the fact that there may be some more interesting species of birds available in the region. This observation has come to the forefront owing to recent research conducted by a certain Dr. David Lohman, who is an assistant professor of biology with the City College of New York. As per his findings, the nation of Philippines may actually be much more of a 'biodiversity hotspot' than it has been given credit for. If his studies hold ground with authorities, then it might be high time that there are some serious changes made in the process of conservation practices.

A number of animal species that are otherwise found in the country of Philippines are known to be endemic to this particular nation. This nation is ideally made up of 7100 islands and is known to be home to a lot of species that are found only in Philippines. For instance, about 64% of the land mammal species and about 77% of its amphibian population cannot be found anywhere else in the world.

In order to test whether or not the bird population of Philippines could include certain unrecognized species, Prof. Lohman began research on around 7 smaller species of birds, which fell under the category of perching birds. He then went on to conduct some genetic tests and tried to reconstruct the evolutionary histories of the different sorts of birds. According to his findings, the samples derived from the populations inhabiting Philippines were said to be distinctly different from the ones found elsewhere in Southeast Asia.

The genetic lineage of these birds was definitely seen to be unique. There is need for more research to be conducted in order to determine whether or not these birds make for totally unknown species.

Earlier, the taxonomists would use plumage color in order to identify different species of the birds. But what they wouldn't realize half of the times was that species that are closely related, but distinct in reality, might actually end up looking uncannily similar. There continues to be a healthy amount of debate surrounding whether or not the newly discovered findings would imply that these are wholly new species; but one thing remains clear - these are unique genetic lineages that weren't known of earlier.

However, Lohman himself claims that a lot of study has to be conducted before any reports are printed about these so-called new species. He does, however, stress on the fact that conservation practices in Philippines need renewal at the earliest, lest we lose some newer species to extinction.

Shark Bay, Australia - The Ideal Natural World Heritage Site

Shark Bay could be considered the western most point of Australia and is said to be made up of a conglomeration of islands and the lands that surround it. The vast sea beds spell 'green' and are perhaps, the largest and the richest in the world. The dugong, nicknamed the sea cow, is native to these waters. The stromatolites make for quite an interesting sight. The region of Shark Bay is also said to house five species of animals that are listed under the 'endangered' list.

The Census of Marine Life Throws Up Surprises

The Census of Marine Life which took about ten years to complete is said to have thrown up some interesting surprises that has taken scientists, researchers and marine life enthusiasts by surprise. National Geographic News spoke about the closing of the Census on Monday, 4th of October, 2010. Here's a look at some of some of the discoveries made by the decade long inventory.

Extinct Species Get Rediscovered

The two centuries that have gone by are said to have witnessed accelerated rates of extinction of certain animal species. There has been endangerment that has taken place alongside the industrial progress and there has been rapid growth of the human population.

Naturally speaking, the concept of 'background extinction' has been in play for a very long time now. However, it is estimated that the extinction rates in current times are said to be about 1000 times the background extinction rates that were known earlier.

Most of this animal extinction can be relegated to two causes - human demand for animal resources; or human demand for natural resources which may contain the habitat of certain animals.

5

Moving Towards Rural Tourism

Rural tourism focuses on participating in a rural lifestyle. It can be a variant of ecotourism. Any village can be a tourist attraction, and many villagers are very hospitable. Agriculture is becoming highly mechanized and therefore requires less manual labor. This is causing economic pressure on some villages, leading to an exodus of young people to urban areas. Rural tourism allows the creation of an alternative source of income in the non-agricultural sector for rural dwellers. The added income from rural tourism can contribute to the revival of lost folk art and handicrafts. It is an ideal and natural method of rural and urban economic exchange.

Tourism growth potential can be harnessed as a strategy for Rural Development. The development of a strong platform around the concept of Rural tourism is definitely useful for a country like India, where almost 74% of the population resides in its 7 million villages. Across the world the trends of industrialization and development have had an urban centric approach. Alongside, the stresses of urban lifestyles have led to a "counter-urbanization" syndrome. This has led to growing interest in the rural areas. At the same time this trend of urbanization has led to falling income levels, lesser job opportunities in the rural areas leading to an urbanization syndrome in the rural areas. Rural Tourism is one of the few activities which can provide a solution to these problems. Besides, there are other factors which are shifting the trend towards rural tourism like increasing levels of awareness, growing interest in heritage and culture and improved accessibility, and environmental consciousness. In the developed countries, this has resulted in a new style of tourism of visiting village settings to experience and live a relaxed and healthy lifestyle. This concept has taken the shape of a formal kind of Rural Tourism. Under this Scheme, thrust is to promote village tourism as the primary tourism product to spread tourism and its socio-economic benefits to rural and its new geographic regions. Key geographic regions are identified for development and promotion of Rural Tourism. The implementation is done through a Convergence Committee headed by the District Collector. Activities like improving the environment, hygiene, infrastructure etc. are covered for assistance. Apart from providing financial assistance, the focus is to tap the resources available under different schemes of Department. of Rural Development, State Governments and other concerned Departments of the Government of India.

Any form of tourism that showcases the rural life, art, culture and heritage at rural locations, thereby benefiting the local community economically and socially as well as enabling interaction between the tourists and the locals for a more enriching tourism experience can be termed as rural tourism. Rural tourism is essentially an activity which takes place in the countryside. It is multi-faceted and may entail farm/agricultural tourism, cultural tourism, nature tourism, adventure tourism, and eco-tourism. As against conventional tourism, rural tourism has certain typical characteristics like; it is experience oriented, the locations are sparsely populated, it is predominantly in natural environment, it meshes with seasonality and local events and is based on preservation of culture, heritage and traditions.

Identification of villages : Each State/UT Govt. would be requested to furnish one proposal for promotion of Rural tourism. Based on the merits and after a joint inspection by the

Deptt. Of Tourism, and the State/UT Govt. if required ten proposals would be identified for implementation in the country.

Preparation of detailed plan for implementation of the project : After shortlisting the proposals, the State/UT Govts would be requested to draw up a detailed plan of action. The thrust here would be to achieve convergence between the different schemes of the Govt. of India and the State Govts. It should be ensured that atleast 50% of the project should be implemented through achieving convergence of different schemes. Assistance upto Rs. 3 lakhs would be provided to the State Govt. for engaging an expert for preparing the project report.

Assistance under the Scheme : A maximum of Rs. 50 lakhs would be sanctioned under this scheme. The activities listed under the para 5 could be taken up.

Permissible activities : The following works may be taken up under the Scheme-

1. Improvement of the surroundings of the village. This would include activities like landscaping, development of parks, fencing, compound wall etc.
2. Improvements to roads within the Panchayat limits. This shall not include any major road which connects the village.
3. Illumination in the village.
4. Providing for improvement in solid waste management and sewerage management.
5. Construction of Wayside Amenities.
6. Procurement of equipments directly related to tourism, like Water Sports, Adventure Sports, Eco-friendly modes of transport for moving within the tourism zone.
7. Refurbishment of the Monuments. (66:33 basis, i.e. CFA of 66%)
8. Signages.
9. Reception Centres.
10. Other work/activities directly related to tourism.

11. Tourist Accommodation.

Constitution of a Convergence Committee : A Convergence Committee would be set up under the Collector to oversee the implementation of the project.

Execution of the works : The execution of the work would be entrusted to any Central Govt./State Govt. agency and the funds would be released directly to the implementing agency by the Govt. of India as recommended by the State Govt.

Installments of release : On sanction of a work the first installment of 30% of the sanctioned amount of CFA will be released. The second installment of 50% would be released on submission of the UC for the first installment. The balance would be released on the completion of the work.

Following codal formalities : The executing agency shall follow all codal formalities while awarding contracts and procurement of equipments and ensure complete transparency in its transactions.

Management of assets created : The infrastructure and assets created will be maintained and managed by the State/ UT Governments or their agencies with no financial commitment to Govt. of India except those assets created in the protected areas of ASI.

Prescription of the Schedule of Rates : While executing the works the executing agency shall follow the Schedule of rates prescribed by the CPWD or the State PWD.

Submission of the Utilisation Certificates : The executing agency shall furnish the Utilisation Certificate through the State Government for release of the second installment. A Completion Certificate has also to be furnished through the State Govt. before the release of the final installment.

Relevance in Developing Nations

Rural tourism is particularly relevant in developing nations wherein farmland has become fragmented due to population growth.

Relevance in Developed Nations

Rural tourism exists in developed nations in the form of providing accommodation in a scenic location ideal for rest and relaxation.

United States: Niche Tourism in Rural Areas

Many niche tourism programs are located in rural areas. From wine tours and eco-tourism, to agritourism and seasonal events, tourism can be a viable economic component in rural community development. According the USDA, Cooperative State, Education and Extension Service, "Tourism is becoming increasingly important to the U.S. economy. A conservative estimate from the Federal Reserve Board in Kansas, based on 2000 data, shows that basic travel and tourism industries accounted for 3.6 percent of all U.S. employment. Even more telling, data from the Travel Industry Association of America indicate that 1 out of every 18 people in the U.S. has a job directly resulting from travel expenditures."

The publication Promoting Tourism in Rural America explains the need for planning and marketing rural community and to weigh the pros and cons of the impacts of tourism. Local citizen participation is helpful and should be included in starting any kind of a tourism program. Being prepared by planning tourism can assist in a successful program that enhances the community.

Growing Rural Tourism Opportunities

The northern Great Plains region is characterized by a semi-arid climate and an extensive agricultural economy based on dryland farming and range livestock production. In recent decades, combinations of economic forces and ecological trends have placed farm operators and agriculturally dependent communities in this region under substantial economic stress. Production agriculture in the northern Great Plains region has long been characterized by uncertainty, stemming both from climatic factors and from volatile commodity prices

(Dhuyvetter, Thompson, Norwood, & Halvorson, 1996). Periodic droughts have resulted in severe economic stress for the region's farmers and ranchers (Leistritz, Ekstrom, Wanzek, & Mortensen, 1989). Further, some observers question whether some of the lands of this region can be cropped on a sustained-yield basis. As a consequence, some of the region's farm and ranch operators have been considering alternative enterprises to increase and stabilize their incomes.

Farm families in the northern Great Plains region have faced serious economic challenges. In 2002, net cash farm income for North Dakota averaged $31,129 per farm (USDA, 2004). For the neighboring northern Great Plains states of South Dakota and Montana, net cash farm income averaged $26,763 and $10,715, respectively. Net cash farm income is the farm's cash receipts less cash expenses. From this amount, the farm family must make any principal payments on long-term debt and also provide for capital replacement [depreciation] and family living expenses. Given the relatively low levels of net farm/ranch income, farm and ranch families have become increasingly reliant on off-farm earnings. For example, over the period 1993-2002, off-farm wages and salaries of North Dakota farm households more than doubled (Swenson, 2003).

In the face of these conditions, many farm and ranch operators have examined the possibility of adding new enterprises to diversify and enhance their incomes. One of the fastest growing forms of new enterprise has been nature-based or agri-tourism (Schroeder, 2004; Leistritz, Hodur, & Wolfe, 2004). Many farm and ranch operators are creating new on-farm tourism (agritourism) enterprises, hoping to attract some of the out-of-state visitors to their business. Types of new on-farm businesses range from trails to guided hunting and fishing to corn mazes and wineries, and the timing could not be better. There is a growing national touring population that is looking for new, educational, physical, and authentic cultural hands-on experiences (Wilkerson, 2003; Gartner, 2005).

While North Dakota and other Great Plains and Midwestern states have not traditionally been major tourist destinations, entrepreneurs have increasingly discovered opportunities to launch successful enterprises. North Dakota State University (NDSU) Extension and the North Dakota Agricultural Experiment Station have attempted to respond to the needs of this clientele, and the efforts and activities undertaken in doing so offer a case study that may be of wider interest.

This article briefly describes an integrated research and Extension program developed by North Dakota State University to support development of the agritourism and nature-based tourism sector in the Great Plains and other rural regions. This was a challenging undertaking because the state's rural tourism sector has only recently begun to develop, and little information was available regarding the attributes of either the state's agritourism and nature tourism businesses or of the visitors who make up their clientele. The North Dakota experience may be of particular interest to Extension personnel in states where the rural tourism sector has developed only recently and where the information base and support infrastructure for the sector is limited.

Initial Programming

In response to numerous requests for information about how to start on-farm tourism businesses, NDSU Extension began offering programs in agritourism enterprise development for farm/ranch families in 1999. At that time there was little information and only a few successful examples of rural tourism businesses in the state. The North Dakota Extension Service, with the assistance of a Montana State University Extension specialist David Sharpe, delivered an innovative educational program to assist farm and ranch families who were considering starting tourism related businesses. North Dakota State University Extension also identified and introduced a network of agencies and partners that could assist those considering a business start-up. This network continues to grow. A typical agenda for the 1-day workshop contained the following key components.

- Panel of successful agritourism entrepreneurs
- Discussion and information on tourist needs and expectations
- Discussion of appropriate facilities
- Agency panel for funding and business assistance
- Agency presentations: tax department, health department, and state tourism
- Financial feasibility
- Legal issues
- Marketing strategies

A total of 486 participants attended the Extension programs, and several new businesses were launched. In 2005, 24 of 53 workshop participants (45%) responding to a survey indicated that they had started a business as a result of the program. One successful example of a business that participated in the Extension program and responded to the survey is West Bay Resort, LLC.

Need for Research

While the program was successful and NDSU Extension specialists knew that the number of agritourism ventures was growing, better information on current attributes, outlook, and perceived needs of rural tourism business operators was needed in order to facilitate future Extension program development in the state and region. A statewide survey of agritourism and nature-based tourism operators was conducted by the NDSU Department of Agribusiness & Applied Economics to meet these program needs. Information was obtained from 194 tourism business operators (approximately 47% of the active agritourism and nature-based tourism businesses in the state).

A hunting-related service (guiding, hunting lodges) was the most common business focus, while lodging and/or a meal was the service most often provided (Hodur, Leistritz, & Wolfe, 2004). Only 28% of the businesses had paid employees, but a majority (52%) had unpaid family members who helped with the business. Most of the businesses operated seasonally, with only 36% reporting operating year round. Most of the businesses were relatively recent start-ups, and 85% had begun operations since 1990.

Most of the businesses (58%) reported 100 or fewer customer days during their most recent year of operation. The median number of customer days was 90, up from 74 2 years earlier. The bulk of the clientele (69%) were from out of state. Most of the businesses (71%) reported net revenue of $10,000 or less; the median value of $2,000 is likely representative. These income levels were consistent with the seasonal nature and relatively small scale of most of these businesses.

Most operators felt that demand for their type of business had increased in the past 3 years (72% agreed) and that more customers were needed to operate at full capacity (64% agreed). Less than one-third of respondents reported difficulty attracting new customers. More than three-fourths of the respondents (78%) felt that outdoor recreation-based tourism activities offered rural areas economic development opportunities (Hodur, Leistritz, & Wolfe, 2004). Finally, more than three-fourths of respondents felt that there should be more promotion of the state as a tourism destination.

Affordable liability insurance was frequently identified as a critical issue for the tourism business operators. While only 13% indicated they were unable to purchase liability and/or comprehensive insurance, 51% believed liability insurance was prohibitively expensive.

The issues critical to North Dakota rural tourism operators are issues in other states as well. Insurance issues are beginning to be addressed through changes in state law. For example, Texas has established a liability cap or limit for agritourism operators who have liability insurance up to the liability cap amount. Nebraska and other rural states are considering similar approaches.

Developing the Nature and Rural Tourism Sector

New business operators soon discovered that starting an agritourism business is the easy part. In follow-up discussions with new business owners in North Dakota, it was found that they needed to network with others with similar interests and business operations across the state to become more efficient and effective at attracting tourists to their individual businesses. However, networking was impossible because the operators did not know each other and no database existed to help them. In response, the NDSU Extension Center for Community Vitality facilitated, along with the Garrison Conservancy District, the creation of the North Dakota Nature and Rural Tourism Association in 2004. The association created an environment for sharing and learning to take place.

The members of the new association quickly identified two issues that required action, affordable insurance and cooperative marketing. As a result of the association's recommendations and lobbying for affordable liability insurance, the North Dakota legislature in 2005 directed the North Dakota Insurance Department to conduct a study to examine the cost and availability of liability insurance for recreation and agritourism related businesses. The study has been completed, and the results were reported to the 2007 legislature. Cooperative marketing efforts using visitor packages, Web sites, and brochures have become more prevalent.

Research and Extension personnel continue to actively support the North Dakota Nature and Rural Tourism Association by providing research and educational programming. For example, in response to the growing interest in birding festivals, researchers from the Department of Agribusiness and Applied Economics surveyed participants in a rural birding festival (Hodur, Leistritz, & Wolfe, 2005). They found that more than three-fourths of participants were visitors to the area, with most coming from out of state. Visitors came from locations as distant as Oregon and Tennessee, and spent an average of $235 per person during the course of the 4-day event.

Visitors were asked how they had learned of the event. More than two-thirds of out-of-state visitors mentioned a birding magazine as their source of information. On the other hand, visitors from within North Dakota much more often learned of the event through local media or from a brochure distributed by the festival organizers. This information was used by the organizers to plan their future marketing efforts.

As interest in organizing birding festivals and other agricultural and tourist-related events has grown in rural communities, the NDSU Extension Center for Community Vitality and Cass County Extension Office offered a 6-day University of Minnesota Extension certification training in Festival and Events Management. Because the potential economic impact of visitor spending is often an important local issue in planning festivals and events, the program was augmented to include a seminar by Dr. Larry Leistritz and Nancy Hodur of the NDSU Department of Agribusiness and Applied Economics on the principles of estimating the economic impact of events and festivals.

They first developed a conceptual framework for estimating an event's contribution to the local economy (e.g., visitors' spending would generally be counted as part of the economic contribution or impact, whereas local residents' spending generally would not). They applied this framework to various types of events in both rural and urban settings (e.g., a Birding Festival held in central North Dakota, various events held at the FARGODOME in North Dakota's largest city). Their presentation emphasized key issues that event organizers need to consider when estimating the local impact of their event. A major message was that a well-designed survey of event participants can provide the information needed to estimate local economic impact, as well as providing insights that can aid in planning and marketing future events (Hodur, Leistritz, & Wolfe, 2005).

ERTD

ERTD is a collaborative partnership between 13 training institutions and public/private agencies drawn from 5 countries across Europe. The project is supported by the European Union through the Leonardo da Vinci programme, aimed at improving the vocational education systems of Europe.

Aim-The aim of the project is to develop and pilot new learning materials and a new course in rural tourism development which will be delivered on-line to course participants via a virtual campus. The programme will incorporate a variety of learning tasks, including the research, design and promotion of new rural tourism itineraries incorporating case studies to facilitate the learning process. The learning programmes will ensure skills and knowledge of participants meet the needs of the rural tourism sector and new opportunities for employment within it.

Target Group-The new learning programme developed within this pilot initiative is aimed at the following groups of participants

* Those owner/managers and employees involved in rural tourism activities, eg bed & breakfast, self catering holidays, agro-tourism
* Young people training in Leisure and Tourism
* Those people seeking to set up business within the rural tourism sector including the unemployed and those wishing to change direction

Primary Outcomes of the Project-* New learning programmes, course materials, to meet the needs of rural tourism enterprises which will be piloted, tested and evaluated across participating European countries

* The new courses will be developed using e-learning methodologies and will lead to a 'European' accreditation and certification offering participants recognition of the skills and competencies acquired. Certification will be secured in the following
* Management in Rural Tourism
* Development of Rural Tourist Attractions

Rural Destinations in India

With the rise in the eco-tourism of the state it has also brought in the good effects of growing Rural Tourism that has potentially hyped the tourism growth in the state. The serenity and the quaintness the hills have also proved a step forward taken in carving out rural tourism in Tripura. The economic phase is on rise with the development in the tourism field. The stretches of paddy fields, criss-cross of the writhing lakes, picturesque hilly landscapes, lush green forests and the thatched bamboo houses pinned against this background has become a plethora of divinity playing in lap of nature. The wildlife along with the culture, socio-economic life and handicrafts sings the purity of the state. This aesthetics senses satisfy the tourists and their knack towards handloom and handicrafts call them to run out to the sate. The state has become and is on constant ride to become a growing hub of rural tourism besides the eco-tourism activities as rendered by the Tourism Development Corporation.

- **Anegundi**-Anegundi is a small, traditional village set in the background of an ancient cultural heritage site in the Koppaldistrict of Karnataka, across the Tungabhadra river from the Hampi World Heritage Site. It was linked with the first administrative centres of Vijayanagara which was an empire of the golden age of India, reaching its zenith during 1510-1542 AD. It has a population of 3018, most of whom live in small whitewashed houses with wooden pillars lining the street. The small cosmos like valleys created by boulder hills are full of paddy and banana fields which are fed by the canals constructed during the Vijayanagara period that still function. Anegundi, home of the Devarayas, is located right on the banks of river Tungabhadra, which flows to the south and to the east of the village. It is surrounded by granite hills on three sides and is bordered by river Tungabhadra on the other. The river curves many times flowing from the west to east. According to the ancient scripture of the Purana, this location is called scared land or Punya Bhoomi. Anegundi was also the cradle city of 'Kishkinda', the monkey kingdom mentioned in the Ramayana, and Hanuman's birth place. Sri Ranganatha, a form of 'lord Vishnu in his cosmic sleep' is the presiding deity of the village.

- **Ballavpur Danga**-Ballavpur Danga is 3 km from Shantiniketan, the celebrated home of Nobel laureates Rabindranath Tagore and Amartya Sen. It is a Santhal Adivasi tribal community, framed in the rustic beauty of rural Bengal. The Sonajhuri forest lies to the east and the Ballavpur Avayaranya forest area and bird sanctuary is to its south. Santhali art, craft and culture is woven into the community's life. Attractive designs adorn the walls and floors of their homes, with colours made from red earth and cowdung. Tribal dances unfold in the open air, with fire, to the rhythmic beats of the madal, their traditional musical instrument, while oral Adivasi myths and history remain etched in song and recitation.
- **Chougan**-If Rudyard Kipling had to name a home for Mowglie and his friends, it would definitely be Chaugan on the edge of the alluring Narmada River in Madhya Pradesh. This picturesque tribal settlementwith the Baiga and Gond communities is about 32 km from Mandla, close to the route for Kanha National Park which inspired Kipling to chronicle his famous 'Jungle Book'. The local community has a rich heritage, complemented by their art and culture. This village will offer the visitor an experience of life among the tribal community, away from the bustle of the city.
- **Chitrakote**-Chitrakote is situated 38 km from Jagdalpur, the district headquarters of Bastar district in Chhattisgarh, 340 km from the state capital Raipur and 350 km from Visakhapattanam in Andhra PradeshTucked away in the centre of Bastar district, in the south of the newly created state of Chhattisgarh, amidst barren rocky terrain dotted with patches of mixed deciduous forest, the Indravati river takes a plunge of 100 feet and creates what the local tribes call as Chitrakote Ghoomer or the abode of spotted deer,

waterfall. The serene natural beauty of the waterfall and its surroundings transports you to a different world where you stand alone, far from the madding crowd.

- **Durgapur(Assam)**- Durgapur has all the ingredients of the Assamese rural essence; thatched houses, expert craftsmen and skilled weavers, proximity to Kaziranga National Park World Heritage Site, with innovatively styled accommodation nearby. Virtually every household harvests silk and weaves it, using local dyes. The village has three fishing ponds for traditional fishing practices and even its individually owned tea gardens, eri and muga silk and betel nut plantations. Bamboo mats are woven in almost all homes. Assamese festivals, especially Bihu, are celebrated with gaiety. Traditional musical instruments, namely 'dhol', 'pepa' and 'gogona' are prevalent. The village reflects a clean environment, neatly divided by lanes on both sides.

- **Jageshwar**-Jageshwar village lies at 1870 meters on the Jatganga stream in an attractive narrow valley, forested with deodars, 34 km by road from Almora, and 386 km from Delhi. Believed to be the abode of 12 jyotirlingas, it has 124 temples and many statues dating to the 11th century AD, finely crafted. A 3 km climb to Vridha jageshwar on the high ridge above provides a panoramic vew of the snow peaks surrounding Nanda Devi, the presiding deity of Kumaon and Garhwal. A dozen Khukrne wood craftsmen retain the traditional local skill used for the ornate Jaegshwari dwellling facades. The community's dwelling idiom consists of single or double storeyed homes, mud plastered with slate-tiled sloping roofs, carved wooden windows and doorways. Nearby outings include a 10 km trek to Shokiathal and Mritola Ashram, which also enlists overseas disciples. Prominent fairs are held during Shivaratri and Saavan, when visitor inflow peaks. The region abutts the buffer zone of the Binsar Reserve Forest and adjoining tracts, characterised by a diverse, though fragile Himalayan environment.

- **Kazhugumalai**-About 50 km inland from the Thoothukudi port, Kazhugumalai is a place of archaeological importance, with the centuries' old Jain rock carvings that are attractions for both tourists and scholars. The Thoothukudi coastline nearby defines the rural milieu in a marine eco-system, home to several forms of folk art, palm and banana based products and traditional fishing practices. Two distinct farming systems are practised: agro farming, supported by the Tamiraparani river system and coastal farming dominated by coconuts and palmyra. Visitors can experience the fragile eco-system of coral, the reefs being only a 50-minute boat-ride from the coast. Also at hand are artificial reefs and reef restorations. During the Pongal festival, the area is a visual treat. Farmstead stays can be arranged while long 'Silambattam'
- **Kumbalanghi**-A canvas of nature's most captivating brush strokes, Kumbalanghi is an island for simple joys, just off Kochi. The village has retained its rural ambience and is the perfect getaway from urban chaos. Laze around the expansive Vembanad Lake, go for a leisurely boat ride in the canals and backwaters, exclaim at the variety of mangroves, drop jaw at the neat chequered paddy fields and coconut plantations, understand boat building, and bid at the traditional auction for fish, prawn and crab. Then, with your senses satiated, allow your hosts to feed you from a wide range of traditional recipes. Sit in the backyard of your home-stay and enjoy the unforgettable sunrise or sunset. If local culture interests you, ask for a performance of the foot stomping Chavittunadakam, the valorous Parisamuttukali, Kolkali, Margamkali or the gentle Thiruvathira
- **Lachen**-110 km from Gangtok, Lachen is a scenic Himalayan village of migrant Buddhist Bhutia yak herders called Lachenpas, in the North district of Sikkim. The world's third highest mountain, Kangchendzonga, rises alongside, lending its name to India's high altitude Kangchendzonga National Park. The hospitable Lachenpas

greet or bid visitors farewell with the traditional 'khada' scarf. Blankets made from sheep wool or chuktuk, carved woodwork, furniture, signs, symbols and blankets are the handicrafts of Lachen. A number of hot springs, lakes and trek routes dot the vicinity of Lachen. Every season is distinct - from the flowering of rhododendronds in spring to swirling monsoon mists, the afterglow of autumn and the severity of winter when the snow settles in. Local fauna listings show the elusive snow leopard, musk deer and Himalayan black bear.

- **Mana**-At an altitude of 3420 meters on the confluence of the Saraswati and the Alaknanda streams, Mana is 525 km from Delhi. Onwards, it is only 3 km beyond Badrinath, one of the world's oldest and most frequented pilgrimages. Mana is also the last Indian village, 48 km ahead of which lies the Mana pass on the old trade route to Tibet, disused after the border was sealed in 1962. The Border Roads Organisation has extended the road another 10 km to Musapani, from where the Inner line is 2 km away at Ghastoli. Mana's Bhutia tribal community is migratory, their life pattern linked to the Badrinath shrine. The community's dwelling idiom consists of stone cottages, single or double storeyed, mud plastered with slate-tiled sloping roofs, built into the hillside, some with carved wooden windows and doorway facades. Women are the real keepers of the indigenous knowledge of making natural dyes. The also collect wild plant raw materials. The Mana Bhutias are known for their expertise in making a range of woollen garments and materials, besides processing and colouring of wool. Mana, like many Garhwal villages, is thus not just a human settlement but a micro-ecosystem encompassing the local community, livestock, physical and organic resources.
- **Mukutmanipur**-The signature view of Mukutmanipur is its large water-body, heaving gently away from the tribal hamlets, suggestive of that tranquil mood. The surrounding greenery serves to raise the de-stress bar. A short stroll brings up the confluence of the Kangsabati and Kumari

rivers, not far from Pareshnath Hill. Stone images of Parsvanath Swami, made of chlorite stone, and Shiva await discovery at the top. Three or four verdant green islands of varying sizes in this lake including the one with a deer park, Banpukuria Mrigadab, beckon in the distance. Boating in the lake and visiting these islands is a worthwhile experience. Mukutmanipur's undulating forested landscape marked by the vibrant colours of Palash and Sonajhuri trees is refreshing and invigorating for the body and mind. It is marked by the prominent hillock about 200metres high, locally named "Baroghutu" (Baro- twelve, ghutu-/stones/hill). The tribal hamlets of Baroghutu, Jambeda, Kumorbahal, Dhagora and Mukutmanipur encircle this hillock. With a landscape that seems naturally designed for adventure, Mukutmanipur offers opportunities in rock climbing, trekking and a variety of water sports. The local festivals, Tusu, Bhadu, Sahrai and Badna are symbolized by much music and dance, and strengthen the Mukutmanipur experience, laden with the relaxed air of nature in the heartland.

- **Nagarnar**-Nagarnar is situated 18 km from the Bastar district headquarters at Jagdalpur, and well connected by road with Raipur, the state capital of Chhattisgarh. Nagarnar is renowned for terracotta handicrafts created by the local craftsmen who have acquired international acclaim. High skill levels are also evident in weaving, carpentry and metal crafts in mediums such as bell metal and wrought iron. The village homes are made of stone and mud with thatched roofs or stone slabs and placed symmetrically in clusters where the residents express pride in their art.
- **Naggar**-The heritage village of Naggar is situated in the Beas valley of Kullu District in the Western Himalaya, on the left bank of the river. Standing majestically at a height of 1851 meters, the village, surrounded by Deodar trees, provides a picturesque view of snow-clad mountains on the north and the glitening Beas river powering its way

deep down. Enthusiastic local families offer home-stays for visitors. Naggar is renowned for its impressive cultural heritage, a rich architectural style using local materials and skills, and an extensive handicraft range. There are centuries old temples that bear traditional stone and wood carvings...not forgetting the enduring artefacts in the Roerich Art Gallery. There are also several options for treks and adventure sports for enthusiasts.

- **Pipili**-Pipili is synonymous with applique, the stitching of colourful cloth pieces on a fabric base. The result is bright decorative motifs of gods and goddesses, animals and stories from the epics. Said to be named after a Muslim saint Pir Palli, Pipili falls on Orissa's Golden Triangle connecting the state capital Bhubaneswar (20 km) and Puri (40 km) with the Konark Sun Temple World Heritage Site (50 km), extended to the Chilika Lake (90 km). Pipili is thus the gateway to these attractions of coastal Orissa.
- **Pocham**-pally Spread over an attractive corner of the Deccan plateau, Pochampalli is 50 km from Hyderabad. It is the largest centre for Ikkat, the intricate tie-and-dye craft for silk and cotton weaving. Ikkat is the process of resist dyeing with the sequence of wrapping and dyeing sections of bundled yarn to a predetermined colour pattern, prior to weaving. Gurukul learning of Ikkat will specially interest the visitor, seeking a live experience of the craft, combined with local culture and cuisine. Pochampalli was also the launch pad for Acharya Vinoba Bhave's Bhoodan (donation of land for community use) movement. The Acharya's Ashram, bordering a large waterbody, is open to visitors and as indeed is the local community's warm disposition.
- **Raghurajpur**-Raghurajpur has resurrected itself to a living, sylvan visage of Orissa's mural painting tradition. Only mineral and earth colours are used in the paintings, together with plant gums for binders. The grinding and preparation of pigments and binders is done by the women. Red Ochre and Cinnabar (red), Lamp black (black), conch shell (white) and Orpiment (yellow) are the only pigments

used. Though patachitra is its best known, Raghurajpur's households proudly display other accomplishments in palm leaf inscriptions, papier mache, sodhai work, mural painting, cow dung toys, coir, screw pine leaf and wood work, filigree, applique, terracotta and bell metal work. Alongside, the Gotipua Gurukul Academy has nurtured Raghurajpur's illustrious Odissi dance tradition of Guru Kelucharan Mohapatra. The artistry is heady...not to be missed and easily reached!

- **Sualkuchi**-Sualkuchi is barely 30 km by road and 12 km by river ferry from Guwahati on the north bank of the Brahmaputra. The picturesque Sualkuchi forest range on the opposite side, well-tended agricultural fields and the village fishing pond complete the rustic picture...fauna and all. Sualkuchi combines the ethnic setting of weaving skills in white and golden Assam silk, indigenously called Pat and Muga, together with agriculture and fishing in the neighbouring villages. The established regional tourist circuit includes the Kamakhya Temple and North Guwahati, noted for its archaeological heritage, temples and the sacerd Hajo. Local residents welcome visitors and can facilitate extension of their stay by arranging bullock cart rides, village walks, and Gurukul learning programmes in traditional weaving, fishing, agriculture, brewing, treks, cruises and cultural performances.
- **Thadiyankudissai**-Thadiyankudissai is also an atarctive node in the Spice Circuitand is surrounded by high ranges. Nature here is at its purest, the sky verdant and the tress imparting a unique fragrance...heightened with medicinal herbs, pepper plants, aromatic cardamom and coffee, jack fruit, butter fruit, star fruit and pineapple, each blessed by perennial streams, brooks and falls.Thadiyankudisai is truly a gift of nature. The tribal life style of the local community includes musical instruments and dwellings that take us back three hundred years, echoing the mosaic of the hills, birds and animals, coconut groves, evergreen forests and the warmth of these wonderful people...naturally a must for nature lovers...

6

MOVING TOWARDS MUSLIM TOURISM

It was one of these curious moments in history. On the very morning of 11.9.2001 just a few hours before the terror attacks in the USA, a new bilingual Arab/English tourist magazine was presented in Damascus at an international conference organized by the UNESCO on cultural tourism: namely, "Islamic Tourism", a London based "quarterly magazine of tourism in the Islamic world". The magazine itself is neither theoretic nor scientific. It is rather oriented to a board public, with easy-to-read reports and lots of pictures. The main new aspect is the "Islamic-shaped" language of the magazine. This is even more interesting than the choice of topics and locations, which are all located in Muslim countries or connected to Muslim locations worldwide. The publisher, Abdel-Sahib Al-Shakry, explains what the meaning of "Islamic" in the context of tourism in nine points, which can be summarized in three main blocks: first, the revival of Islamic cultures and the spread of Islamic values; second, economic benefit for Islamic societies; and third the strengthening of Islamic self-confidence, identity and beliefs in the face of negative stereotyping in comparison to other cultures and lifestyles. While counterproductive binarisms like "Islamic capabilities" versus "popular arts" or "attacks from other cultures" versus "spiritual beliefs of Muslims and Arabs" are openly mentioned, the positive and progressive open-minded elements and attitudes are revealed.

For example, the intention of Islamic-tourism is "not to replace existing tourist activity in our [Arabic/Muslim] areas but to open up new and exciting opportunities for growth, as well as to market a new type of commodity for which we are convinced there is an urgent need" or that Islamic tourism "will restrict sectarian and disagreement among Islamic schools of thought and opinion, and among people generally". The magazine takes a part in reflecting the discussions about an "Islamic" tourism that started before September 2001, but which have new dimensions and intensity after the attacks.

Concepts of Muslim Tourism

The various suggested ideas, models and comprehension of what an "Islamic" tourism could be are reflected in three major concepts: economic, cultural and religious-conservative concepts.

1. The Economic Concept—The economic concept for Islamic tourism is an extension and expansion oriented concept which focuses on the importance of intra-Muslim and intra-Arab tourism in terms of inclusion of new tourist markets and tourist destinations. Its precept understands the intra-Muslim tourism either as new markets to be integrated in the existing tourism strategy, or as a possible re-placement of the floundering and problematic European and North American markets after 2001. The economic concept is the most wide-spread and widely discussed in the Arab and Muslim worlds at different levels. It considers the Muslim countries as one of the emerging tourist markets of the future with huge economic, demographic and destination potentials. In the strategic working papers and recovery recommendations of the World Tourism Organization (WTO), Recovery Tourism Committee (RTC) and in many other official treaties as well as in workshops and symposia discussions, the economic concept is to be found in at least one of its numerous modifications.

The importance of the intra-Arab tourism was clearly to be seen after the huge crash of the international tourist markets after 9.11. On the one hand, countries like Egypt, Lebanon, Syria,

Bahrain and UAE were able right quickly to re-cover from the crisis due either to their ability to attract more tourists from Arab countries or to their less dependence on European and American Markets. One the other hand, countries like Tunisia, Morocco and Yemen, which are totally dependent on the European markets had collapsed (Table 1). Of course the further terror attacks in Jerba and Casa Blanca as well as the Moroccan-Spanish conflict on the Laila-Island and the unstable security situation in Yemen have massively strengthened the negative trends.

While the main "recovery effect" came from the shift towards more Arab and Muslim tourists in the structure of the international income tourists (Table 2), the Arab and Muslim countries have being trying to re-direct their strategies towards more intensification of the intra-Arab and intra-Muslim co-operation and co-ordination in tourist sector. The Islamic Conference for Ministers of Tourism (ICMT) and the Arab Counsel of Ministers of Tourism (ACMT) are examples of such intesification. The first meeting of the ICMT took place in October, 2000, in Iran and the second meeting in October, 2001, in Malaysia. The third meeting is Riyadh, in October, 2002, presented a new quality in the history of the ICMT. Fifty seven country were present at the meeting and the adopted "Riyadh Declaration" presented indeed a pragmatic and future-oriented working program. The main points of the declaration aims to ease the visa, investment and cash-flow restrictions in and between the Muslim countries. Joint marketing, financial support, experts' meetings, revival of Islamic cultural heritage and common codes of behavior are on the agenda as well.

The inclusion of new markets and the development of new tourist destinations are the major elements of the economic concept. Turkey, Iran and the middle Asian countries are becoming important export tourist markets to UAE and Egypt. The Arab golf countries are becoming important export tourist markets to Malaysia and Indonesia. Traditional Arab-, and Muslim-oriented destinations are booming (Cairo, Beirut, Bahrain) and new ones aim to place themselves on the Arab and Muslim tourist maps (Sharjah, Ain Sukhna, Singapore, Kuala Lumpur).

The Cultural Concept

The cultural concept for Islamic tourism includes visions and ideas that outline the inclusion of Islamic religious-cultural sites in tourism programs with "pedagogical" and self-confidence-building elements. It tries to encourage a re-orientation inside the tourist destinations towards less consumption and "western-culture" loaded sites towards more Islamic historical, religious and cultural sites. The re-discovering by tourism authorities and tour operators of second ranging marks of Islamic cultural heritage, such as shrines, tombs, old battle sites, ancient pilgrim routes etc., and including them in special tourism programs, is one of the examples of the new development. A very special place in this concept is played by the new "tourist" interpretations of pilgrimage and the efforts to merge religious and leisure tourism in joint programs. Saudi Arabia is developing a new strategy for tourism that is based on a new interpretation of pilgrimage that includes leisure activities besides the traditional pilgrim visits to the holy sites. Tourism promoters in other Muslim countries are offering or working on similar programs. Islamic sites such as Mu'ta and Mazar in Jordan, Qum in Iran, Islamic missionary routs in Oman, various shrines in Morocco, old mosques in Bosnia and the historic cities of Samarkand and Bukhara are already addressed in tourist promotions programs in Arab and Muslim countries. The cultural concept attempts to revive the Islamic and Arabic cultures in the discourse of tourism as a counterpart to the process of cultural globalization dominated by "McDonaldization" or "Cocalization". According to Al-Aidi, "marketing national Arab tourism as Arab in character and dominated by Arab features, with its own tradition and costumes, is also convenient for the requirements of Arab tourist". The cultural "Arabization" and/or the "Islamization" of tourism are only to be understood as a reaction of the (much) weaker part in the aggressive process of cultural globalization, to define and to protect one's own culture and cultural heritage. The challenge is whether the tourism industry is indeed capable and skilled enough to implement such a task or even to contribute to a solution. Kevin Meethan suggests that tourism will globally "commodificate" the national cultures into exotic and "consumptional" goods, and doing this it will help saving them.The commodification of native and national cultures is one of the most controversial topics of understanding tourism in the era of the aggressive neo-liberal globalization.

The Religious-Conservative Concept

The religious-conservative concept for Islamic tourism has not yet been theoretically articulated. But various opinions and remarks in the discussions on the future of tourism in the Arab and Islam worlds as well as some practices of hotel's managements indicate that articulations and implementations are just a matter of time. The whole idea is based on the conservative interpretation and understanding of Islam. Merging elements of the extremely conservative Islamic lifestyle with the modern tourism industry could indeed present new tourism options, spaces, and spheres. Excluding the fundamental isolationistic views which reject practically any tourism activities beyond pilgrimage, the religious-conservative concepts may be described as "community tourism". Islamic resorts and hotels as well as Islamic destinations and programs are shaping some tourist activities; Islamic resorts funded and owned by Islamic finance institutions, alcohol-free accommodations, no in-door disco/ nightlife hotels, gender-segregated fitness and sport facilities, conservative in-door dress-codex, availability of prayer-rooms on site, women floors and "Islamic" entertainment programs. Many elements of this concept are indeed implemented in the domestic tourism in Saudi Arabia and Iran. Nevertheless, the luxurious hotels and resorts, where the share of international tourism is significant, are less controlled and have a more liberal atmosphere even in these both countries. For a benefit oriented hotel business, the implementation of elements of the conservative-religious is just an adjustment to a new market segment and to new demands (praying room in JW Marriot/ Deira, dry law in the hotels in Sharjah, planned women floor in Pearl Movenpick/Dubai Media City, female hours in spa are widely speared, alcohol free restaurants). For a growing conservative intra-Arab and intra-Muslim tourism market, the implementation of a religious-conservative concept in tourism planning as an extra-option, as an insertion into the existing main-stream tourism could indeed have a positive economic and social effect. The exclusion of a noteworthy and growing group of population from the tourism market, leads to the alienation of the tourism industry by the religious-conservatives. Being under durable "lifestyle" pressure in liberal and "west-style" tourism locations, if religious-conservative families and individuals ever decide to vacation in such locations, it could lead to the negative affects of "never again" or simply "frustration". The discussions in Saudi Arabia about opening the country for international tourism and about tourism with Islamic values are steps in the right direction. Here, though, one must not lose sight of the fact that other types of tourism, for liberal-Muslims and non-Muslims, must be an option as well. The example of Dubai/Sharja is interesting in this context; Dubai is an international, liberal, shopping-, events- ,and leisure oriented destination, while Sharja, a city located just a few kilometers to the north, has an alcohol-free accommodation rules and a more conservative cultural and leisure tourism concept.

The Global Islamic Tourism Conference & Exhibition

The Global Islamic Tourism Conference & Exhibition (GITC) is an annual forum for the global Islamic tourism industry to gather leading relevant regional and international travel and tourism professionals to network and unlock the business potential within the Islamic tourism industry around the world. This is the second exhibition and conference of such nature for Malaysia which proudly has long historical ties with Muslims all over the world.

The GITC event focuses on exploring and celebrating the countries and cultures of the Islamic world and also features attractions in countries where Islam is practiced, though in a much smaller scale such as Japan, South Korea, the United Kingdom and Australia, among others.

The Hosted Buyer Programme at Global Islamic Tourism Conference & Exhibition (GITC) brings exhibitors together with tour operators, leisure buyers as well as the industry's most influential meetings, incentive and corporate buyers.

Running simultaneously as the exhibition is a 1-day international conference where speakers will share their views and findings on Islamic Tourism and its various definitions. The first conference was a success which led to the establishment of a World Islamic Tourism Secretariat with the role objective of maximizing efforts at facilitating tourism promotion and value creation. This second GITC will also include a Food Festival and will be themed as the Global Islamic Food Festival@GITC to show the correlation between tourism and food.

The exhibitions, conferences, press conferences, networking luncheons, dinners, cocktail receptions, food-tasting, celebrities cook-off, media culinary event and free food seminars are just a few of the scheduled activities trade visitors attending the event can also expect to experience.

Products and Services

Airlines, Car Hire Companies, Coach Operators, Conference/Incentive/Meeting Venues, Cruise/Ferry Companies, Ground handlers, Health Resorts & Spas, Hotel/ Accommodation Providers, Internet Support Services, Reservation Systems, Special Internet Holidays, Telecommunication/Technology, Tourism Developments, Tourist Attractions, Tourist Boards/Associations, Developers, Restaurants, Confectioneries, Manufacturers.

Trade Visitors Profile

Associations, Business Travel Agents, Conference Organizers, Eco Tourism/Adventure Travel, Ground handlers, Group Travel Organizers, Holiday Specialists, Hotels/Hotel Groups, Inbound Tour Operators, Online/Internet Travel Services, Outbound Tour Operators, Retail Travel Agents, Sporting Holiday Specialists, Technology/Environment/

Reservation Systems, Transport Air, Road, Rail and Shipping Companies, Restaurateur's.

The Muslim Heritage of Our World

Bali

The tourism industry is primarily focused in the south, while significant in the other parts of the island as well. The main tourist locations are the town of Kuta (with its beach), and its outer suburbs of Legian and Seminyak (which were once independent townships), the east coast town of Sanur (once the only tourist hub), in the center of the island Ubud, to the south of the Ngurah Rai International Airport, Jimbaran, and the newer development of Nusa Dua and Pecatu.

The American government lifted its travel warnings in 2008. As of 2009, the Australian government still rates it at a 4 danger level (the same as several countries in central Africa) on a scale of 5.

An offshoot of tourism is the growing real estate industry. Bali real estate has been rapidly developing in the main tourist areas of Kuta, Legian, Seminyak and Oberoi. Most recently, high-end 5 star projects are under development on the Bukit peninsula, on the south side of the island. Million dollar villas are being developed along the cliff sides of south Bali, commanding panoramic ocean views. Foreign and domestic (many Jakarta individuals and companies are fairly active) investment into other areas of the island also continues to grow. Land prices, despite the worldwide economic crisis, have remained stable.

In the last half of 2008, Indonesia's currency had dropped approximately 30% against the US dollar, providing many overseas visitors value for their currencies. Visitor arrivals for 2009 were forecast to drop 8% (which would be higher than 2007 levels), due to the worldwide economic crisis which has also affected the global tourist industry, but not due to any travel warnings.

Bali's tourism economy survived the terrorist bombings of 2002 and 2005, and the tourism industry has in fact slowly recovered and surpassed its pre-terrorist bombing levels; the longterm trend has been a steady increase of visitor arrivals. At 2010, Bali received 2.57 million foreign tourists. It is surpassed the target of 2.0-2.3 million tourists. The average occupancy of starred hotels achieved 65 percent (last year 60.8 percent), so still capable for accommodates tourists for next some years without any addition of new rooms/hotels, although at the peak season some of them are fully booked.

Bali received the Best Island award from Travel and Leisure in 2010. The award was presented in the show "World's Best Awards 2010" in New York, on 21 July. Hotel Four Seasons Resort Bali at Jimbaran also received an award in the category of "World Best Hotel Spas in Asia 2010". The award was based on a survey of travel magazine Travel + Leisure readers between 15 December 2009 through 31 March 2010, and was judged on several criteria. The Ayana Resort received the designation; #1 Spa in the world by Conde Naste's Traveller Magazine for 2010 by their readers poll . The island of Bali won because of its attractive surroundings (both mountain and coastal areas), diverse tourist attractions, excellent international and local restaurants, and the friendliness of the local people.

The Ngurah Rai International Airport is located near Jimbaran, on the isthmus at the southernmost part of the island. Lt.Col. Wisnu Airfield is found in north-west Bali.

A coastal road surrounds the island, and three major two-lane arteries cross the central mountains at passes reaching to 1,750m in height (at Penelokan). The Ngurah Rai Bypass is a four-lane expressway that partly encircles Denpasar and enables cars to travel quickly in the heavily populated south. Bali has no railway lines.

December 2010: Government of Indonesia has invited investors to build Tanah Ampo Cruise Terminal at Karangasem, Bali amounted $30 million.

A Memorandum of Understanding has been signed by 2 ministers, Bali's Governor and Indonesian Train Company to build 565 kilometers railway along the coast around the island. It will be operated since 2015.

Cairo

On September 17, five Islamic monuments were officially inaugurated in the Al-Darb Al-Ahmar area of Cairo. The Al-Imam mosque, the Al-Laythmosque, the Al-Set Meska mosque, the Ali Labib house and the well zone of Youssef at the Salah El-Din Citadel have all been undergoing restoration work, which cost around LE 9.5 million. These monuments including the first phase construction of the new lighting system of the Salah El-Din Citadel were inaugurated at the ceremony. The ceremony took place at the Salah El-Din Citadel.

Dr. Zahi Hawass, the Secretary General of the Supreme Council of Antiquities (SCA), Dr. Hamdi Zaqzouq, the Minister of Endowment, and Cairo Governor Abdel Azim Waziri inaugurated the special ceremony along with top governmental officials.

The restoration of these important historical edifices is a part of the Supreme Council of Antiquities' dedication to preserve Egypt's Islamic heritage.

The most outstanding restoration-conversion attraction, amid the decrepit villages of the Egyptian capital unfamiliar to visitors, one extremely ambitious project has been undertaken with the creation of a vast, green open space in a once run-down area of Cairo. Interestingly since the project was started, another dimension has been added -a rehabilitation of the surrounding residential district called Darb Al Ahmar, so impoverished it needed the Aga Khan to give it a facelift.

For years, tourists have long been kept off the area by the virtually unofficial wasteland or rubbish dump lying alongside the derelict eastern rim of old Cairo's medieval city walls. From its early beginnings as the massive wastebasket to a gigantic mountain pile of dirt, it ended up obscuring residents' views of the fortress wall and pretty minarets nearby through the years. It has become, in a sense, irreverent that it lies beside the walled old cemetery known as the City Of the Dead, where scores of homeless Cairenes have found shelter in tombs housing urns of the more-privileged.

In 2004, on the metropolis shared by the living and the dead, where dust, debris and garbage have collected through the millennium, arose a $45 million project the Aga Khan Development Network designed to complete in 7 years to uplift the destitute.

Four years after unexplained shoveling, digging and earth-moving the contractors were doing much to the perplexity of locals, the project finally took shape. Out of the barren 30-hectare Darassa Hills came a lush, green park overlooking Cairo's Islamic city. It would bring hundreds of jobs, a place for the busy Cairenes to de-stress, open views of the Citadel never there before; notwithstanding, give people hope in a hometown that had never produced them profits.

Opened to the public end on a trial basis, it welcomed the first guests. Once the city built in ancient times by the Fatimids and named Al Quahire or the victorious, the previous 20 percent devoted to open space now had tourists flocking to it. From Easter till end of September, for about 5 and a half weeks, the park construction concentrated on the finer details of what would become an interesting rehab site inaugurated September 17 during a special event at the Citadel.

Istanbul

The city consists of three separate elements - the old Turkish town (Eminönöü, Aksaray, Fatih), in the form of an almost equilateral triangle, which extends from the right bank of the Golden Horn to the Sea of Marmara; linked with the old town by the Galata and Atatürk Bridges, the district of Beyoglu with its suburbs of Galata and

Harbiye, largely inhabited by foreigners, on the slopes between the Golden Horn and the Bosporus; and the district of Üsküdar, with its suburbs, on the Asiatic side of the Bosporus. Istanbul is a unique and unforgettable sight with its towers and its palaces and the numerous domes and minarets of the 35 large and over a hundred smaller mosques rising above the water. Little is left of the colorful Oriental life of the old capital of the Sultans, and the people now wear European dress. Street names and shop signs are in the Latin alphabet; and the old rows of brown timber houses with red roofs and latticed kafes (bow-windows) have given place in the central areas to stone and reinforced-concrete blocks.

The climate of Istanbul is marked by sharp contrasts. In the evening it is frequently cool, even in summer. Among the city's numerous birds visitors will be impressed particularly by the black kites and, on the Bosporus, the black cormorants. Dolphins are a frequent sight in the Bosporus and the Sea of Marmara.

About 660 B.C. Dorian Greeks founded on what is now Seraglio Point the city of Byzantion (in Latin Byzantium), which controlled access to the Black Sea at the entrance to the Bosporus. In 513 B.C. the town was captured by the Persian King Darius I. During the sixth and fifth century it was a member of the first and second Attic Leagues. In 148 B.C. the free city of Byzantion entered into an alliance with Rome, and thereafter it several times lost and then regained its freedom. In A.D. 196 the city was captured and harshly treated by Septimius Severus, but soon recovered. In 324, after his victory over Licinius, Constantine I (306-37) resolved to make a second capital of the Empire.

In the autumn of 326 a beginning was made with the construction of a line of town walls taking in an area which extended far to the west, and on May 11th 330 the new city was solemnly inaugurated, under the name of Nova Roma or New Rome, soon to be changed to Constantinopolis. Like Rome the new city was divided into fourteen regions, and even had its seven hills. After the division of the Empire in 395 Constantinople became the capital of the Eastern Roman Empire. In the reign of Justinian (527-65) who rebuilt the city in greater magnificence after much of it had been reduced to ashes during the Nika Insurrection, it enjoyed its period of greatest splendor. Late Greek and Roman culture developed into the distinctive Byzantine culture, which found expression in the Greek language.

Soon afterwards, however, the Empire was torn by domestic and external conflicts. The city was harried by the Avars and Persians (627) and by the Arabs under the Omayyad caliphs; in 813 and again in 924 it was besieged by the Bulgars; and in 907 and 1048 Russian fleets appeared off Constantinople. Finally came the catastrophe of 1204, when, following disputes over the succession to the Imperial throne, the Crusaders captured the city and founded a Latin Empire.

After the Ottoman conquest of Asia Minor in the 13th century and the transfer of the capital from Bursa to Edirne (Adrianople) Constantinople was increasingly encircled by Turks. In 1453 Mehmet II Fatih (the Conqueror) took the city, which now became the Ottoman capital under the name of Istanbul. There was a great wave of building by the Sultans and Turkish grandees, particularly by Selim I (1512-20) and Süleiman the Magnificent (1520-66). Many major buildings were also erected in the 17th and 18th century During the 19th century Western influences began to make themselves felt in the city's architecture.

After the First World War, in which Turkey had been allied with the Central Powers, Istanbul was occupied by the Allies. In 1922, following Turkey's victory in the War of Independence, Turkish troops re-entered the city. In 1923 the Sultanate and Caliphate were abolished and Turkey became a Republic and its first President, Mustafa Kemal Atatürk, moved the capital to Ankara. In a drastic program of reform Atatürk banned the fez, the wearing of veils by women, the Order of Dervishes and polygamy and introduced the Latin alphabet, the metric system and regular surnames. The aspect of Istanbul has since then been increasingly Europeanized by the driving of wide modern streets through the old town, the pulling down of the old wooden houses and their replacement by new blocks of flats and offices, the establishment of a new commercial and business center north of Taksim Square and the development of whole new districts of the city.

Istanbul made a bid to host the 27th Summer Olympic Games in the year 2000.

Copt (Coptic) Spots

A Copt (Coptic) is a native Egyptian Christian. Copts form a major ethno-religious group that has ancient origins. Copts are Egyptians whose ancestors embraced Christianity in the first centuries after Christ. The word "Coptic" was originally used to refer to Egyptians in general (see etymology section), but it has undergone a semantic shift over the centuries to mean more specifically Egyptian Christian. This semantic shift dates back to the time when Christians became an Egyptian minority, after the Muslim conquest of Egypt in the 7th century.

Egypt's Coptic Church is one of Christianity's earliest, brought here by Mark, writer of the oldest New Testament gospel. The liturgy closely resembles those seen in other Eastern Orthodox churches, though the Copts' leader, or pope, has always been based in Egypt. This church was actually built in the 1990s, a tribute to its ancient heritage, modern engineering, and the affluence of some in Egypt's Coptic minority. But that wealth is in small pockets of Egypt's upper class and a Copt diaspora in rich countries.

The Coptic Church developed separately from other Eastern churches. The Coptic Church's clerical hierarchy had evolved by the sixth century. A patriarch, referred to as the pope, heads the church. A synod or council of senior priests (people who have attained the status of bishops) is responsible for electing or removing popes. Members of the Coptic Church worldwide (about 1 million Copts lived outside of Egypt as of 1990) recognize the pope as their spiritual leader. The pope, traditionally based in Alexandria, also serves as the chief administrator of the church. The administrator's functionaries includes hundreds of priests serving urban and rural parishes, friars in monasteries, and nuns in convents.

The main language in the eastern part of the Roman Empire was Greek, also used by the Egyptian Christians

(Copts). Some Egyptians had started to write their own language using Greek letters (old Coptic) before the advent of Christianity; Coptic later became the principal script and language of Christian Egypt below the official Greek (then Arabic) level, and it remains alive today in the Coptic Church, for liturgical use. Greek was the state language used for administration and education, until replaced by Arabic at the end of the 7th century. In the first century after the Moslem annexation of Egypt, documents might be produced in three languages, Greek, Coptic and Arabic. Coptic enjoyed a revival under Islam: most of the Coptic books in collections today date to the Islamic Period. Contrary to the common perception that Coptic was only used for liturgy, there are many Coptic texts in medicine, mathematics, and alchemy. From the 11th century onwards, Arabic was used to write Christian material often side by side with Coptic, producing bilingual texts which were instrumental in the process of the European decipherment of Egyptian language by Kircher and successors such as Champollion.

Following Islam's spread through Egypt, Muslims alternately tolerated and persecuted the Copts. Heavy taxation of Christians encouraged mass conversions to Islam, and within two centuries, Copts had become a distinct minority. By the tenth century, Arabic had replaced Coptic as the primary spoken language, and Coptic was relegated to a liturgical language.

Historic Egyptian Copt (Coptic) Spots

St.Catherine's Monastery Sinai

The oldest Christian monastery still in existence in the world and houses also the richest collection of icons and precious manuscripts. St Cathrine's basilica is through a massive 12th- century entry door, in the Fatimid style: this door opens directly onto the narthex where, under thick protective glass, is displayed a marvelous collection of icons dating from the 5th to 7th centuries

Coptic Museum

Founded in 1910, it contains the finest extant collection of Coptic art: the collections belonged to Marcos Smaika Pasha . The Museum consists of two pavilions and a square court: the older one contains ornamental latticework (the "musharabiya") and wooden ceilings from the oldest Coptic palaces, as well as fountains, windows in stucco and mosaics, marble and stone columns . The Museum has thirty rooms containing frescoes, wooden sheathing, worked metals, vases, objects in glass, tapestries, papyrus scrolls, manuscripts, icons and ivory sculpture. There is also a library with seven thousand books and manuscripts, mostly in the Coptic language.

The Holy Family's journey to Egypt

The advent of the Holy Family to Egypt, seeking refuge, is an event of the utmost significance in our dear country's long, long history. The tortuous trails they followed in their passage across Sinai, and their subsequent travels within Egypt After their short, but all-too-felt, stay in Old Cairo, the Holy Family moved in a southerly direction, reaching Cairo suburb of Maadi which, in earliest Pharaonic times was an outlying district of Memphis, the capital of Egypt then they boarded El Sorian Monastery "Wadi El Natroun"In the earliest decades of Christianity, the desert expanses of Wadi el-Natroun became the site of anchoretic settlement and, later, of many monasteries, in spiritual commemoration of the Holy Family's passage through the Valley. Virgen Mary Church "Zeitoun"is one of the Holy Family's remarkable stops along Egypt.

The Hanging Church

Built at the close of the Century and beginning of the 5th Century. So called because it was built on the southern tower of the Babylon Castle, headquarters of the Byzantine army in Misr al Qadima (Old Cairo). It is built in the Basilica style.

LARNACA, CYPRUS

Though Larnaca is part of Cyprus and an important port for the country at that, it would appear that the city belongs to all mankind, preserving our collective inheritance as residents of this planet. It is said that the city was built by Noah's grandson, and the important Neolithic settlement in the area and the migratory birds from distant lands that grace the Salt Lake, combine to give telling credence to this. Christianity and Islam both have deep imprints on the city and tourists can combine a vacation with deep religious experiences in Larnaca's monumental Churches and the shrine built to honor the Aunt of the Prophet himself. Situated as it is at the confluence of Europe and Asia, the city gives every visitor a truly remarkable experience.

Larnaca provides a unique expose to history. It is a delight for those who relish the past but can also kindle a spark in the most hardened modernist. It is fascinating to walk through the city, as rarely can one be transported in such realistic manner back several centuries, in the midst of a modern urban center with cafes and other trappings of spots that all vacationers love. The combination of a calm atmosphere and a warm people will calm the most stressed nerves as will a day on the pristine sands of the Mackenzie beach. There are many cities by the sea but few have kept them with as much love and spirit as you find in Larnaca. You can spend quality time just strolling along the palm fringed avenue, stopping to savor the scene over some beverage at a café.

An important landmark of Larnaca is the Stavrovouni Monastry. It was founded in the 4th century, reportedly with a fragment of the Holy Cross. It has a majestic location on the top of a rocky hill with a commanding view of the countryside. The monks have a rich tradition of icon painting. Women and photography are prohibited and men must be properly dressed if they wish to visit.

Larnaca has many well kept records of its past from the 8th to the 10th century. The Agia Phaneromeni Church is a fine piece of architecture from this period. The Ayios Lazarus is a 9th century Church built on the tomb of St. Lazarus, Larnaca's first Bishop, after his resurrection by Lord Jesus. The architectural highlight of this splendid structure is the decoration of icons on the main doors of entrance. The Church is also worth a visit for its rare museum collection of art, apart from its imposing bell tower. The latter, though of relatively recent origin, is still 150 years old. The Kition archeological site is another experience without which no tourist should return to the city's modern airport! The site has temples and settlements from the 10th century.

Reasons that only accomplished historians can explain, make one jump from the 10th to the 17th century, in the journey along Larnaca's past. The Larnaca Castle, used as a prison by the British, has splendid views and an absorbing collection in its museum. The city does have a range of museums as one might expect, and it is possible to spend days on end browsing amongst rare treasures and still leave much unseen. The 18th century Kamares aqueduct is worth a visit for its imposing and characteristic sweep of the landscape.

A visit to the Lefkara village sets a suitable tone for the end of a Larnaca visit. It is known for lace and silver, and while the handicrafts can be sourced from one's hotel shopping mall or an up-market boutique, purchases from the friendly craftspeople leaves lasting fragrance on your souvenirs.

Saudi Arabia

Saudi Arabia, although many would not think so, actually has a thriving tourism industry and there is a lot to see in this very historic country full of culture and intrest to many.

Mecca

This is the most holy place to all Muslims and pilgrims are always present here all year round. This is also a popular tourist spot in Saudi Arabia for non-Muslims where they got to witness the different events and festivals held in Mecca. There are also the Mountain of Light, the Holy Mosque, and the Grand

Mosque where you could truly appreciate the wonderful Islam religion.

Al Masjid Al Nabawi

A major tourist spot in Saudi Arabia and considered by the Muslims as the second holiest mosque in the world. The place was once the residence of Prophet Muhammad and now has become the focal point for religious instructions. This is an important landmark in the rich heritage of the country of Saudi Arabia.

Masjid al Qiblatain

A top tourist spot in Saudi Arabia that displays the rich architecture of the country. The mosque is among the list of the world's oldest mosques that was once a small building and now renovated to receive 2,000 people all at once. This mosque plays an important role in the history of Islam religion.

Quba Mosque

Quba Mosque is the holiest of all the mosques found in Madina and is also the world's oldest mosque. This ancient mosque is part of the most famous tourist spot in Saudi Arabia. It is a belief that the first stones of the edifice were put in place personally by the Prophet himself. The architectural design of the mosque is also very interesting.

Jawatha Mosque

This tourist spot in Saudi Arabia is among the oldest religious mosques within the country. It was built during the seventh century by the Bani Abdul Qais tribe and was believed to be the first of all the mosques within the eastern section of Saudi Arabia. Within its ruins, you will be able to view the past glorious days of the mosque.

Dumat al Jundal

A tourist spot in Saudi Arabia that will let you encounter romance within its ancient ruins. This mystical city of Dumat al Jundal will take you back to the time of the tenth century

B.C. and lets you discover the interesting history of Saudi Arabia. The place is located within a beautiful oasis on the northern part of the Great Nafud Desert.

Tayma

Don't miss out this fascinating tourist spot in Saudi Arabia where a very prosperous settlement of the Jews once inhabit the area. You need to spend enough time in order to thoroughly seek the wondrous scattered in the area and learn the interesting history that comes with them.

Medain Saleh

A tourist spot in Saudi Arabia that is not just beautiful but also important in the history of the country. Scattered within the area are about 131 tombs and the total land area of the place is estimated to be 13.4 kilometers. Aside from the tombs, there are also towers, walls, houses, and other kinds of ruined structures.

Rock Carving Site

There are a number of rock carving sites in Saudi Arabia and the most notable of them all is Jubbah. Travel through time as you learn the ancient art of the primeval folks and understand the way of their life during the prehistoric era. These arts in the ancient rocks are truly intriguing and fascinating.

Al Ula

An interesting tourist spot in Saudi Arabia that was once an active site of the commerce and trade activities. The place has been the heart of the Saudi Arabian Civilization until the first century B.C. Surrounding Al Ula are wonderful carved tombs and other ancient structures.

Brunei

Brunei can be deceiving in all its riches available for tourists. Don't be fooled and know what awaits the gambling tourist who is looking for a new and exciting place to visit. So here are the top ten tourist spots for Brunei which all should visit if traveling in this historic country.

Jame'Asr Hassanil Bolkiah Mosque

Brunei has a lot of cultural and religious tourist attractions. That should be expected due to the 600 year rule of sultans in the country. A lot of these religious sites have become historic as the years have gone by. The Jame'Asr Hassanil Bolkiah Mosque is by far the most splendid one of them all. It is also one of the most important religious sites in the country.

It is located in Kampong Kiarong, which is quite close to the nation's capital. Though it is mainly a place of worship among Muslims, it is open to visits by those not of the faith during Thursdays. You'll definitely enjoy the architectural masterpieces to be witnessed here.

Royal Regalia Museum

A tour of the many tourist attractions of Brunei will give you various glimpses into the royal buildings and cultural centers. Not only do they speak of the architectural prowess of the country, they also speak volumes regarding the people's history.

The Royal Regalia Museum is one of the most culturally significant places to visit if you want to understand the people's culture and history. The collections you will find here portray the regal life of the royal dynasties that ruled the land, which also reflects the political aspects of the nation.

Brunei History Center

600 years worth of history is preserved in the Brunei History Center. Historical edifices are preserved here for the perusal and appreciation of generations to come. It was built in 1982 under the consent of the reigning sultan of the time. If you want to take a crash course into the country's history then this History Center place will give you quite a comprehensive introduction.

Kampong Ayer

Kampong Ayer is locally dubbed as the Venice of the East. It is one of the tourist attractions in the country that you shouldn't miss. This place is sometimes called the 'water village'. It is quite interesting that the moniker 'Venice of the East' wasn't coined by one of the locals but was given by a foreign visitor.

Omar Ali Saifuddin Mosque

One of the important mosques in the country is the Omar Ali Saifuddin Mosque. This mosque is quite picturesque being situated on an artificial lagoon near the Brunei River. This religious site has become quite popular in South East Asia being known for it transient beauty. Incidentally, this mosque was named after the country's 28th sultan.

Istana Nurul Iman

The residence of the nation's sultan, Istana Nurul Iman, is a spectacular place to visit. In fact, it is the biggest palace in the whole country. The palace was designed by the Philippines' national artist for architecture, Leandro V. Locsin. Unfortunately, the palace itself isn't usually open to visitors. You can only adore the lavish residence during the annual Hari Raya Puasa Festival.

Jerudong Theme Park

This is one of the most popular tourist attractions in the country. It is often frequented by a lot of visitors all year round. It is open to the public and visitors are not required to purchase any ticket to gain entry. It's a great place to have a picnic or just spend a relaxing afternoon. There are rides for visitors and food kiosks in case you get hungry.

Drottningholm

This tourist attraction is actually where the country's royal family resides. The very first palace built in this site was constructed in the 16th century. However, it was destroyed in

1961 and a new palace was constructed the following year. The place is quite charming and reflects the country's glory.

Religious Pilgrimage

The main religion of this nation is Islam. And as such, one of the highlights to any visit here would be a religious pilgrimage. People come here not only to admire the beautifully crafted mosques but also to worship. The architecture of these religious buildings is already a welcome treat to any visitor.

Visiting the Royal Residences

One of the big attractions of Brunei is the lavishly decorated and designed royal residences. The members of the sultanate's royalty live in regal homes that are wonderfully decorated and fashioned. Some of these places are also historic sites as well.

Yemen

For those looking for something new, the tourist spots in Yemen will appeal to your sense of exploration and adventure. That they're not as famous and crowded as the tourist sights in other countries makes them all the more appealing.

Aden

Situated by the Arabian Sea, it is filled with numerous fortresses and tunnels. Two of the most vital historical landmarks are the Water Reservoirs of Al-Taweelah and the Fort of Jabal 'Aly. Most of the monuments are situated in the Old city of Aden and the surrounding area.

Crater

This ancient city is famous for its ancient mosques, most notably the Mosque of Abban. The Lighthouse in Crater is another major sightseeing spot. The city is also famous for its markets, including the Al-Taweel, Za'afaran and the Buhara Market.

Taiz City

One of the upcoming tourist spots in Yemen, the city is 256 km from Sana. The most distinguishable landmarks are the Al Ma'tabiyyah dome and the Al Muzaffar mosque. There is also a museum housing artifacts and relics.

Tomb of Sheikh Ahmad

One of the most famous tombs in the country is that of Sheikh Ahmad Bin Alwan, a Sufist who lived c. 1300 AD. His tomb is located just to the southwest of Taiz. The tomb is under a mosque and draws scores of visitors annually.

Al Mocha

The city is west to Taiz (approximately 94 km). The most conspicuous landmark here is the Shazli mosque. Dating back 500 years, it is one of the most remarkable tourist spots in Yemen. Other sightseeing spots include the Malik Beach, Yakhtal Beach and the many palm trees in the area.

Al Janad

It was here the first mosque in Yemen was built in 630 AD. Landmarks include the ancient mosque set at the mountains. There are also water canals by the mountain. Also part of the attraction is the Weekly Souks or markets.

Hudedah

The main attractions in this city are the beaches along the western end, ideal for swimming or fishing. There are also several valleys here including the Wadi Surdud and the Wadi Zabid valleys. Bura Mountain is the tallest in the vicinity at 2,400 m. Rass Mountain reaches a height of 2,000 m above sea level.

Mukalla City

The fishing center of the country, the city is one of the most beautiful tourist spots in Yemen due to the sultan palace.

This was built by Omar bin Awad Al-Qu'aity. The Al-Ghuweizy Castle, the public markets and museum are other attractions.

Al Shehir City

The olden part of the city is filled with ancient landmarks including old walls and gates. The newer section is renowned for the white stones used on the buildings. The city is also known for its jewelry shops, boats and markets.

The Hadramout Valley

At 160 km, it is the longest in the entire Arabian Peninsula. It goes all the way to Thamoud up to the Masila Valley. In some areas there are palm trees and plants surrounding it. The tourist spots in Yemen are both remarkable and distinctive. What the sites may lack in popularity is made up for by their notable appearance.

Bahrain

The tourist spots in Bahrain constitute some of the finest sightseeing locations in the Middle East. Today, people from all over the world are coming to Bahrain to get a glimpse of Arab culture and architecture.

Al Fateh Mosque

Set near King Faisal Highway, the Al Fateh Mosque is one of the biggest mosques in the world, with room for 7,000 worshippers. The 60 ton dome is made entirely of fiberglass and draws tourists and religious devotees by the thousands.

Al Khamis Mosque

This mosque is regarded as one of the most ancient in all of Islam. The foundation was set down in 692 AD during the time of Caliph Umar II. Its most distinguishing traits are the twin minarets.

Arad Fort

No list of the tourist spots in Bahrain would be complete without mentioning the Arad Fort. Built sometime in the 15th century, very little is known of its past. Today however, it is one of the visually striking sights in Bahrain, especially at night.

Bab Al Bahrain

Situated at Manama's business district, it is the site of the Bahrain financial harbor. The monument has been renovated and now sports Islamic inspired designs. In the vicinity are the Gold City shopping mall and a handicraft shop.

Bahrain Fort

A UNESCO World Heritage site, the fort is composed of mounds made by the primitive peoples in 2300 BC. It is one of the most highly regarded tourist spots in Bahrain, as it used to be the seat of the Dilmun civilization. The name actually means Bahrain Castle.

The Bahrain National Museum

Located near King Faisal Highway, it is the largest museum in Bahrain. The $30 million complex encompasses 6,000 years of the land's history. Apart from historical artifacts, other halls focus on Bahrain culture and life. Exhibits of flora and fauna are also to be found there.

The Dilmun Burial Mounds

This burial ground dates back to the time of the Dilmun civilization. The mounds come in a variety of sizes but most of them are 15 by 30 ft (4.5 by 9 m). Because the bodies were buried with some items, it has proven to be a valuable archaeological resource.

Riffa Fort

This tourist spot in Bahrain offers some of the finest views of Hunanaiya valley. During the 1860s, the fort was the seat of power in the area. Today the structure offers glimpses of royal life and architecture in the 19th century.

The Barbar Temple

The temple is an archaeological site in the village of Barbar. To date, three of these temples have been unearthed, the oldest going back to 3000 BC. Tools and assorted weapons have been found along the site too.

Tree of Life

This tree can be found 2 km from the Jebel Dukhan, the highest peak in Bahrain. It is a 100 year old tree and stands alone. What makes it fascinating is the entire area is free of water.

The tourist spots in Bahrain are not just fine examples of Arab architecture and history. It also offers first time visitors the chance to understand a different culture.

Kosovo

Discovering the best tourist areas in Kosovo is the easiest and best way to experience this grand and ancient country which is quickly becoming a great place for tourism.

Prishtina

The capital city of the country is also a great tourist spot in Kosovo. Take a walking tour of the city as you visit one building to another like museums, mosques, monuments, and government buildings. It is also quite interesting to have a visit to the offices of Kosovo's important international organizations.

Drini River Waterfall

This tourist spot in Kosovo is a fantastic place during the summer months. The waterfall is located behind the village of Berdynaj in the northern part of Pec. The road going to the river is already amazing aside from the great view of the waterfall.

The Pec Patriarchy

Located about two kilometers away from the center of Pec City in the northwest direction. This is where the foundation of the Serbian Orthodox Church Patriarchy is located since 1302. This tourist spot in Kosovo is a gorgeous monastery full of amazing paintings.

The Rugova Gorge

Driving further from the Pec Patriarchy is the Rugova Gorge. A tourist spot in Kosovo that is a canyon composed of very steep walls. The highest reach of the walls of the gorge is about 300 meters.

The Gjakova Old Bazaar

This tourist spot in Kosovo is an ancient and very attractive shopping center that dates back to 17th century. The place has been reconstructed after it was damaged by fire during the battle in 1999. An ancient mosque that was constructed during the 15th century is found at the center of the shopping center.

The Mitrovica Bridge

This tourist spot in Kosovo is a fascinating representation of the division between the populace of the country. The bridge serves as a dividing path between Albanians and Serbs in Mitrovica. Approaching and taking a good look at the bridge is always safe except when political situation becomes worse.

Prizren

Of all the cities in Kosovo, Prizren is the most historical since it has lots of lovely Islamic architecture. This tourist spot in Kosovo is a home of monasteries and mosques that dates back to the fourteenth century. Tour around the city and admire the wonderful mosques spread across the city and the most notable of them is the Mosque of Sinan Pasha.

Brod

A very spectacular village in the country of the Balkans and the place is inhabited by the Gorani people. Walking around the village is very ideal to really see the uniqueness of the place. Their houses are made of mountain rocks and other materials from their immediate area. A horse ride going to the mountains is a wonderful opportunity to see the beauty of nature in this part of the world.

Novo Brdo

A tourist spot in Kosovo that was a metropolis during the year 1326 according to historical documents. The place has a large medieval fortress that was constructed on the peak of the cone of an extinct volcano. Taking a visit to the ruins of the fortress will give you a good experience to cherish.

Ulpiana

A tourist spot in Kosovo that was once an ancient city of the Romans. Located in Lipljan, the remains of this once great city are significant for the history of the country. Mosaics, basilica, and tombstones were unearthed from the area including ceramics, coins, jewelry, and weapons.

Afghanistan

One of the countries in South-Central Asia, Afghanistan has an improving tourism. The tourism industry is an important contributor to the country's economic growth. To enjoy the tourists' vacations in the country, they should spend time visiting the top 10 tourist spots in Afghanistan.

Masjet-e-Jam

Also known as the Friday Mosque, the Masjet-e-Jam in Heart is one of the finest and most popular Islamic sites in the world. Inside the mosque, tourists can see a big bronze cauldron as well as a Sherbet receptacle. Moreover, the place features Sultan Ghiyas-ud-din's tomb.

Gardens of Babur

The Gardens of Babur in Kabul features several plant species. The tourist destination is also the place where the remains Moghul Emperor Babur were buried. In the gardens, people can find a small but attractive mosque.

Bot-e-Bambiyan

The Bot-e-Bambiyan features popular Buddha statues from the 3rd century and the 5th century. The heights of the statues are 36 meters and 53 meters. This place is considered as one of the major archaeological places in Afghanistan.

The Mausoleum of Ahmed Shah Durrani

Found in Kandahar, the Mausoleum of Ahmed Shah Durrani is one of the significant historical monuments in the place. Ahmed Shah Durrani played an essential role in the history of the country because he led numerous territorial campaigns from 1747 to 1772.

Sultan Masood Palace

The Sultan Masood Palace in Ghazni was constructed in 112 A.D. Inside the palace, people can find antique furnishings. The palace has soldiers' quarters, government offices and a throne room. It also features several small but beautiful gardens.

The Museum of Islamic Art

The Museum of Islamic Art in Ghazni became open to the public in 1966. This tourist spot displays the Timurid architecture. Numerous collections of artifacts and antique items are stored and featured at the site such as bronzes and ceramic tiles. The remains of Sultan Abdul Razaq were buried in the museum.

The Shrine of Baba Wali

Located in Heart, the Shrine of Baba Wali provides a relaxing view of the Arghandab River. Near the shrine, tourists can find other attractive tourist spots including the Elephant Mountain. The site is open to public seven days a week.

Shahr-e-Gholgola

Also called as the Town of Noise, Shahr-e-Gholgola in Bamiyan features the ruins of a wealthy city that existed in the 5th century and 7th century. One of the nice attractions at the town is the historic citadel where the massac~e of the residents in the place led by Genghis Khan started.

Mousallah Complex

The Mousallah Complex in Heart features the ruins of the ancient madrassa. At the site, people can find 12 minarets. In addition, this tourist destination is also the place where Gaur Shad's mausoleum were constructed.

Kabul Bala Hisar

The Kabul Bala Hisar is a historic town that has a very strong and complex defensive system. One of the interesting places in the town is the fortress, which was used as a military college since 1939. Within the premises of the town, people can find the residences of popular emperors and Afghan rulers.

Afghanistan features numerous historic and archaeological sites. To have a notable travel to the country, it is beneficial if foreigners visit these tourist destinations.

7

Moving Towards Luxury Tourism

Luxury tourists are wiling to pay expensively for their holidays. For this they demand satisfaction, exclusivity, high quality and impeccable service. Although extreme, it is useful to consider the example of Bill Fischer, 'secret travel agent' of stars and celebrities like.Tom Cruise, Stalone etc. Fischer Travel charges an "entry fee" of $ 10.000 and an annual subscription of $ 5.000. Additionally it only accepts clients upon recommendation. It is, however, in a position to fulfil any wish, no matter how strange, its clients have.

The luxury tourist does not seek the best price but the best product. The product does not relate only to accommodation (hotel) but the complete spectrum of tourist services, i.e.:

- o Service from the travel agencies
- o Airport service and transfer from and to them
- o Activities and services outside the hotel
- o Public infrastructure (roads, parks, beaches etc.).

Hence, to attract this market, it is not enough to build isolated luxury units but it is necessary to have an integrated approach by all involved in the tourist product. The complete spectrum of services must be covered:

- o from the moment the tourist gets in touch with a travel agency specialized in handling luxury travel, continuing with

- o (air-)transportation from his origin to his destination and vv., including the situation at the airport / port etc
- o and transfer to and from the hotel. For a considerable part of this market the unavailability of a limo or a helicopter to pick them up from the airport is unacceptable;
- o services within the hotel;
- o activities outside the hotel (e.g. shopping, entertainment, culture etc.);
- o and last, but not least, the services offered by other tourist enterprises (restaurants, bars, entertainment areas, rent-a-car, guides etc) as well as Local Authorities (cleanliness, condition of roads and pavements, parks, beaches etc.).

The little data that exists is shows a great potential for Greece. For example, Britain, which is its largest source market, sends 8.7% of its mass market to Greece but only 1.7% of its FITs.

The luxury market is not a market that can be developed fast or cheaply. It is, however, a market that can bring higher profits with fewer visitors. For example, according to Hotel Study 2003, both the ADR and the GOPPAR of luxury hotels in Greece is 2 to 3 times higher than that of A Class hotels. Furthermore they employ more than double the number of staff per room.

LUXURY TRAVEL AND LIFESTYLE TRENDS

Luxury travel markets will continue to expand, while consumers of high-end products will hone their tastes ever more pointedly. The urge for self expression will spread, while a new ethical and environmental consciousness will take a firmer hold. These are among the many forces that will help dictate luxury tourism trends and lifestyle trends.

Traditional demographics won't define luxury consumers. Buying behavior, geography, interests and connoisseurship will become the new definition of wealth, particularly in emerging markets where luxury status will be displayed outwardly via symbols: luxury goods and labels such as Louis Vuitton handbags or Chanel cuffs, ubiquitous among their peers.

Mature affluents are gravitating to "stealth wealth." They seek luxury travel products that express personal interests and style, and those which require connoisseurship. They prize uniqueness and limited-edition luxe: originals, one-of-a-kind objects, which are expensive and highly collectible. Think men's shirts with the monograms inside the sleeves, bespoke Hermes and non-branded, one-of-a-kind hotels that reflect the owner's exquisite taste, selectivity and demanding standards. To know and appreciate these products, one must savor subtle details and be in the loop.

Relationships with family and friends take center stage. Accelerating since 9/11 and fueled by a backlash against 24/7 work schedules and dehumanizing technology, a tourism trend that is growing at a faster rate than all other sectors is family travel. A recent survey of American Express travel agents revealed a significant rise in luxury travel among families; 82% wanted high-end hotels with kids programs and 56% were traveling with nannies. Parents, grandparents and friends are looking to travel as a way to reunite, and to celebrate life's landmark events. Business trips with the whole family will become as common as tag-along spouses, while high-end business hotels and resorts will get on board with family travel trends, rolling out the red carpet with special suites and villas.

Creativity checks in. As Thomas Friedman writes in "The World is Flat," we are living in the Talent Age. Companies will need to innovate to set themselves apart by finding new solutions and alliances to tap into fresh talent. The right side of the brain will trump the left as creativity and design sell. Look to more companies to follow the lead of Richemont, a Swiss luxury goods conglomerate (Cartier, Montblanc, Dunhill and others), which established The Creative Academy, its own international Master of Arts in Design school, an alliance that bears creative fruits.

Concierges are king. A lack of time and information overload for the affluent to sort through, and they will pay experts to create lives they desire. As a lifestyle trend, personal concierges are all the rage. They're curators for sourcing flowers, a home or even friends, even helping clients define their own tastes and style.

In retail, it's "curated consumption" - stores offering the finest designs, already individually selected by the proprietor for buyers of electronics, fashion, furniture, etc. There's an online model - www.couturelab.com - a brilliant webzine that promises to be the template for other luxury products. Luxury travel brands will be expected to go beyond providing just luxury service and hospitality in their hotel, cruise ship or airline. They will be pressed to offer quality, inside-track information and time-saving services, such as Virgin Atlantic's Upper Class Wing - a fast track security channel to get passengers from limo to lounge in ten minutes or less.

Altruism and social responsibility are a big lifestyle trend. Differing from the cause-related marketing of the 90s, today's wealthy want to believe their consumption is helping to save the planet or has an altruistic motive behind it. In a recent HSBC luxury goods report, a graphic of American psychologist Abraham Maslow detailed an emotional needs hierarchy. The top, being linked to a higher cause. He said: "The future of luxury will be about imparting real meaning into a product." The product itself must be sustainable and show a genuine sensitivity to community. The operative words here, as succinctly put by London's Future Laboratory, are the three "T"s: truth, transparency and trust. A good example of the future's responsible luxury, courtesy of Jeffrey Miller, consultant and columnist for Luxury Briefing: a Gucci Green Car.

Health, well-being and looking good continue to move up in financial priorities. The New York Times recently documented the lives and beauty budgets of three women in different parts of the country. One, a real estate agent from Los Angeles, admitted she regularly spent several thousand dollars monthly just for "maintenance," just to "be in the game." Lifestyle trends such as this fueled the spa and medical tourism boom in 2007. Spas are going well beyond the dedicated spa outlet or the home spa, and branching out into mobile spas, "macho" spas for men, and even pets. We are seeing the advent of medical real estate, where entire communities are in the works, such as Cooper Life at Craig Ranch in Texas. Monthly fees provide luxuries, including annual physical examinations and doctor house calls. Five star hotels are increasingly offering medi-healthy packages in alliance with neighboring medical facilities. Next? The buzzword will be "age management" programs to help the rich look and feel young.

Saving time is the greatest luxury among travel trends. Any service that achieves this will be a big winner (as evidenced by the number of jet sales and private jet charter companies serving time-starved travelers. Major airports are becoming luxury travel/shopping destinations, targeting power spenders on layovers. Aside from the bevy of high-end watches and handbags, Heathrow's Terminal 5, set to open in March 2008, will have a two-story Harrod's department store, stocking only luxury brands. Additionally, numerous companies are springing up to train armies of professional household and estate managers (butlers, maids, personal chefs, wine stewards, etc.). There's even a new real estate development in Umbria that offers farmhouses with onsite architect, contractors, artisans and maintenance staff, so the owner can move in with just a suitcase. Lenovo just introduced its ThinkPad Reserved Edition ($4999) that comes with supple leather case and in-person assistance on call, guaranteed within four hours.

Big money follows culture and is big news. From Miami's burgeoning Art Basel to the celeb-filled Sundance Film Festival, publicity seekers should take note of the international coverage that cultural events are receiving. Art tie-ins also make good financial sense: Sotheby's introduced a co-branded World Elite MasterCard, giving cardholders VIP access to cultural events and receptions, even guided tours of newly excavated, private areas of Angkor Wat. More and more hotels are realizing that art attracts a certain art-savvy clientele, who are happy to spend freely on suites, spa treatments and fine wines. We will continue to see hotels become houses of culture, with in-house museums, curators, artists as interior designers, and stepped up marketing efforts that embrace culture. We will see more luxury retail and commercial spaces being treated as curatorial, artistic projects, such as Ferragamo's flagship in New York: a boutique, corporate office and museum under one roof. Seen, too, are online sites such as Artipolis, a private members club for individuals who meet on- and off-line to share their passion for the arts.

The affluent are sated with product and look to unique experiences. Luxury travel is being redefined as experiences as consumers are inundated with products. Today's well-traveled affluents want new, exciting experiences; to be intrigued, entertained and enlightened. They will spend top dollar to be first, or reach the most remote, exotic places. Witness how quickly suborbital flights and space travel took off. Taking advantage of lifestyle trends, marketers need to think big by turning any product into a life-enhancing experience. This can mean asking how visitors could have interactive experiences instead of passively visiting the Forum in Rome or the pyramids of Teotihuacán. When selling multi-million-dollar condos, marketers must go beyond touting professional style kitchens, but throw in a dinner party cooked by a personal chef when the buyer receives the keys, or a personal training session in a state-of-the-art triathlete fitness center. A travel trend that rates highly is acquiring knowledge and expressing one's creative side. Hotels, resorts and destination management companies are going well beyond cooking classes to offer everything from videography to tea ceremonies and instruction in the visual arts; even gallantry at Paris' Belle Ecole.

Space, space and more space is luxury. I recall what contemporary music composer John Cage said: the greatest luxuries are time and space. Especially when it comes to first class travel, airlines are vying to outdo rivals in offering the world's largest airplane bed. Witness Singapore Airlines' new private suites with double beds that sleep two. It will mean over-sizing hotel guest rooms and ship cabins, not just plush interior furnishings and amenities. Top hotel suites will get larger and pricier, appealing to the super wealthy accustomed to homes of 10,000 sq.ft. or more.

THE FUNDAMENTAL EVENT FOR THE LUXURY TRAVEL SECTOR

Meeting Luxury - International Luxury Travel Exhibition is the trade exhibition entirely dedicated to the luxury travel segment, the only qualified marketplace in the heart of Europe where the international offer of this exclusive sector meets the worldwide demand.

Also the next edition of Meeting Luxury, which will be held from March 31st to April 2nd 2011, will take place in the beautiful Lugano, Switzerland: an important financial marketplace and cosmopolitan city that welcomes visitors with a Mediterranean flair.

In two editions only, Meeting Luxury has managed to become the fundamental business to business event for the entire industry: the exhibition has in fact already hosted over 220 exhibitors belonging exclusively to the luxury tourism segment, more than 500 worldwide luxury buyers and over 800 international trade visitors, generating more than 30,000 meetings with representatives of 60 different countries.

The elegant design furnishing of the exhibition, the professionalism and know-how of the organizing company have helped Meeting Luxury to become an event even more exclusive, an appointment offering its exhibitors a tailor-made service always related to the needs of the sellers.

THE AWARD FOR THE STARS OF LUXURY

The Luxury Tourism Awards are the prestigious awards that will be given to the most luxurious destinations worldwide and institutions working for the valorization and promotion as well as for a continuous redefinition of the luxury tourism concept.

The awards are assigned by an esteemed Scientific Committee and announced during the event MeetingLuxury, the annual appointment entirely dedicated to the world of Luxury Tourism. Amongst the destinations, who won the international recognition in the last editions, are the Sultanate of Oman, Tenerife Island, Cape Town, Bermuda Islands...

The Luxury Tourism Awards are a prestigious showcase in the world of luxury travel: competing for the Luxury Tourism Awards is a synonymous of prestige, refinement, high standards in quality, luxury, design, protection of the environment, wellness and all the values that embody luxury today.

Luxury Holiday

Luxury holidays are all the rage. Most people expect to stay in far better standard accommodation than that in which they live at home. On holiday we feel that we deserve the very best, and a special treat. However with 'luxury' being one of the most overused terms in marketing its getting harder to understand what luxury actually means. While luxury is often just a short hand for expensive, even cheap products - such as toilet paper - are marketed as luxury. Luxury may in fact just be a relative term.

For some a hotel with a flat screen TV and Sky is luxury, but an increasing number of people leading very hectic, urban lives put a premium on tranquility, wide open spaces, abundant nature, and privacy from other people.

For them wilderness is the new luxury. At the extreme end Ted Turner is recreating the open American prairie with buffalo herds at his ranch. Celebrities such as Jade Jagger are just as likely to be found in remote retreats as larging it up in Monaco.

Tourists seeking to experience some of the world's last wilderness areas are prepared to pay for the privilege of eco-chic lodges and resorts - but wilderness conservation also comes at a price. Many wilderness areas have been managed by man for centuries - did you know that there is only one forest in Europe with no evidence of being managed by man? Conservation of vast pristine areas is very expensive.

Secondly some wilderness areas are only kept pristine because local people use them wisely and sustainably. For example in developing countries parks and wilderness areas often have the best firewood, grazing and water - by not denuding parks of these resources local people pay what is called an 'opportunity cost.'

If they are not rewarded for this - beyond the knowledge that they are conserving their natural heritage - then very poor communities face no alternative but to support their families in any way that they can, often to the detriment of the wilderness.

So while you are nourishing your soul at a wilderness retreat, then make sure that your holiday is also nourishing conservation and local people.

If you are paying top dollar for an eco chic resort then the least you should expect is that they are looking after it and local people.

Case Study

Luxury Tourism : Thailand

Thailand is a land of endless surprises-a truly amazing destination with a wide array of unforgettable experiences that anyone can enjoy to the extent of his or her own discretion. You will find the world's finest luxury hotels, endless shopping delights, and extraordinarily delicious local and international cuisine, all presented with inimitable Thai panache, complete with a most graceful wai and world-renowned smiles. Begin your luxurious experiences today!

Plush Accommodations

Lavish bungalows on secluded sun-drenched islands with white powder beaches, luxurious villas atop a mountain awash in lush tropical greenery, or ultra-exclusive penthouse suites atop glittering skyscrapers... Whatever you desire, it's all here.

Bangkok

- o The Oriental, a world-class romantic riverside setting with luxurious and unparalleled services
- o The Peninsula Bangkok, one of the finest addresses in Bangkok, with spectacular panoramic views
- o Sukhothai, an authentic hospitality with blends of tradition and contemporary living
- o Metropolitan, an urban ultramodern haven with Zen-like tranquility in the central business area
- o The Banyan Tree, the tallest suite luxury hotel in Bangkok, with its renowned spa suites
- o Conrad Bangkok, the cutting edge in design, cuisine, and service in the heart of Bangkok

Chiang Mai

- o Mandarin Oriental Dhara Dhevi, 60 acres of serene and natural landscapes, with a myriad of facilities, including the world class Dheva spa, a Thai Cooking School, and an authentic Thai shopping village
- o The Chedi, an elegant retreat in the heart of the historical city with its contemporary Asian nostalgic appeal

Chiang Rai

- o Four Seasons Tented Camp Golden Triangle, a one-of-a kind experience at the legendary Golden Triangle
- o Phu Chaisai Resort & Spa, the perfect place to rejuvenate and relax amidst the breathtaking landscape and exotic culture
- o Legend Chiang Rai, a comfort and class with modern Asian decor

Hua Hin

- o The Barai Suites, an exclusive stay and private spa indulgence

- o Anantara Hua Hin, an ancient Thai village with lush tropical gardens
- o Let's Sea, a spacious retreat with unforgettable vantage points
- o Asara Villa & Suite, maximum comfort with privacy in mind
- o Putahracsa, with unique stylish character and friendly professional service

Koh Kood

- o Soneva Kiri & Six Senses Spa, a luxury resort with private spa suites and personal spa butlers

Samui

- o The Renaissance Koh Samui Resort & Spa, a perfect holiday atmosphere, with private jet transfer from Singapore, Hong Kong, and Bangkok
- o The Signature Collection of Samui Villas & Homes, a luxury holiday villa in your own private paradise
- o The Thongsai Bay, a pure luxury with nature's own offerings
- o Four Seasons Resort, Koh Samui, a veritable 'Garden of Eden' with all the modern amenities
- o Napasai, a contemporary Thai village with modern elegance and luxury
- o Sila Evason Hideaway Samui, stunning views of the Gulf of Thailand and the surrounding islands
- o Zazen Boutique Resort & Spa, a comfortable and cozy boutique resort
- o The Villa Lawana Resort, a distinct character with private pools and all amenities

Krabi

- o Rayavadee, features award-winning architecture and tropical landscaping with an atmosphere of a Southern Thai Village

- o Pimalai Resort and Spa, offers the sights and sounds of virgin tropical rainforest
- o Zeavola, a haven of relaxation and comfort on the secluded northern tip of Phi Phi

Phuket

- o Amanpuri, features beautifully decorated Thai style pavilions
- o Aleenta, a sanctuary of mind and body, with its signature 'Outside Living In' design philosophy
- o Trisara, a sanctuary of privacy, space, and simple good taste
- o Banyan Tree Phuket, a palace of luxury and romance, with the finest facilities and ambience
- o The Villa Zolitude, a hideaway resort with a touch of Moroccan inspiration, with a perfect blend of privacy, functionality, and design
- o Sri Panwa Phuket Resort, commands a panoramic view and an exclusive private beach
- o Rising Sun Residence, a serene and natural setting with a bird's eye view of the island's lowlands and surrounding sea
- o Cape Yamu, an exclusive hotel-within-the-hotel, designed by Phillipe Starck of YOO and Jean-Michel Gathy of Aman Resorts

Fine Dining & Entertainment

Thailand keeps extremely high standards for its amazing food. There is no lack of fine dining options for both Thai and international cuisine, offering world-class cuisine to connoisseurs. Here are some of the highlights:

Bangkok

- o A dinner cruise down the Chao Phraya River on the Manohra, the Marriott's beautifully restored authentic rice barge

- o Sip on after-dinner cocktails with a breathtaking view at the Sirocco at the Dome
- o Luxury-class Asian-style seafood and BBQ over the vertical views from the 52nd floor of the Breeze
- o A fine dining experience at The Oriental Bangkok's Le Normandie, Bangkok's best French restaurant
- o A charming dining experience featuring Thai traditional dances at the Blue Elephant
- o A unique blend of Japanese cuisine at the JW Marriott's Tsunami
- o Indian and Thai cuisine with a classy bar, pastry shop, and café at The Face
- o A dinner under the stars at the celebrated Mahanaga, a converted colonial house with a lush garden courtyard
- o Night time favorites at The Met Bar - Metropolitan Hotel, Diplomat Bar - Conrad Hotel, and Bamboo Bar - The Oriental Bangkok

Samui

- o Fine Mediterranean cuisine along with Thai cuisine selections and seafood at The Cliff Bar & Grill
- o World-class Italian cuisine set in a timeless and stylish atmosphere at Prego

Shopping

Thailand is a shopper's paradise, world famous for its incredible range of fun and wonderful treasures. It's no wonder why many tourists come to Thailand specifically for a shopping excursion. Here are some of the best shopping venues:

Bangkok

- o Gaysorn, Thailand's most exclusive shopping center, specializing in luxury designer brands, with the flagship stores of Prada, Gucci, and Louis Vuitton, as well as Thailand's most innovative designers

- o Central World, the largest lifestyle-shopping complex in Southeast Asia
- o Siam Paragon, a world-class destination for supreme shopping and entertainment; features an assortment of fine dining, designer boutiques, Thailand's largest department store, and Asia's biggest aquarium
- o The Emporium, a shopper's paradise, with three floors dedicated solely to fashion
- o Playground! The Inspiration Store, a multi-store with cutting-edge fashion, art, and funky homewares
- o Erawan Bangkok, a boutique mall to shop with luxurious comfort

Phuket

- o Jungceylon, one of Thailand's most spectacular shopping and entertainment zones, with international retailers, high quality restaurants, pubs, and clubs
- o Soul of Asia, the largest western art gallery in Asia, including a special collection of Chigall, Dali, Picasso and Warhol

Spa

Thailand's legendary hospitality extends to some of the world's finest spa treatments. Whether it is for beauty, peace of mind, or health benefits, there are numerous luxurious options to satisfy mind, body, and soul. Here are those that are not to be missed:

Bangkok

- o Nibhana Spa, with the charm of Oriental ambience surrounded by a rich décor of culture and wisdom
- o S Medical Spa, a unique combination of Eastern traditional healing and spa arts, plus the modern science of the West
- o TRIA Integrative Wellness, featuring a wide range of treatment options ranging from modern medicine to traditional medicine, exercise, and nutrition treatment

- The Bodhi, a wellness center with advanced equipment and a team of in-house specialists

Chiang Mai

- Dheva Spa at Mandarin Oriental Dhara Devi, a world-class destination spa with an extensive range of holistic therapy, healing treatments, wellness programs, and a world-renowned Ayurvedic treatment center
- The Spa at the Chedi, features a diverse range of healing traditions designed for ultimate relaxation
- Palm Spa Village, a serene sanctuary with holistic therapies honoring East-meets-West healing rituals to promote rejuvenation and relaxation

Hua Hin

- Chiva-Som, a center of unparalleled world beauty and serenity, with extensive fitness, spa, and holistic health facilities combining ancient therapies of the East with the latest Western techniques
- The Barai Spa at the Hyatt Hua Hin, offers a delightful feeling of peace and tranquility through custom-designed treatments echoing and satisfying personal needs and desires
- Six Senses Spa at the Evason Hua Hin, a truly relaxing experience with therapeutic treatments to rejuvenate all the senses

Samui

- Tamarind Springs Tropical Spa, a fantastic unique, exotic design in an idyllic setting amongst a coconut jungle
- Kamalaya Wellness Sanctuary and Holistic Spa, blends Eastern treatments to homeopathy and metabolic detoxification in a five-star tropical luxury setting
- Natural Wing Health Spa, offers a combination of Thai massage, natural detoxification, and spa cuisine

Phuket

- o Six Sense Erawan, an unequalled spa treatment in a luxurious private atmosphere

Transportation

SGA Airlines: a speedy and comfortable alternative from Bangkok to Hua Hin by a 12-seat Cessna Grand Caravan

Destination Air: a shuttle service ferrying passengers around the Andaman Islands aboard a nine-seat Cessna 208 and a four-seat Cessna 206

Asia Marine: crewed yachts and catamarans for exciting daytrips, headlined by the opulent chartered yacht Blue Gold, accommodating 8 to 10 live-on-board passengers for longer nautical adventures

Tawan Cruises: chartered motor yachts with state-of-the-art entertainment systems, along with generous dining and seating facilities

Golf Courses

Santiburi Samui Country Club & Golf Course: a breathtaking par 72 championship course blended into the natural peaks and valleys of Samui

Blue Canyon Country Club: two award-winning 18-hole championship golf courses cradled in Phuket's secluded and verdant valley, set against a magnificent backdrop of the majestic mountains and Andaman Sea

Red Mountain Golf Course: one of Asia's most exciting new courses, with the largest lake on any golf course in Phuket

Siam Country Club: in Chonburi, the first privately-owned golf course in Thailand and home of Honda LPGA

Amata Spring Country Club: a world-class golf course in Chonburi and home to the Royal Trophy - Europe vs. Asia Golf Championship

Ayodhya Links: a championship golf course within a gracious private club in Ayutthaya

Las Vegas Luxury Tourism

Tourism is undisputedly the main industry in Las Vegas. And with such a vast array of hotels, lodgings, displays, events, restaurants and casinos, it is obvious that each location would appeal to different income levels and different tastes. But for the purpose of this site, we are going to speak solely about Las Vegas luxury tourism. So if you like posh surroundings, expensive entertainment, exotic cars, and the biggest, most luxurious limos on the road, then you have to come to the right place.

Luxury tourism in Las Vegas is a total package. Stay in the finest hotels in Vegas and ride in the most expensive vehicles. Even the nightclubs are classed in categories from dives to luxury entertainment. In addition to the accommodations and nightlife, Las Vegas is home to luxury shopping centers, complete with all the right designer boutiques and the most expensive labels in the world. Rare champagne, gourmet foods, divine spas and salons, first-class entertainment from the world's biggest stars, and sprawling casinos are integral components of the Las Vegas luxury tourism market.

Indeed, Las Vegas is all about illusion. And these luxury resorts cater to both the rich and the not-so-wealthy who splurge to look good. Take for example the exotic car rental businesses. Being able to rent a Ferrari for two hours to cruise The Strip is the chance of a lifetime for someone who may never aspire to own this sexy and powerful vehicle. But in Vegas, all is possible, and if someone wants to appear wealthy for an hour or two, then so be it. Las Vegas luxury tourism caters to these kinds of dreams.

Luxury is also about getting into the right Las Vegas nightclubs and having the monetary influence to secure the best tables inside the venue. Valets park Mercedes, Lamborghinis and Bugattis, while limousines whisk club-hoppers between the most famous and most desirable parties. No expense is spared in Vegas and any dream can be fulfilled for a price. That is true luxury and Sin City knows how to please.

Las Vegas has also become the city known for the most celebrity chefs in one place. The allure of all those visitors and all that money was too much to pass up. Gourmet chefs arrived in numbers to push their culinary fare. Upper scale restaurants boast menus of delectable treats, catering to patrons who can afford the hundred dollar plate dinners and specialty wines from private cellars.

Undoubtedly, Vegas appears to have the best of everything. Luxuries are the staple of this massive tourist attraction. Cigar lounges, oasis-like ambiance, opulent hotels, and trendy shopping, are among the finer things in life that are readily offered by Las Vegas Luxury Tourism.

8

Moving Towards Tourism Tips Guide

It's always important to take care of your health, but there are additional concerns to keep in mind when you're traveling. Whether you're taking a quick trip with your family or studying abroad for several months, it's easier to get sick when you're in a new place because your body hasn't had a chance to adjust to the food, water, and air in a new environment. Traveling can bring you in contact with things that your body isn't used to. Here are some tips on keeping your travel experience as healthy as possible.

The stress and excitement of travel can make you more likely to get sick, but if you follow a few simple tips, you're more likely to stay healthy throughout your trip - and your trip will definitely be more enjoyable. The good news is that as a teen, your immune system is as strong as an adult's, but lack of sleep and a poor diet can make it easier for you to become sick.

The first thing you should do if you're heading overseas is to find out what kinds of vaccinations you'll need in advance because different countries have different requirements. In the United States, contact your doctor or the Centers for Disease Control and Prevention (CDC) for a list of necessary vaccinations. You'll want to allow plenty of time for this step in case you need to get vaccines that require more than one dose.

COMMON TRAVEL TROUBLES

Three of the most common health problems that you may experience when traveling are jet lag, altitude sickness, and diarrhea. When you fly across time zones, the differing amounts of light can change your internal body clock, resulting in a condition known as jet lag. Jet lag may cause some symptoms that are bummers on a fun trip, including upset stomach, insomnia, and tiredness.

There are some things you can do to combat jet lag; for example, if you're traveling from west to east, you should stay out of the sun until the day after your arrival. If you're flying from east to west, go for a brisk walk as soon as possible after you arrive.

Altitude sickness is caused by dry air, a decrease in oxygen, and low barometric pressure when you travel to a higher altitude than you're used to. As a result, you may have problems, such as headaches, dehydration, and shortness of breath. Some people are affected at 5,000 feet (1,524 meters), but others aren't affected until they reach altitudes of 10,000 feet (3,048 meters) or more. Find out what altitude you're traveling to before you go to see if altitude sickness could be a problem.

The best prevention for altitude sickness is to gradually increase your altitude every day to get used to it. If that isn't possible, a drug known as acetazolamide can help relieve and even prevent symptoms of altitude sickness. If you think that you might get altitude sickness, talk with your doctor before you leave home.

The topic of diarrhea may seem gross, but it can be a serious problem. Traveler's diarrhea, known as turista, often occurs when a foreign type of bacteria enters your digestive tract, usually when you eat contaminated food or water. The best way to prevent turista is to be very careful of the food you eat and the water you drink on the road.

World Weather & Climate Information

Get all the latest updates on weather around the world. Our Weather Information section offers climate conditions and temperature throughout the globe.

World Time Converter

London, Reykjavic and Dakar are all on Greenwich Mean Time which makes it easy enough for them, but for others in different time zones, here's the global Time Converter. Anywhere, at all times, at the click of a mouse.

Safe Eats and Drinks

So what foods are safe to eat? Any foods that have been boiled are generally safe, as well as fruits and vegetables that have to be peeled before eating. Avoid eating uncooked or undercooked meat or meat that is not cooked just prior to serving.

Stay away from foods that require a lot of handling before serving. Here's an example: Nine friends ate at a restaurant when on a school trip overseas; eight had diarrhea the next day. The one who didn't get sick was the only one who had ordered a dish that didn't need to be touched by human hands right before serving.

One of your favorite foods at home is on the safe list on the road - pizza! Pizza dough, sauce, and cheese are foods that are less likely to spoil than others, and the high heat of a pizza oven tends to kill any harmful bacteria in the food.

You've probably heard that you shouldn't drink the water in some countries overseas, but did you know why? Water supplies in many developing countries are not treated in the same way as water supplies in developed countries; various bacteria, viruses, and parasites are commonly found in the water. Many experts suggest you drink only bottled water when traveling. If you need to use tap water, you should boil it first or purify it with an iodine tablet. Even if you're brushing your teeth, rinsing contact lenses, drinking a small glass of water to wash down pills, or adding ice to your drink, first take precautions to ensure the water is safe.

You Can Take It With You

When you're packing, you'll want to include any medications and other medical supplies you use on a daily basis because they may be hard to find in another country if you run out. Even if you can find them, there's a good chance the formulations will be stronger or weaker than the ones you're used to. These may include any prescriptions you already take, such as inhalers, allergy medication, and insulin, as well as contact lens cleaners and vitamins.

Packing an over-the-counter pain medication like acetaminophen and diarrhea medication is also a good idea. And pack some OTC allergy medication even if you don't take it at home. People sometimes unexpectedly develop allergic reactions to the pollens and other allergens found in a new environment. Those with asthma or other allergies can unexpectedly react to these new substances.

Basic Safety

It's easy to let your guard down when you travel. After all, you're more relaxed and there are so many new sights to focus on. In addition to paying attention to your personal safety (avoiding secluded places and not walking alone after dark), you'll need to reset your thinking when it comes to traffic safety, too. The rules of the road aren't the same overseas as they are at home. In some countries, people drive on the opposite side of the road and you'll need to be aware of this before you cross the street - look in the opposite direction from the one you're used to. Pedestrians don't always have the right of way overseas, either. Be sure there are no cars coming when you step into the street: If there are, they may not stop for you!

Travelling Light

Technical advancement in the telecommunications industry has created a very cheap way to keep in touch while traveling. International phone cards are a cheap way to help you keep in touch while travelling. Selection of the right prepaid calling card can save up to 95% on the long distance phone costs.

Remember to carry a voltage converter so that all your electrical gadgets are compatible with electrical outlets in foreign destinations.

Equip yourself with a Swiss knife or a penknife. A watertight wallet is a good idea if you're travelling to the sea - side.

Instead of carrying an iron that takes up a lot of place in your suitcase, carry a spray for your business suits and evening dresses. You'll find it in most travel shops. You can also avoid wrinkling your clothes if you roll and pack them.

Most hotels frown on guests doing their own laundry in the bathrooms, but if you do need to wash some smalls, carry a length of nylon twine to improvise a clothesline.

On long-haul trips, stick to lightweight, drip-dry garments that require little ironing and maintenance.

When choosing your travel wardrobe, remember that dirt doesn't show up as easily on busy prints, dark colours and polyester fabrics, so prefer these to light-coloured solids unless you're planning to do a lot of laundry!

Medicine Box

Pack a small first - aid kit of over the counter medicines equipped to deal with small health hazards. A tube of antiseptic, bandaids, pills for migraines, headaches and stomach upsets are essential.

Carry a medical prescription if you suffer from any chronic illness. make sure that you have the generic name of the drug, as brand names differ in countries.

If you're allergic to a particular drug, it's advisable to keep a note in your wallet.

Carry water purifying pills if you're planning to travel into rural areas where you might not get bottled or purified water.

Just drop one into the water and that will ensure that you're stomach stays fine.

Contact lenses: carry an extra pair of prescription glasses plus a copy of your lens prescription. Carrying a torch makes those floor crawling search exercises easier.

If you are on the floor looking for your contact lenses with a torch, remember to keep the beam parallel to the ground.

Bags & Baggage

Tie a coloured ribbon or a luggage belt around your suitcase so you can easily identify it on the conveyor belt.

Travelling light is a boon especially if you have a long wait at the airport between flights. You are less likely to set down light baggage and leave it unattended while you browse through an airport shop or use the toilet.

Planning to shop on your travels? Just flatten an empty airbag at the bottom of your suitcase. Use this to stuff dirty linen at the end of your trip, and voila! You have an extra bag! Make sure the bag has double zip pulls for a padlock.

Popular Hotels Information

VirtualTourist hotel reviews can help you find the best value 5 star luxury hotels, 2 and 3 star hotels, motels, and even specialty lodgings around the world. All the members on VirtualTourist are real travelers and locals whose genuine insight, advice, and helpful tips make finding the perfect hotel easy. Read reviews, meet the community, and add your own tips and photos too.

- Paris Hotels
- New York City Hotels
- London Hotels
- Sharm El Sheikh Hotels
- Las Vegas Hotels
- Rome Hotels

- Dubai Hotels
- Orlando Hotels
- Barcelona Hotels
- Cancún Hotels
- Singapore Hotels
- Kuala Lumpur Hotels
- San Francisco Hotels
- Chicago Hotels
- Negril Hotels
- Antalya Hotels
- Venice Hotels
- Istanbul Hotels
- Honolulu Hotels
- Bangkok Hotels
- Punta Cana Hotels
- Amsterdam Hotels
- New Orleans Hotels
- Toronto Hotels
- Phuket Hotels
- Cairo Hotels
- Manila Hotels
- Beijing Hotels
- Playa del Carmen Hotels
- Key West Hotels
- San Diego Hotels
- Vienna Hotels
- Montreal Hotels
- Los Angeles Hotels
- Berlin Hotels
- San Antonio Hotels

- Sydney Hotels
- San Juan Hotels
- Myrtle Beach Hotels
- Marmaris Hotels
- Fort Lauderdale Hotels
- Tokyo Hotels
- Vancouver Hotels
- Melbourne Hotels
- Boston Hotels
- Prague Hotels
- Goa Hotels
- Houston Hotels
- Dublin Hotels
- Nassau Hotels
- Madrid Hotels
- Hurghada Hotels
- Rio de Janeiro Hotels
- Buenos Aires Hotels
- Montego Bay Hotels
- Anaheim Hotels
- Penang Hotels
- Miami Hotels
- Florence Hotels
- Hong Kong Hotels
- Miami Beach Hotels
- Shanghai Hotels
- Seattle Hotels
- Budapest Hotels
- Atlanta Hotels
- Puerto Vallarta Hotels

POPULAR DESTINATIONS

Whether your next trip means a family vacation to Florida, a trip to Europe, or an off the beaten path beach vacation in Thailand, the VirtualTourist community of real travelers is there to help. Our travel guides and forums feature the best tips, photos and reviews on 70,000 travel destinations. It's all offered by a friendly, global community of 1 million fellow travelers.

- Paris
- Singapore
- New York City
- Amsterdam
- Barcelona
- Los Angeles
- Rome
- Kuala Lumpur
- Las Vegas
- Chicago
- Bangkok
- Beijing
- Florence
- New Orleans
- Hong Kong
- Ho Chi Minh City
- Tokyo
- Seoul
- Istanbul
- San Francisco
- Boston
- Toronto

- Cairo
- Montreal
- Buenos Aires
- Stockholm
- Dublin
- Madrid
- Orlando
- Philadelphia
- Munich
- Sharm El Sheikh
- Vancouver
- Vienna
- Dubai

General Tips

- To beat jetlag, book an overnight flight or one that arrives in the evening when travelling east so you can either catch your sleep on the flight or as soon as you get in to your destination.
- To prevent the swelling of feet as is wont to happen on long flights, walk in the aisle at intervals and try not to take off your shoes.
- Refrain from OD-ing on the free booze when on a flight, as too much alcohol causes dehydration. Tank up instead on aqua-pura.
- When making flight reservation, remember to request for special meals if you have any food restrictions.
- After September 11, airlines follow very strict security procedures. So make sure you reach the airport for check in well before departure time. Its best to check with the airline regarding how much in advance you should be at the airport.

If your baggage does not arrive on the same flight as you, fill out a Property Irregularity Report (PIR), with a description of the baggage, a list of contents and address to which it should be forwarded. If your baggage does not arrive at all, place a claim with the airline within 21 days.

- Overbooking is a fact of life in the airline industry. If you are not in a particular hurry to get to your destination then volunteer to give your seat up and take the next flight. The airline will provide you a hotel room and other frills, so you can end up having an extended vacation at the airlines expense!
- Do not accept any package from a stranger.
- For a smooth ride on a plane, choose the seats located near the wings as if the plane hits an air pocket, this is where you will get the least amount of bumps.
- If you are planning to watch the in flight movie, choose the fourth or fifth row from the screen to avoid getting a neck cramp.
- If you are prone to motion sickness, take an anti sickness pill before the flight. The pill won't help much, if you have it after you have started feeling sick!
- Abide by the list of items prohibited on board and carry most items like skis/cues/walking canes/sticks/Swiss knives in checked in baggage - this smoothens the check-in process plus avoids the risk of confiscation and unnecessary delays.
- Last and this is equally important - report any unattended items in the airport or aircraft to the nearest airport or airline personnel.

9

Moving Towards Tourism Planning

Planning is the dynamic process of determining goals, systematically selecting alternative courses of actions to achieve those goals, implementing the chosen alternatives and evaluating the choice to determine if it if successful. The planning process regards the environment which includes political, physical, social and economic elements as interrelated and interdependent components which should be taken into account in considering the future of a destination area.

Tourism is one of many activities in a community or region that requires planning and coordination. This bulletin provides a simple structure and basic guidelines for comprehensive tourism planning at a community or regional level. Planning is the process of identifying objectives and defining and evaluating methods of achieving them. By comprehensive planning we mean planning which considers all of the tourism resources, organizations, markets, and programs within a region. Comprehensive planning also considers economic, environmental, social, and institutional aspects of tourism development.

Tourism planning has evolved from two related but distinct sets of planning philosophies and methods. On the one hand, tourism is one of many activities in an area that must be considered as part of physical, environmental, social, and economic planning. Therefore, it is common to find tourism addressed, at least partially, in a regional land use, transportation, recreation, economic development, or comprehensive plan. The degree to which tourism is addressed in such plans depends upon the relative importance of tourism to the community or region and how sensitive the planning authority is to tourism activities.

Tourism may also be viewed as a business in which a community or region chooses to engage. Individual tourism businesses conduct a variety of planning activities including feasibility, marketing, product development, promotion, forecasting, and strategic planning. If tourism is a significant component of an area's economy or development plans, regional or community-wide marketing plans are needed to coordinate the development and marketing activities of different tourism interests in the community.

A comprehensive approach integrates a strategic marketing plan with more traditional public planning activities. This ensures a balance between serving the needs and wants of the tourists versus the needs and wants of local residents. A formal tourism plan provides a vehicle for the various interests within a community to coordinate their activities and work toward common goals. It also is a means of coordinating tourism with other community activities.

Planned Development

The serious situation caused by haphazard development has made people and the governments aware of the need for planning of tourism development based on scientific research of the requirements of the travel market and the capacity of the area to take in the tourists. The need for planning is paramount. We do not provide more seats to a plane or rooms in a hotel beyond its maximum capacity, taking into account the passenger's comforts. Why should a resort or an area be choked with people?

Planning of tourism development, however, is of recent origin. It was specially taken note of during the last 65 years after public voices were heard against the unplanned invasion of tourism. In 1950, Gerhard Noble called mass tourism "one of the great western plagues hardly less evil in effects than the epidemics of the middle ages." In a conference held in Limuru, Kenya, the tourist inflow was referred to "as a dangerous invasion." These remarks, however, may be exaggerated apprehensions of the environmentalists. But no one disputes the fact that where modern industrial life makes inroads into ancient societies, traditional values begin to totter. Tourism is a form of social industrialisation with all its advantages and disadvantages. Its advantages have to be grasped and utilised with care so that the impact of the disadvantages is minimised. It is here that planning comes in. Planning is of greater benefit to developing societies where tourism is a new phenomenon and has had little or no adverse effect so far. The World Bank warned us as early as 1972:

In many areas of the world, tourism development has produced great disparities in the standards of amenities provided for the visitors and for the local population. This cannot be entirely avoided, but in the long run, the improvement of standards for the local population is probably a condition of successful tourism development. The development of a new resort by the provision of infrastructure costing perhaps millions of dollars has a great impact on land values in the area affected. Were these benefits to accrue largely to a few private landowners, the Bank would have difficulty in financing such a project. The acquisition of land by government or a public agency prior to development... eases the problems of planning on an integrated basis, and of enforcing proper zoning and building regulations. It also helps to ensure that windfall gains do not accrue solely to private landowners and provides the opportunity for the public agency to offer serviced sites to hotel developers at prices which can include, if necessary, an incentive element. There is a very close relationship between land prices and building densities, and by appropriate land pricing the development authority can help to ensure that acceptable physical planning and density standards are maintained.

The statement makes two significant points:

(a) Planning should be integrated to avoid as far as possible, disparities in the standards of amenities for the visitors and local population.

(b) Tourism planning should not be left totally to private enterprise in search of profit. Government must actively participate in it.

In the past, tourism planning was looked at from a simplistic point of view. Planning simply implied that new hotel construction should be encouraged, more airlines should start operation, promotional campaigns may be launched within the country and abroad and border crossing must be eased. Although it worked to some extent, it was at best an erratic method of planning tourism. That is how most developing countries started their own tourism planning, resulting in a number of mistakes.

Tourism has become a major industry in many countries of the world and has thus a pervasive effect on the economy of the nations as well as their social structure. Unplanned tourism can hamper a nation in getting maximum benefits from its development.

The development of the tourism sector is one of the several options before a government, making claims on its resources which, in most cases, are limited. It is, therefore, necessary for tourism planners to place their case before the government in justifiable terms listing anticipated contribution to the economic development of the country through tourism development. The two economic arguments in favour of developing tourism are:

(a) the contribution in terms of foreign exchange; and

(b) multiple employment potential of the tourism industry. Tourism development has to be planned in relation to the total development of the country and the available resources.

Initially, in the fifties and sixties, most countries except USA were interested in measuring international tourism because this was what mattered to them in economic terms. Meanwhile,

USA and subsequently Europe discovered the value of domestic tourism. Its effect on economy was as good as international tourism. In fact, it provided more regional balance than international tourism. In several countries, an annual survey of domestic tourism is conducted and its findings are available to travel industry. Similarly, US Database, a travel research organisation of the USA, has been gathering all kinds of data on domestic and international tourism for more than two decades.

Presently, almost all National Tourist Organisations in developing countries have divisions dealing with domestic tourism. But, only feeble attempts have been made to quantify domestic tourism. For instance, the Government of India has not yet ordered an all-India survey to determine the size and magnitude of domestic tourism. A few Tourism Departments of the State Governments have set up their research sections to quantify the size of domestic tourism in their states.

The following are some reasons for the need of statistical measurement of tourism:

1. Statistical measurement is necessary to evaluate scale and magnitude of tourism to a destination. It can relate to a country, region or a city. The research helps a country forecast future demand over a long period-say, ten years.
2. The results of these researches are important to take decisions relating to physical planning and area development, keeping in view the requirements of the visitors and the local population. In the absence of timely research, a lot more investments will be needed for future expansion. In the sixties, the Government of India built a new airport in Calcutta and by the time it was completed, it was already short of requirements. It was built without adequate research on future demand.
3. Statistical information is required for marketing and destination promotion. The people in charge of marketing want to know which are their prime markets, how market profiles change, information about the emerging new markets, etc.

Process of Planning

Tourism is part of the services industry. Its importance - economic and social - has to be balanced by a government in relation to the competing priorities of a nation.

A government must take a decision as to whether tourism is important for its economic, social and political interests. And, if the decision is positive, planning based on indepth research is imperative. The economic advantages of tourism are so overpowering that decision in most cases has been favourable. The erstwhile USSR under Joseph Stalin was forbidden to foreign visitors till 1960, but it opened up with a vengeance when Stalin died. The new Russian state immediately switched to international tourism to get its share of the tourist dollar. Other East European states and the newly independent Republics which once-formed part of the Soviet Union are now trying to attract travellers. China was a closed society a decade ago. Now, it is one of the top 15 among the tourist receiving countries, thanks to the massive foreign investments it received from multi-national companies.

While tourism planning is usually thought in terms of developers and promoters in specific projects, it must be seen from national, regional and local levels. Tourism planning and development has to be seen from two levels:

(1) The geographical level within which the tourism activity occurs - the destination.

(2) At the level of individual operator - resort or a hotel.

Steps in the Planning Process

Like any planning, tourism planning is goal-oriented, striving to achieve certain objectives by matching available resources and programs with the needs and wants of people. Comprehensive planning requires a systematic approach, usually involving a series of steps. The process is best viewed as an iterative and on-going one, with each step subject to modification and refinement at any stage of the planning process.

There are six steps in the planning process:

1. Define goals and objectives.
2. Identify the tourism system.
   a) Resources
   b) Organizations
   c) Markets
3. Generate alternatives.
4. Evaluate alternatives.
5. Select and implement.
6. Monitor and evaluate.

STEP ONE: Defining Goals and objectives. Obtaining clear statements of goals and objectives is difficult, but important. Ideally, tourism development goals should flow from more general community goals and objectives. It is important to understand how a tourism plan serves these broader purposes. Is the community seeking a broader tax base, increased employment opportunities, expanded recreation facilities, better educational programs, a higher quality of life? How can tourism contribute to these objectives?

If tourism is identified as a means of serving broader community goals, it makes sense to develop plans with more specific tourism development objectives. These are generally defined through a continuing process in which various groups and organizations in a community work together toward common goals. A local planning authority, chamber of commerce, visitors bureau, or similar group should assume a leadership role to develop an initial plan and obtain broad involvement of tourism interests in the community. Public support for the planning process and plan is also important.

Having a good understanding of tourism and the tourism system in your community is the first step toward defining goals and objectives for tourism development. The types of goals that are appropriate and the precision with which you are able to define them will depend upon how long your community has been involved in tourism and tourism planning.

In the early stages of tourism development, goals may involve establishing organizational structures and collecting information to better identify the tourism system in the community. Later, more precise objectives can be formulated and more specific development and marketing strategies evaluated.

STEP TWO: Identifying Your Tourism System When planning for any type of activity, it is important to first define its scope and characteristics. Be clear about exactly what your plan encompasses. A good initial question is, "What do you mean by tourism?" Tourism is defined in many ways. Generally, tourism involves people traveling outside of their community for pleasure. Definitions differ on the specifics of how far people must travel, whether or not they must stay overnight, for how long, and what exactly is included under traveling for "pleasure". Do you want your tourism plan to include day visitors, conventioneers, business travelers, people visiting friends and relatives, people passing through, or seasonal residents?

Which community resources and organizations serve tourists or could serve tourists? Generally, tourists share community resources with local residents and businesses. Many organizations serve both tourists and locals. This complicates tourism planning and argues for a clear idea of what your tourism plan entails. You can begin to clarify the tourism system by breaking it down into three subsystems:

(1) tourism resources,

(2) tourism organizations, and

(3) tourism markets.

An initial task in developing a tourism plan is to identify, inventory, and classify the objects within each of these subsystems.

Supply and Demand

Tourism development is a complex phenomenon requiring indepth study of resource and demand pattern in each country.

The local visitors have their own preferences regarding what they want to do during their holidays. In Great Britain, a 1990 study revealed that 60 per cent of domestic visitors go to the sea for their holiday which is accessible in a few hours from any part of the country. Fortunately, for Britain, most overseas visitors are not interested in sea holidays. For them, London is a tourist 'Mecca'. Some 10 million foreign visitors add to the congestion of London, annually, along with another 15 million domestic visitors. The French also prefer the sea. In the case of France, the sea is also the focus of attention of the foreign visitors adding to the congestion on its beaches. The Italians prefer the lakes, while the visitors opt for the history and culture of Rome and many other cities of Italy spreading millions of visitors thinly all over the country.

India, as a large country, is in a position to distribute the tourists evenly though Delhi and Bombay have pressure in peak winter months.

The pattern of traffic has to be kept in mind while planning the development of tourism in a destination, specially at the supply side as it is not flexible. Hotels are not built in a day nor are the airports. It took Los Angeles several years to expand its airport to host the Olympics in 1984. For successful tourism planning, current and future supply has to be correlated to current and future demand.

Influencing Factors

The following are some of the factors which influence tourism development in a destination area:

1. Size of the existing population.
2. Diversity and vitality of already existing tourist activity.
3. Whether the facilities were planned and planted in the area or grew spontaneously because of some man-made or national attraction.
4. Availability of land and finance.
5. Impact on the local community-benefits and social costs.
6. Attitude of the local people towards the tourism projects.

7. Magnitude and speed of development.
8. State of the local economy - options of alternate development.
9. Availability of local manpower - a dynamic population.
10. Whether the area is extensive for future expansion or only limited expansion is possible.

Resentment by local population against tourism projects, however beneficial to the community, can create problems, as it happened in Australia. Yeppon is a small town on the coast of central Queensland-Australia's sunshine state described by its 6,000 inhabitants as 'Paradise'. It has beautiful views and miles of glorious beaches. A Japanese businessman saw the area and fell in love with it, deciding to develop it into a resort. The beach here is 10 times longer and wider than Waikiki in Honolulu. He bought 20,000 acres to develop it into an international resort, building a number of hotels, guest houses, wildlife parks and several other attractive features.

The scheme was approved by the Australian Government but the local residents did not like it. They could not tolerate the idea of thousands of tourists crowding their beaches all the year round.

The investor tried to woo the local population, offering them millions of dollars to build a retirement home and other facilities. In November 1981, a bomb exploded under a motel under construction destroying property.

This is an example of the type of problems a developer can face - if local cooperation is not sought.

A Precondition

As discussed earlier, research is a precondition for planning in tourism. It is surprising that in the tourism field, an insignificant amount of money is spent on research compared to total turnover of tourism earnings.

The spectacular tourism development in certain areas like Majorda in Spain or Hawaii in the United States was due to the fact that these were some of the first areas developed for a particular type of holiday. Today, they are no longer alone in the field. The sun, sea, sand and reasonable prices are available at other places too. Fast jets have made inexpensive travel possible to distant lands - like Sri Lanka, India, the Maldives, Thailand and Malaysia - where prices are much lower. Therefore, for any new resort development, planning, both physical as well as economic considerations, are essential.

A country which decides to develop tourism should take a hard look at places offering similar attraction, study their economics and call for specialists to prepare a tourism development plan. Competition must be identified.

Technical assistance from foreign experts is useful as they can provide an objective assessment of the tourist resources of a country. Among the aspects to be studied are:

1. Characteristics of the land available for development, and the price structure.
2. Speed of construction to attract public investment.
3. Composition of the facilities to be provided - hotels, non-hotels and other services, industries like restaurants, stores and beach services.
4. Total cost of infrastructure and superstructure in the area proposed to be developed. Infrastructure includes all forms of construction on and below the ground, that is, roads and parking areas, railway lines, airports, water supply, power houses and sewage disposal. Superstructure consists of hotels, motels, restaurants, entertainment, and shopping facilities.
5. Possibility of direct and indirect taxes from tourism- related activities to justify public investment.

Planning Levels

Planning has to be done on two levels - national and local. At the national level, the central government will be involved in developing selected areas on the basis of research and study. The guiding principles in the selection of the areas are their marketability as tourist spots to international and domestic travellers, anticipated receipts from the tourism sector, and projections of future demand. The national plan shall also lay down the broad framework for development at local and regional levels.

The detailed planning of the local needs has to be done at the local level though the central government may give financial assistance or subsidies to some of the activities. This arrangement is prevalent in countries where tourism is not highly developed and the state has to play a pivotal role. In India, although the government is involved in tourism planning, the private sector plays a significant role in developing tourist facilities. Some of the facilities are planned, developed and managed solely by the state. Now, most countries including China have opened their tourism sector for private participation.

It may, however, be understood that a government cannot afford to do everything at once. They have to select priority areas for development where some infrastructure may exist and whose tourist attractions are relatively better known. The development of completely new areas, though a worthwhile proposition in time, has to take its turn depending upon the resources of the country and the political will to develop tourism on the part of the government.

In October 1977, the World Tourism Organisation published an inventory of tourism development plans of various countries. Out of the forty-three member-countries, which replied to the WTO questionnaire, thirty-seven had an integrated planning system at the national level. But in majority of the cases, the plans remained on paper and when these were acted upon, action was half-hearted or partial implementation. Some countries, like the United States and Canada, have, strictly speaking, no national tourism plans. In the USA, a study for making federal policy and programme involvement in tourism more coherent and responsive to national interest was undertaken only in 1976. After six years of intensive efforts by the travel industry, President Ronald Reagan signed into law a National Tourism Policy Act on October 16,1981. Under this Act, the US Congress created the US Travel and Tourism Administration to 'optimise' the contribution of tourism and recreation industries to economic prosperity, full employment and international balance of payments to the US. In 1996 USTTA has been axed in an economy drive by Clinton Administration. In Canada, each of the ten provinces and two territories are involved in tourism development planning. In USA, states are more actively involved in the promotion of tourism even more than the federal government. France has a full-fledged Ministry of Free Time which deals with tourism and leisure affairs.

Integrated Planning

There has been little coordination and regulation in physical planning for tourism development. Resorts have developed in attractive settings while ancillary facilities like transportation were created belatedly to meet the demand. Industrial and commercial cities found themselves receiving more visitors. The new, substantial facilities created were shared by foreign visitors and the local people. Existing infrastructure designed for the requirements of a relatively static age came under the strain of a new and mobile society. The need for replanning of the existing use of land and planning of new areas became paramount. This realisation, however, came only in the second half of the twentieth century. Simultaneously, the transport revolution opened new parts of the world for touristic exploration.

The tourism planners, therefore, had two different tasks - one of physical planning in new areas with potential but with little or no existing touristic activity, and the other of re-shaping the areas where tourism already existed. Two, replanning of existing high density tourist areas.

Where should the planners begin? The first thing is to analyse different types of national or other tourist resources - of which each country has many - that could attract tourists. These may be of scenic beauty, history, a mystique, and so on.

An inventory of all these resources of the country has to be made. Then, there are cities like London and Paris which have their own natural draw for visitors. London, the biggest tourist attraction in the world, is visited by over 10 million tourists and Paris by about 20 million foreign visitors annually.

After preparing the inventory, areas have to be selected for tourism development keeping in view the economic resources available. While taking up the areas for development in a city, it is necessary to define the minimum urban planning parameters which, if respected, may prevent the degradation of the environment through unregulated building activity. The Mediterranean seacoast is an example of such unregulated development leading to ugliness and confusion.

The basic parameters in planning a sea resort should indicate (a) the space between buildings, (b) the distance of the road from the beach; and (c) the capacity of tourist accommodation on the beach or off the beach.

The guidelines should also give building specifications, length, suggested dimensions, and characteristics of the road network providing access to the sea. The creation and development of a green belt should be clearly marked. No unregulated or unplanned structures should be allowed in the area proposed to be developed. Similarly, the tourism development plan of an area with historical monuments as a major attraction requires that the view of the monuments should not be concealed by any haphazard construction in the area surrounding the, monument. For instance, no new construction should be allowed near the Taj Mahal, which may obstruct its view.

To sum up, the following must be considered in any area planning:

1. Preparation of overall inventory of national tourist resources.
2. Determination of broad parameters of urban planning and architectural specifications.
3. Cost benefit studies of the proposed projects.

4. Exploration of possibilities of investment in private and public sectors.

Investment and Income in Tourism Development : When a tourism project is taken up for implementation, the time relation between investment requirements and revenue expectation has to be kept in mind. The chart on this relationship and the involvement of the public sector in this chapter explains the position.

The following 8-point project structure for tourism planning and development is recommended:

1. Establishment of goals after a feasibility study.
2. Market and resources analysis.
3. Conceptual planning.
4. Approval of the plan.
5. Master planning.
6. Staged implementation programme.
7. Evaluation and direction.
8. Monitoring operations to ensure quality of services and operational success.

Systems must be set up to provide continuing feedback on volume of tourism and levels of satisfaction provided. Such programmes are directed against decline of a destination.

Environment and Government Tourism

The control of planning of physical environment in tourism is imperative. The following points must be taken into consideration:

(a) What facilities should be erected and when?

(b) Alternative uses of land

(c) Pollution

(d) Serenity of atmosphere

(e) Integrity of landscape

(f) Cost of land and its ratio to building and development costs.

(g) Traffic circulation

(h) Zoning and density

(i) Services - water, electricity, gas, sewerage, etc.

Architectural style, building regulations, site-layout density, and preservation of the natural features of the land are part of the environmental control. Protecting lakes, hills, beaches, rivers and historical monument from the onslaught of large masses of visitors are also the responsibility of the government.

A couplet in the Atharvaveda says: "Whatever I take from the Earth may that have quick growth again. O Purifier! may we not injure the vitals of Thy heart."

The Atharvaveda pronounced these words of wisdom more than five thousand years ago when Indian culture was being formed in the magnificent forests teeming with wildlife. It is remarkable that people in that age realised that the resources of the earth were not something which could be damaged at will. The following words of philosopher Krishna Chaitanya provide another warning:

If we do not realise that the beauty and variety of the earth are autonomous values in their own right, if we believe that we have life and health on earth and not with the earth, we will exploit it greedily and come to ruin speedily. If we treat the earth without reverence and ruin its beauty and order, the end will be the failure of the earth to produce any food for us.

Demands for tourism are as diverse as the resources. It is not easy to match the supply with the demand, for tourism can create pressure on local facilities; can affect the landscape and the lifestyle of the people.

The problems of conservation were taken note of in the early stages of tourism development. America established the Yellow Stone Park within an area of 3,350 square miles in 1872. The British founded a national trust for places of historic interest and national beauty in 1895. A separate Ministry of Town and Country Planning was created in 1943 in Great Britain. National Physical Planning began in the United Kingdom as early as in 1947 with the passing of Town and Planning Act. The National Park Access to the Countryside Act in 1949 established a National Park Commission with the objective of natural beauty and provision of opportunities for open-air recreation. The ten national parks created in England covered nine per cent of the land area. In 1971, a Department of Environment was set up in England. In India, too, a Ministry of Environment and Forests was set up when Rajiv Gandhi took over as Prime Minister in 1985.

The concern for preservation of ecological balance was not confined to the USA and the UK; it has its worldwide impact. In 1968, the Council of Europe launched the Air Pollution and Water Charter and Water Conservation Campaign. The African convention for conservation of nature took place in the same year. In the USA, the Council of Environmental Quality was established in 1970 and President Nixon promulgated a 37-point programme of preservation of environmental quality.

India is already facing problems relating to environment mainly due to pressure of population and only partly due to tourism. The case of Dal Lake in Srinagar (Kashmir) proves our point.

Tourism can be a boon to any country, especially to a developing country like India. But tourism planning has to ensure that India preserves the Himalayas in their original glory, and the wide variety of wildlife, which is a great asset for tourism. The government took a wise decision in banning the hunting of tiger, panther and other species which were in danger of becoming extinct due to wanton killing. The Tourist Development Council, an advisory body of the Government of India, in a resolution passed as early as 1972 at Goa, requested the Government of India to take steps to ensure that:

(a) Any new construction in the vicinity of monuments should meet aesthetic requirements.

(b) Any unnecessary interference from electric lines, power plants, petrol stations, advertisement hoardings be avoided.

(c) Special care should be taken to prevent pollution of water and air, working of mines and quarries, dumping of domestic, commercial and industrial waste in the vicinity of monuments.

(d) Deforestation of the area around monuments be avoided.

(e) Financial assistance be given by the state governments, local bodies to improve and beautify roads and environment of monuments and other places of tourist interest.

(f) To avoid haphazard peripheral growth, the location of facilities like canteens, bookshops, curio shops, etc., in the vicinity of important monuments may be done only after clearance from the Archaeological Survey of India and the Department of Tourism.

As a follow-up on this resolution, the Department of Tourism selected ten archaeological complexes of tourist importance comprising thirty archaeological centres. Master plans for these have already been prepared.

Tourism Concerns

As part of the concern for tourism in relation to environment, WTO conducted a survey of tour operators in United Kingdom about their views on environments.

To a question whether tourists were concerned about the environmental quality of the destination they visit, 63 per cent of the tour-operators surveyed answered yes.

In reply to another question whether they offered any products that might be classed "environmental friendly" or "Green", 61 said yes. Seventy-nine per cent of the group said that they offered green products in Europe, 16 per cent in Asia Pacific, 13 per cent in Americas and 37 per cent in Africa.

It seems that tour-operators were taking their business to alternate destinations from areas where environmental degradation was accentuating. Fifty-nine per cent said that they were moving their business from areas where environment was not safe.

10

MOVING TOWARDS TOURISM MANAGEMENT

Tourism Management is the leading international journal for all those concerned with the planning and management of travel and tourism. Management in all business and organizational activities is the act of getting people together to accomplish desired goals and objectives using available resources efficiently and effectively. Management comprises planning, organizing, staffing, leading or directing, and controlling an organization (a group of one or more people or entities) or effort for the purpose of accomplishing a goal. Resourcing encompasses the deployment and manipulation of human resources, financial resources, technological resources, and natural resources. Because organizations can be viewed as systems, management can also be defined as human action, including design, to facilitate the production of useful outcomes from a system. This view opens the opportunity to 'manage' oneself, a pre-requisite to attempting to manage others.

Managing tourism destinations is an important part of controlling tourism's environmental impacts. Destination management can include land use planning, business permits and zoning controls, environmental and other regulations, business association initiatives, and a host of other techniques to shape the development and daily operation of tourism-related activities.

The term "destination" refers broadly to an area where tourism is a relatively important activity and where the economy may be significantly influenced by tourism revenues. Destination management is complicated by the fact that a single, recognizable destination may include several municipalities, provinces, or other government entities - in island environments it may be the entire country.

Participating governance structures led by local authorities, with the involvement of local NGOs, community and indigenous representatives, academia, and local chambers of commerce, make up what are known as "Destination Management Organizations" (DMOs). Often DMOs take the form of local tourism boards, councils, or development organizations. The network of local tourism businesses (hotels, attractions, transportation services, service providers such as guides and equipment rentals, restaurants, etc.) are also a significant part of a destination.

Destination Management Approach

The needs, expectations and anticipated benefits of tourism vary greatly from one destination to the next, and there is certainly no "one size fits all" approach to destination management. As local communities living in regions with tourism potential develop a vision for what kind of tourism they want to facilitate, a comprehensive planning framework such as Local Agenda 21 has proved useful and is being used more and more often. Promoting sustainable tourism within Local Agenda 21 processes is a way to strengthen local stewardship of the environment.

Tourism Organisation

Having determined what makes people travel, we can look at the organisation of tourism in the world. The travel agents act as coordinators of different segments of travel.

Travel has become a massive business enterprise. In some countries it has assumed the shape of mass tourism. Imagine,

Spain with a population of ten million-had forty-eight million foreign visitors in 2000) had Even in Asia, Singapore has a population of 2.4 million and foreign visitors were seven million in 2000.

Government's Role : Governments, therefore, have to play a key role in the planning, development, regulation and marketing of tourism. Tourism helps every government because it provides employment to the citizens and earns foreign currency for the country. Therefore, practically every government in the world, irrespective of its size, has a NTA. It may be called a Department of Tourism as in the case of India, a Tourist Promotion Board as in the case of Singapore, a Tourism Authority as in the UK and Thailand or a Tourism Ministry as in the Philippines. The NTAs are involved in planning, development, promotion and administration of tourism. While planning a beach or mountain resort, an NTA tries to make sure that there is no overcrowding, pollution and destruction of historic or archaeological landmarks as a result of the new area development for tourism. To promote tourism, an NTA opens tourist offices overseas to attract foreign tourists to their shores. They also have tourist information offices within their own countries, to provide information to foreign visitors on arrival and also to domestic travellers who wish to travel within their own country.

In India, the Central Department of Tourism has eleven tourist offices in foreign countries and twenty-one within India. In large countries like India, there are several Government tourist organisations. For instance, almost all the twenty-eight State Governments of India and seven Union Territories have their Departments of Tourism and majority of them have Government-owned State Tourism Development Corporations. They operate at State levels. Although most States have their Departments of Tourism and Tourism Development Corporations, the level of tourism development has been uneven. Tourism is a State subject and the Centre cannot enforce its decisions unilaterally on all the States. It was in this context that the National Committee on Tourism (NCT), suggested in 1988 that tourism should be brought on the concurrent list of the Constitution of India. The advantage would be that the Central Government could initiate a legislation in the tourism field for All-India application. Initially State Governments were not interested in tourism development. The Centre had to subsidise the State Governments to open such departments for promotion of tourism. Now most of them are reasonably active and are no longer subsidised by the Centre. The Centre, however, assists them financially to strengthen or streamline their infrastructure where needed.

At the All-India level, there is the public sector-India Tourism Development Corporation (ITDC), with a network of hotels all over India, transport units in various states, a chain of duty-free shops at the international airports and undertaking other tourism-related jobs. Several States have followed the ITDC pattern at their level. Now, a decision has been taken at the Centre that the Government should leave the tourism business to private sector. ITDC is, therefore, in the process of privatisation and the State Governments too are thinking on similar lines. In fact, these Corporations with so much public investments have become a burden on public exchequer, as they are no longer profitable. The Government has to put in money to run them.

Establishment of World Tourism Organisation (WTO) : In the organisational chart of tourism, World Tourism Organisation (WTO) is the apex body-representing at world level, the tourism interests of NTAs and working as an affiliate of the United Nations Organisation (UNO). Started as the International Union of Official Travel Organisation (IUOTO) in the first half of the twentieth century, it became an inter-governmental organisation in 1975 and named World Tourism Organisation WTO, for short. Presently, it has a membership of one hundred and thirty-seven countries and territories. Besides, there are some three hundred and fifty affiliate members like airlines, travel agencies, etc.

WTO provides many services to its members-principal one being the compilation of travel statistics and the publication of books and reports, to help member Governments to plan and develop their tourism. It works closely with several other international organisation with the objectives of helping develop tourism in the world. It offers expert help to developing countries to plan, develop and reorganise their tourism. It strives to improve the quality of tourism education. Presently, its focus is to create environment for sustainable tourism.

India is one of its founding members and is often elected to its Executive Council. Its Chief Executive is called Secretary General. WTO aims to create favourable conditions for free movement of travel in the world. For this purpose, it favours the passport-free travel in the world. To some extent, it has been achieved in all the European Countries (EU), where the citizens can travel without visa and passport. Besides, they have introduced a common currency called Euro making travel hassle-free. At present, if a visitor gets visa for one of the eleven European countries, it is valid for all the eleven member countries. WTO is based in Madrid, Spain.

Establishment of Pacific Asia Travel Association (PATA) : Among other world bodies which sustain and promote international tourism, Pacific Asia Travel Association (PATA) is notable. Although its active members are from the Pacific region, extending from Canada to the Indian sub-continent, (hundred governments, sixty-six airlines and cruise lines. Its presence, etc., worldwide is felt through its more than eighty chapters (seventeen thousand members). It is primarily a marketing organisation, promoting tourism to the Pacific region and assisting member countries in various ways.

Originally established in Hawaii in 1951, it was later headquartered in San Francisco for four decades and is now based in Bangkok, with divisional offices in USA, Australia, Singapore and Europe. It membership exceeds 2000 and consists of governments, airlines, steamship companies, cruise lines, travel agencies, media, etc.

PATA is headed by a Chief Executive and managed by a large Board of Directors, representing many countries. Its annual conventions are a great draw, attracting some one thousand five hundred industry leaders from all over the world. The 2002 Convention was held in New Delhi.

PATA organisation is actively involved in developing ethos for sustainable tourism.

PATA programmes are designed to meet the needs of members, allowing each to remain competitive in the world market place. PATA offers to its members research and marketing services, product development and a variety of educational seminars and workshops.

Besides the above, there are world organisations representing hotels, travel agencies, airlines, transport, etc.

In the organisation of tourism, transport is an inseparable element. Tourism transport consists of aeroplanes, motor vehicles, railways, cruise lines, etc. Of course, governments are closely involved in the operation and regulation of the transport system.

Another essential element of tourism is accommodation-hotels, motels, inns, tourist bungalows or lodges, youth hostels, etc., where tourists can stay.

Finally, the most important elements are the tourist attractions of a country-scenic beauty, historical monuments, rivers, lakes, parks, mountains, beaches, forests, wildlife, flora and fauna, climate, food and shopping. Tourists come to see and enjoy what a country can offer. Together, all the elements mentioned above, comprise the tourism assets or resources of a country. When these are packaged, the experts call it the 'tourism product' of a country. After all, this is the product a visitor wants to buy. Like manufactured products, the tourism product too has a lot of variety. You can package it in many interesting ways as preferred or demanded by the customers. It may be a holiday on the beaches, a peep into a country's past, a mountain vacation, wildlife viewing or a shopping tour. The visitors have several options and combinations of options at different price ranges.

There is, however, one difference. Tourism is a product which has to be bought unseen. Like manufactured products, you cannot bring them to the customer to see and feel. The customer has to go to it to experience and to feel it. The new technology however, can present to you, on a computer, 'virtual reality' of the tourism product.

Establishment of India's National Tourist Administration (NTA) : As mentioned earlier, every country sets up its National Tourist Administration (NTA) according to its own requirements. All countries or States of the world, have a NTA, supported and sponsored by the Government of the country. In the western world, most NTAs are sponsored and financed by the Government. In a few countries, private sector also supports it financially and is involved, to some extent, in the management of NTAs. This is not so in India.

The Department of Tourism which manages tourism at the Government level, is wholly dependent on the Government for financial support. No attempt has been made to involve the private sector financially in a supporting role. The private sector is not involved even in an advisory role, though it is sometimes consulted at the discretion of the Government.

The argument in favour of private sector participation is that since the private sector is the major beneficiary of tourism promotion undertaken by a Government, it is logical that they share part of the expenditure on tourism promotion and management. The Government of India, in its wisdom, decided not to involve the private sector. Or, when the Government of India mooted the idea of promoting tourism, the private sector was not strong enough to contribute any money. A successful example of the Government and the private sector being actively involved in the NTO affairs is Switzerland, where the private sector contributes almost forty per cent of the expenditure. USA does not have a NTA-it was disbanded in 1995 for economic reasons. Federal Government felt that the private sector should solely promote tourism as they were the primary beneficiaries. And, US tourism has not since looked back.

There were valid reasons for not involving the private sector. When the Department of Tourism was set up in 1958, the travel industry in India was so small and so shy that the

Government did not think that the industry could contribute substantially. So, the idea of charging a fee from the industry did not appeal to the decision-makers.

In fact, the private sector in hoteliering and transport was so reluctant that the Government of India had to set up a company in the public sector to build and operate hotels at tourist centres, where the private sector was not willing to invest. Similarly, at major tourist centres like Khajuraho, Varanasi or Jaipur, there was no adequate tourist transport facilities. The public sector company, ITDC with its headquarters in New Delhi, had to step in to operate public sector transport units to provide good transport fleet.

India, therefore, is a unique case history in tourism development.

During the early years of independence, major business houses, except the house of Tatas, did not consider the operation of hotels and restaurants as an honourable business. There were only a few modern hotels in the country and those too run by foreigners. The Government's intervention became necessary to develop the basic infrastructure at major tourist centres to attract foreign tourists. This led to the Government building and operating hotels and transport units, through its public sector organisation like the ITDC all over India. State Tourism Corporations have followed the same pattern and built budget accommodation and have also operated tourist transport fleets in their respective States.

The tourism scene has changed drastically during the last thirty years and the private sector is now very active in tourism development. Indian hotels in the private sector compare favourably with the best in the world and some of the leading Indian hotel chains are operating hotels in developed countries under their brand name. The Government of India has recognised this fact and decided not to invest any more in the construction of new five-star hotels, leaving the tourism industry totally open to the private sector in India. In fact, there are moves to sell hotels owned by ITDC and Hotel Corporation of India. A few properties were sold in 2002.

India's NTA would, therefore, consists of a Department of Tourism which is a Department of the Ministry of Tourism and also the India Tourism Development Corporation which is a public sector company and implements Government's policy decisions in tourism field. The WTO has a new name for NTOs- the National Tourism Administration-NTAs. They prefer to call it NTA because an Administration has wider ramifications than the Organisation.

The private sector is encouraged by the Department of Tourism to operate tourism facilities under the overall policy guidelines of the Government. In fact, there is an excellent cooperation and understanding between the Department of Tourism and the private sector tour operators, travel agents, transporters and hoteliers in the area of tourism development. Historically, tourism development in India has suffered due to a lack of clear thinking on the part of political decision-makers in the country. Bureaucratic hurdles made it worse.

India became aware of the importance of tourism promotion as early as in 1946. Sir John Sargent, Educational Adviser to the Government of India, headed a committee to survey the potential of tourism in India and recommended that developing tourist traffic, both internal and external, will be beneficial for India. The recommendation led to the establishment of a Tourist Traffic branch in the Ministry of Transport and Communication, with a network of tourist offices in India and abroad. The branch later transformed itself into a department headed by a director general in 1958. The first overseas tourist office was set up in New York as early as in 1952, followed by similar offices in London, Paris, Frankfurt, Colombo, Melbourne and San Francisco. In retrospect, tourist offices overseas were opened too soon at too many foreign cities without providing them adequate budgetary support and without analysing the availability of adequate infrastructure at home, particularly accommodation suitable for foreigners. Besides, travellers from distant countries like USA, Canada, had a poor image of India as a holiday destination.

Establishment of Tourism Logo Department : The establishment of a separate Department of Tourism, helped considerably and the international tourist arrivals which were sixteen thousand in 1951 jumped to over sixteen lakh in 1990, and were twenty-six crore in 2000.

The importance of promotion of tourism for the economic development of India, was realised by the late Prime Minister, Indira Gandhi. She established in 1967, a separate Ministry of Tourism and Civil Aviation under Dr. Karan Singh. It was good to tie up tourism with civil aviation, as fast development of tourism is not possible without the total support of the Civil Aviation Ministry, in a country where ninety-eight per cent of foreign visitors come by air. Subsequently, all kinds of experiments have been done with the Tourism Ministry to suit the political needs of the Government in power. At times, the Ministry of Tourism has been separated from Civil Aviation to work in isolation. Later, it was attached to Commerce which made some sense. In 1991, it was tied to Agriculture which made no sense. In 1991, the Tourism and Civil Aviation ministries were again combined under a Cabinet Minister, Madhavrao Scindia. The Deve Gowda Government linked Tourism Ministry with the Ministry of Parliamentary Affairs in 1996. The BJP Government did the same in 1998. Presently, it is attached to Culture which again makes sense. It seems, tourism portfolio is the least attractive for politicians.

The Director General of Tourism in the Department of Tourism, is of the rank of an Additional Secretary and under him are various heads of divisions like planning, publicity, hotels, market research, supplementary accommodation, etc.

Strategy of Promotion

Since its inception, STPB has involved the travel industry of the country in its promotional efforts. Singapore hotels spend over US$25 million annually on overseas advertising, independently of STPB. Similarly, the National Association of Travel Agents (NATA) and the Retail Shopkeepers Associations are involved in the promotional programmes of their own, complementing the work of the STPB.

Singapore's advertising campaign is an example of cooperative working of Singapore Airlines and the STPB. Their advertising is perhaps most noticeable in the USA and in Europe as compared to that of other Asian destinations. In the UK and USA, Singapore runs television commercials, which not many Asian countries can afford. Although STPB contributes ninety per cent of the advertising funds, their name does not appear in media advertisements. The name is only of the Singapore Airlines, which responds to the enquiries.

Now, they are using Indian TV channels too, for selling Singapore to Indians.

Singapore's tourism promotion budget is the highest in the world according to WTO (above US$100 million in 2000).

STPB is convinced that Singapore by itself cannot be sold as a tourist destination. It has to be a stopover point or an extension to a holiday in the region-average stay is only three days. STPB, therefore, works closely with Malaysia and its other ASEAN neighbours like Thailand, the Philippines and Indonesia. They jointly promote the ASEAN region.

STPB's marketing skills have been applied not only at the selling end of the marketing process, but also at the starting point, with an ambitious product development programme aimed at keeping Singapore in good shape. Promotion and product development have moved hand in hand. The Government encouraged the construction of hotels in the early seventies. It was then felt that Singapore was over-building, but the period of low occupancy was short-lived and hotels soon started enjoying healthy occupancies upto eighty per cent and more.

While modernisation is taking its toll in Singapore, STPB is making earnest efforts to retain the old-world charm of historical institutions, sites and streets as tourist assets of the country. The year 1986 was a momentous year for the Singapore Travel Industry as the US$1 billion Tourist Product Development Plan was launched which has resulted in reviving of the old Bugis Street at a new site near the original one, the redevelopment of Haw Par Villa into the world's first Chinese mythological high-technology park and the revitalisation of historic districts like China Town, Little India, etc. Old buildings have been restored to their original condition and where it was not possible, these have been replaced with exact replicas.

The latest attraction is a Night Safari Park, an artificially developed jungle where hundreds of animals imported from different climes roam in their natural surroundings. The Park opens at night and the animals are visible from windows of a slow-moving train in bright moonlight-again artificially created. Only land-starved Singapore could undertake such a project.

There is no danger of animals straying out of their respective jungle abodes as the high-tech park has fool-proof security.

Singapore has one of the finest airports in Asia. The new Changi International Airport handles take-offs or landings every two minutes, round the clock. Things move very fast at this airport. Customs checks are nominal and immigration clearance even faster. While one is waiting for the baggage, there are courtesy phones from where a person may make a local telephone call without payment. Tourist literature is placed at convenient locations to be picked up by incoming passengers. For visitors taking connecting flights but having time on their hands, short sightseeing trips are available free of charge-courtesy STPB. Such short trips create an interest among the transit passengers to come back for a longer holiday.

Work's Sphere

The activities of the Department of Tourism in India, and for that matter, all NTAs anywhere in the world, can be summed up as under the following broad heads:

- Compilation, collection and dissemination of tourist information in India and abroad; attending to enquiries from international tourists, tour operators and travel industry sectors such as airlines, steamship companies and hotels; production of tourist literature-posters, brochures, information directories, tourist guide maps- for wide distribution. Now, most NTAs including India, have set up their websites for travel information so that the people with internet connections can access this information and make their travel decisions. There website have to be updated from time to time;

- o Cooperation with international travel and tourist organisations at the Government and non-Government levels;
- o Facilitation, such as simplification of frontier formalities in respect of entry of international tourists;
- o Development of tourist activities of interest to international tourists;
- o Publicity at home and abroad with the object of creating an overall awareness of the importance of tourism;
- o Regulation of the activities of various segments of the travel trade, such as hotels, youth hostels, travel agents, wildlife outfitters, guides, tourist car operators and shopkeepers catering to tourist needs; and
- o Compilation of statistics and market research on international tourist traffic to India and on its utilisation for effective tourist promotion. Compilation of domestic tourism statistics.

Recommendations for Reorganisation

In 1987, the Government of India under the late Prime Minister, Rajiv Gandhi, appointed a high-level National Committee on Tourism under the chairmanship of Mr. Mohammed Yunus. The Committee consisted of leading experts on tourism from the Government of India as well as the private sector. A major recommendation of the Committee was the reorganisation of the Department of Tourism, to make it a National Tourism Board like the Railway Board, with considerable autonomy in the implementation of schemes. The other recommendation was to have a cadre of professional tourist officers in the organisation instead of inducting Indian administrative service officers or staff from other ministries.

The recommendations were welcomed by the industry but implementation is not yet on the horizon. The vested interest of the entrenched officers is the major hurdle.

Establishment of India Tourism Development Corporation (ITDC) : Set up in 1966 as an autonomous public sector corporation, ITDC was entrusted with the task of helping to develop a tourist infrastructure and promoting India as a tourist destination. Over the years, ITDC has been playing a crucial, strategic role in ensuring:

- o Proper dispersal of socio-economic benefits of tourism;
- o Promoting national integration and international understanding;
- o Removal of regional imbalances;
- o Generating employment opportunities;
- o Augmenting foreign exchange earnings; and
- o Acting as a catalyst in the development of tourism by opening up new unexplored tourist areas.

ITDC's present range of operations is diverse. The package of tourist services comprises accommodation, catering, transport, publicity services, duty-free shops, an in-house travel agency- the Ashok Travels-entertainment, conferences, and providing management consultancy services within India and abroad.

Accommodation Chain

The Ashok Group, ITDC's accommodation chain, is the largest in the country and offers accommodation in over three thousand and eight hundred rooms in its thirty-three hotels at twenty-six destinations, ranging from luxury suites to modestly furnished rooms and from beach resorts to moderately priced travellers/ forest lodges. ITDC owns twenty-six hotels-six of its hotels are owned by its subsidiaries.

Accommodation is divided into three categories-Elite (six), Classic (sixteen) and Comfort (eleven). A few of the ITDC owned hotels have recently been sold to the private sector. It may be mentioned that a few of the ITDC-owned hotels were sold to private sector in 2002.

The Corporation's scheme of joint ventures/consultancy collaborations with the State Governments/Tourism Corporations, and private entrepreneurs, has had an enthusiastic response. Several States and private sector organisations have entered into agreements with ITDC, with ITDC operating their hotel properties under a management contract.

Duty-Free Shops : To facilitate shopping by international passengers, ITDC operates ten duty-free shops and a tax-free shop. The duty-free shops function in the arrival and departure lounges of the international airports of the country-Delhi, Mumbai, Kolkata, Chennai, Thiruananthapuram and Goa. The only tax-free shop is located at Ashok Hotel, New Delhi. Duty-free shops offer a product portfolio of over fifteen thousand. It is currently one of its few profitable areas, others are loss-making including accommodation.

Facilities of Conferences and Conventions

India's potential for convention tourism has been exploited by ITDC. ITDC's flagship-Ashok Hotel in New Delhi provides good facilities for holding international conferences for a thousand or more people at a time. It is still a popular venue for international conferences in New Delhi.

Network of Ashok : The Ashok Network, a centralised reservation service located at New Delhi, with four regional offices covering north, south, east and west India, ensures instant accommodation and transport confirmations for individuals and groups countrywide. An addition to instant bookings/confirmations is Ashok Internet, a hotel-to-hotel reservation system of the Ashok Group.

Ashok Travels and Tours : To provide back-up support to its hotels, the Corporation has its in-house full service travel agency-the Ashok Travels and Tours (ATT). From eleven units, located in various parts of the country, the ATT operates the largest fleet of coaches, tourist cars and air-conditioned limousines.

Entertainment : The French started a novel experiment in the late fifties-telling the story of old castles and palaces through the medium of sound and light. This was an additional source of entertainment for tourists.

In India, the first Sound & Light Show was mounted at the Red Fort, Delhi, narrating the story of the famous Mughal Fort beginning with the Mughal era and going on to India's Independence.

Subsequently, another show came up at Sabarmati Ashram, Ahmedabad on the life of the "Father of the Nation", Mahatma Gandhi. In the same year, a Sound & Light Show was mounted at Shalimar Gardens, Srinagar, based on the romantic story of the Great Mughal Emperor, Jahangir, and his intelligent and dynamic consort, Noor Jahan. After that, ITDC put up shows at the Cellular Jail (a national monument now) in Andaman and Nicobar Islands and at Golconda Fort in Hyderabad.

Sound & Light Shows provide good, wholesome entertainment and are so very informative. ITDC has now mounted a show at Chandragiri Fort in Chittoor district of Andhra Pradesh. Others in the pipeline are at the Somnath Temple in Veraval district, Gujarat and at the Sun Temple at Konarak, Orissa.

The world heritage site of Hampi in Karnataka-the Capital of the mighty Vijayanagar Empire; as also Katra in Jammu-nestling at the feet of the Goddess Durga, will also see Sound & Light Shows before long.

Modern dramatic techniques of lighting systems, are being used in mounting these shows with the help of digital technology.

Travel Packages : To promote domestic tourism, ITDC operates various tourism packages every year. These packages are moderately priced and sold at all hotels of the Ashok Group in the country.

Publicity Consultancy : ITDC has a publicity division which offers consultancy services to State Governments and other similar organisations. Their services include advertising, publicity and tourism communications.

Financial Success : ITDC with an authorised share capital of Rs 75 crore and paid up capital of Rs 675 crore has six subsidiary companies. It is one of the few public sector undertakings which has been making profits ever since its inception. However, in the late nineties, it started its downhill journey and has been consistently in the red mainly due to over-staffing and unionisation. The Government of India has decided in principle to disinvest in the activities of ITDC and let the private sector run the business of hotel-keeping. It is only a matter of time when ITDC will be out of the hands of the Government. Delay is mainly due to vested interest.

Establishment of India Convention Promotion Bureau (ICPB) : In a bid to promote convention and conference tourism, the Ministry of Tourism has sponsored the establishment of the India

"Wanted Ambassadors for India" : It is estimated that more than 20,000 of India's professional elite, attend over 10,000 conferences worldwide every year. Are you one of them? We need you as an Ambassador.

We need you to go beyond the role of a delegate to that of a dignitary, to present India as the Conference Destination of the 90s.

To bag the next conference at the next international meet you attend, and make India the prestigious venue.

The Booming Conference Business : Over 33,000 conferences are held around the world every year and generate an incredible US dollars 104 billion in revenue.

India's share is minuscule. We host around 170 conferences annually.

Imagine the opportunities and the pivotal role you can play in attracting this immensely prestigious, booming business to India!

India - New Destination : There is an international awakening.

There is a growing realisation that India is much more than a tourist destination. It is an unforgettable learning experience.

Contemporary facilities and the richest legacies.

That is the inimitable beauty of India you can offer with the greatest pride and confidence: Majesty, Mystery, Grandeur and above all our famed warmth and hospitality in comfort and style that will redefine international standards. Assure them of our prestigious conference venues in historic Delhi, in scenic Srinagar and several other centres, each especially planned and developed as a confluence for minds.

Convention Halls for ten to 10,000, Hi-Tech Communication facilities-Fax, Telex, Computers, International Direct Dialling, Administrative and Secretarial help, Staff with convention experience. In essence, you name it, it is there.

India Convention Promotion Bureau (ICPB) redefines you from Delegate to Host : To make you vie with the world.

To provide all the support you need to bid and win. That is the role of ICBP. A non-profit association sponsored by the Ministry of Tourism, Government of India.

In this endeavour, ICBP has the support and resources of its member bodies comprising Airlines, Hotels, Travel Agents, Tour Operators, Tourist Bureaus, Travel Associations, etc.

Count on ICPB to make your conference happen. ICPB is with you all the way.

Right from the ideation stage, discussing ways and means of getting your conference to India, preparing professional bid documents, assisting in the post-bid phase through member organisations, promoters, bookings, management of the event-everything.

If all this sounds amazing, talk to ICBP if you are serious about becoming an Ambassador for India.

ICPB has its office at Room No.233, Ashok Hotel, New Delhi-110021. Tel: 6874318.

Convention Promotion Bureau (ICPB). While a major part of the expenses is borne by the Government of India, the private sector also contributes its share. Its office is located in the Ashoka Hotel, New Delhi. ICPB tries to attract international conferences to India-by making presentations at the conferences regarding the facilities offered by India and the fun that awaits the delegates.

Extracts from the text of an advertisement issued by ICPB in major national magazines are reproduced on the facing page. It explains the ICPB's area of work.

Opening of Overseas Tourist Offices : The Government of India opened its tourist offices overseas, to promote inbound tourism to destination India as early as 1950- now they number seventeen in different parts of the world. Most of them are located in the affluent countries of the west- including the USA, Europe, Japan and Australia. Annual expenditure on the upkeep of these offices and promotion abroad exceeds Rs 75 crore. The expenditure is insignificant as the country earns over Rs 10,000 crore from foreign tourism and this small expense seems justifiable. The entire expenditure is funded by the Government of India-the private sector which benefits from tourism does not contribute to it.

But, there are examples of some successful experiments doing without overseas tourist offices with little adverse effect on their inbound arrivals, e.g., the USA, China and Russia. The USA once had tourist offices abroad but closed them finding that they did not add to the number of arrivals. There are countries like Pakistan, Nepal and others which too do not have overseas offices.

A WTO study done in 1997 revealed that, worldwide, Singapore was the destination which spent most in a year on promotion overseas through its overseas office-US$99 million, followed by the UK, US$78 million; Spain, US$71 million; Thailand, US$66 million and Australia, US$61 million. But, their tourism is much larger than India's.

However, the new technology and the availability of excellent websites of nations has made them redundant. Even at the time, this technology was not available, the percentage of visitors to India who got information from overseas tourist offices or through their advertising was less than two per cent.

Now, it will be much less. Questions, therefore, have been raised by not only the travel industry but also by the Tourism Minister, Finance Minister, etc., about the utility of these offices or at least so many of them. In India, it is not easy to think objectively on subjects where plum jobs are involved-involving extensive foreign travel abroad.

However, in 2002, the Government of India decided to close down five of its sixteen overseas offices.

Explosion of Domestic Tourism : An unfortunate feature of Indian tourism is that policy-makers in the past have always equated tourism with foreign visitors. There were two reasons for it-one, it was traditionally the foreign visitor who occupied hotel rooms, filled airline seats, frequented bars and restaurants and used the recreation and adventure facilities. And, during the days of short supply of foreign exchange, it was the foreign visitor who seem to be purveyor of unlimited money supply. Every aspect of Indian tourism was, therefore, arranged to suit his needs. Even the price mechanism seemed to tie with overseas costs, ignoring the average standards in the country.

There is, however, a hidden dimension to Indian tourism one that has figured little in the policy planning or thinking of most industry and Government players: almost unobstrusive and yet inexorable rise in domestic tourism. In the last ten years, domestic tourism has increased by more than hundred million travellers, up by, from 63.8 million in 1990 to one hundred and seventy-six million in 1999.

The explosion in domestic travel is an inevitable by-product of economic development in the country and various other factors like pilgrimages. An average Indian traveller is an avid sightseer too and his average spending is growing. Soon, many of them will be patronising star hotels.

Personal spending on travel and tourism in 2001, by the residents positions, puts India as the nineteenth largest spender in the world.

The forecast for personal travel tourism growth over the next decade, at 9.7 per cent annually, positions India as the second fastest growing country in this category. Business travel and tourism in India is expected to grow by 7.1 per cent per annum over the coming decade (Source : WTTC), and, that too without much help from the Government.

Careers in Tourism Management

Travel and tourism represents a broad range of related industries. The growth of these industries has opened up many new job opportunities for graduates in areas such as:

- hotels
- restaurants
- retailing
- transportation
- travel agencies
- tour companies
- tourist attractions
- leisure, recreation and sport
- cultural industries

It is interesting to realise that in 1997 travel and tourism provides 10.5% of the total world employment, with up to 25% of all employment, in some areas, such as the Caribbean. It has been estimated that, by 2007, more than 100 million people world-wide will be employed in this sector. Because of this, tourism is now seen to be of importance to most countries of the world.

During this time, the nature of tourism has developed in scope and direction, away from traditional activities, such as the sunshine sand and sea holidays to a wide range of new activities such as cultural tourism, adventure tourism, sports and leisure activities and eco-tourism.

Given the potential for interesting and rewarding careers in these industries many young people are looking for suitable courses which will help prepare them for careers in management within the tourism and hospitality industries. The UK higher education system has a well developed range of courses, at all levels from Higher National Diploma, BA or BSc degrees and MA/MSc/MBA Masters courses and using alternative methods of studying, (including full-time, part-time and distance learning). When looking at courses in hospitality and tourism, there can seem to be a bewildering variety of course titles covering the main employment areas of travel, tourism, hotels and restaurants. Typical titles include:

For hotels and restaurant management:

- hospitality management
- international hospitality management
- hotel and catering management

For travel and tourism:

- tourism management
- tourism studies
- travel and tourism

There are also joint degrees where it is possible to study combinations of subjects, such as tourism and hospitality, tourism and leisure, hospitality and marketing. Most undergraduate courses (HND/BSc/BA) will include a period of work experience as part of the course, varying in length from 6 months to one year. This work experience is seen to be a central part of the course, where the student gets the opportunity to practise what they have learned in college or university. Employers also see great value in this work experience when considering the employment of graduates.

Given the international nature of these industries, another valuable part of any course is the study of languages. Most courses in hospitality and tourism provide access to language courses, either as core components or as options.

Courses at Masters level are becoming increasingly important in tourism and hospitality. These Masters level courses are useful to two groups of people:

- those who have completed a degree course in a subject other than hospitality or tourism but who are looking at ways of getting employment in the industry;

- those who have a degree or sub-degree qualification in hospitality or tourism together with significant management experience within the hospitality or tourism industries and who wish to develop themselves to a higher level or to seek a more senior position in industry. There are many Masters courses in Hospitality Management, Hotel and Catering Management and Tourism Management in universities and colleges in the UK.

In addition to the above courses, there are also more specialised Masters courses in Tourism covering areas such as Cultural Tourism, Tourism Marketing, Tourism Planning, Museum Management, Heritage Management, Cultural Tourism and Sustainable Tourism: these are suitable for people who have an interest in employment in a specific sector of the industry.

Within the UK there are many university and college courses to choose from, but each course will have its own unique characteristics. Before applying, you should think carefully about the type of career you want: if it is in a hotel are you interested in restaurant management or rooms division management? Do you see yourself as a practical hands-on person or someone who is happier to work behind the scenes in a desk based job? Do you aspire to become a general manager of a hotel which is part of one of the major world-wide groups, or do you want to manage your own operation? Are you more interested in one of the functional management areas, such as marketing, human resources, conferences. If you are interested in tourism do you want to work for a travel agency, a tour company, the management of a tourist attraction, or within the public sector-national, regional or local tourism planning organisations. Think about these types of question before consulting the prospectuses or WEB sites so that you can judge each course against your own preferences.

11

Moving Towards Protected Area Tourism

The EDEN award 2009 focused on promoting sustainable tourism in protected areas. Eligible destinations are those protected areas and/or the areas bordering them where an economically viable tourism product has been developed using the protected area as an asset, all the while respecting its protected environment and meeting the needs of local residents and visitors.

The call for proposals was launched by the Commission in March, with 22 countries replying. They have had until May 2009 to select a winning destination from among the candidate destinations. Each destination had to respect the following general award criteria:

1. be "non traditional" (the visitor density rating from "low" to "very low" in comparison with the national average)
2. be based on an area that is part of the Natura 2000 Network or otherwise designated as a "protected area" by national or regional legislation
3. manage its own tourism offer in such a way as to ensure its social, cultural and environmental sustainability, with the management being a partnership between the authorities responsible for managing the protected area and all those involved in tourism in and around the area (e.g. tourist service providers, local communities)

Twenty-two destinations of excellence have been officially awarded at the occasion of the European Tourism Forum on 8th October 2009.

TOURISM IN PROTECTED AREAS INITIATIVE

The Queensland Parks and Wildlife Service (QPWS) manages more than 11 million hectares of public lands across the state. Many of these areas are a key resource for the state's nature-based tourism industry and attract over 16 million visits a year.

Commercial tourism operations make parks more accessible for many visitors, and play a valuable role in enhancing appreciation of these unique areas.

The Tourism in Protected Areas (TIPA) initiative was developed in response to tourism operators' concerns about access to Queensland's protected area network.

A working group of industry and government representatives made 18 key recommendations addressing these issues to the Queensland government.

Benefits of TIPA

The aims of the initiative are to:

- protect key visitor sites better by determining visitor capacity
- provide greater business certainty as a result of longer permit tenure for commercial operators under commercial activity agreements
- introduce alternate pricing and trading arrangements for tour operators
- introduce performance standards, accreditation systems and codes of practice
- use 'expression of interest' processes to allocate access for new capacity.

SUSTAINABLE TOURISM IN PROTECTED AREAS

"Sustainable Tourism in Protected Areas: Guidelines for Planning and Management", a landmark publication jointly published by UNEP, The World Conservation Unit (IUCN) and the World Tourism Organization (WTO) is a contribution to the International Year of Ecotourism 2002.

The publication aims to assist protected area managers and other stakeholders in the planning and management of protected areas based on a wealth of practical case studies and experience.

The main purpose of these Guidelines is to assist protected area managers and other stakeholders in the planning and management of protected areas, visitor recreation and the tourism industry, so that tourism can develop in a sustainable fashion, while respecting local conditions and local communities. A key message is the importance of managing resources and visitors today, so that tomorrow's visitors can also experience quality sites, and the conservation values that these places represent.

The Guidelines also have a number of more detailed objectives:

- To discuss the role of visitor management, including techniques that control and limit impacts of use, while allowing maximum enjoyment of as many visitors as can be accommodated within the limits set by environmental and social conditions;
- To outline approaches to the planning and development of tourism infrastructure and services in protected areas;
- To provide guidance on the definition, measurement, management and use of park tourism data;
- To outline ways of enhancing the quality of the tourism experience;
- To describe positive examples, through a variety of case studies, of how tourism can effectively contribute to the conservation of natural and cultural diversity; and

- To give positive examples, again through the use of case studies, of how tourism can contribute to the development of local communities.

The major questions and issues involved in managing tourism in protected areas are developed for the reader, but the publication does not set out to provide all the detailed answers. Thus a framework is provided to establish principles and guide decisions. There is no "one-size-fits-all" answer to the challenge of tourism in protected areas - indeed an attraction of visiting protected areas is to see how each park manager has developed his or her local situation in a way that projects its uniqueness, while contributing to the common endeavour of conservation. To a large extent, management must be responsive to local conditions.

It may appear that protected area managers have a relatively simple job in achieving the task of conservation and visitor use, but in fact it is not easy at all. Managers have the challenging responsibility of balancing the many competing pressures thrust upon them.

This challenge grows and becomes more complicated with increasing numbers of visitors, changes in patterns of visitor use, and the emergence of an ever more critical public demanding higher standards in conservation management.

The challenge of protected area management, especially that of dealing with the pressures of recreation and tourism, will only be met effectively through building partnerships between all the interested parties. It is hoped that this document, by being available to protected area managers as well as other important stakeholders, such as local communities, tour operators and conservation groups, will help build such partnerships.

Protected areas normally achieve recognition and enhanced protection when sufficient numbers of people visit them, appreciate them, and take political action to assure their survival. Park tourism is a critical component of protected area establishment and management.

These guidelines provide a conceptual background for understanding park tourism and its management. They provide a theoretical basis for management, and they include practical advice to planners and managers.

Sustainable tourism practice within protected areas is a long-term commitment. But while it is important to think long-term, it is also necessary to set realistic short and mid-term goals. Individuals, businesses and organisations must be aware that benefits are long-term, and should not expect to experience them immediately after sustainable practices are implemented. In practice, only a small portion of benefits will arise quickly; most will depend upon many years of continued effort.

It is important for protected area planners to develop incentive measures that will influence decision-making processes within society. It is necessary to create inducements to incite or motivate government, local people, and international organisations to conserve biological and cultural diversity. All existing legislation and economic policies need to be reviewed in order to identify and promote incentives for the conservation and sustainable use of the resources, and to remove or modify those that threaten biological diversity and cultural integrity.

Protected area managers need to make ongoing efforts to communicate with all stakeholders. Only with the broad support of the community will management be successful in the long term. These guidelines suggest that national and international organisations need to encourage governments to make improvements in the following critical areas:

1. Support for effective legislation, with adequate resources for implementation;
2. Creation of national policies on protected areas and the management of tourism (as well as education about the environment and conservation); and
3. Development of a management plan for each protected area, covering all activities, including tourism, to ensure that objectives are achieved and resources are well-used..

At present, the cash flow from tourism often returns largely to urban areas, well away from the protected areas themselves. It is always advantageous to invest and assign some tourism revenue to local communities, so that local people see direct financial benefits from park tourism. Planners and managers should therefore be active in stimulating maximum local economic benefit.

History

Hector Ceballos-Lascurain popularized (and he would say coined) the term 'ecotourism' in July 1983, when he was performing the dual role of Director General of Standards and Technology of SEDUE (the Mexican Ministry of Urban Development and Ecology) and founding president of PRONATURA (an influential Mexican conservationist NGO). PRONATURA was lobbying for the conservation of the wetlands in northern Yucatán as breeding and feeding habitats of the American Flamingo.

Others claim the term was in use earlier: Claus-Dieter (Nick) Hetzer, an academic and adventurer from Forum International in Berkeley, CA, coined the term in 1965 and ran the first ecotours in the Yucatán during the early 1970s.

Ecotourism, responsible tourism, jungle tourism, and sustainable development have become prevalent concepts since the mid 1980s, and ecotourism has experienced arguably the fastest growth of all sub-sectors in the tourism industry. The popularity represents a change in tourist perceptions, increased environmental awareness, and a desire to explore natural environments. At times, such changes become as much a statement affirming one's social identity, educational sophistication, and disposable income as it has about preserving the Amazon rainforest or the Caribbean reef for posterity.

However, in the continuum of tourism activities that stretch from conventional tourism to ecotourism proper, there has been a lot of contention to the limit at which biodiversity preservation, local social-economic benefits, and environmental impact can be considered "ecotourism". For this reason, environmentalists, special interest groups, and governments define ecotourism differently. Environmental organizations have generally insisted that ecotourism is nature-based, sustainably managed, conservation supporting, and environmentally educated. The tourist industry and governments, however, focus more on the product aspect, treating ecotourism as equivalent to any sort of tourism based in nature. As a further complication, many terms are used under the rubric of ecotourism. Nature tourism, low impact tourism, green tourism, bio-tourism, ecologically responsible tourism, and others have been used in literature and marketing, although they are not necessary synonymous with ecotourism.

The problems associated with defining ecotourism have led to confusion among tourists and academics . Definitional problems are also subject of considerable public controversy and concern because of green washing, a trend towards the commercialization of tourism schemes disguised as sustainable, nature based, and environmentally friendly ecotourism. According to McLaren, these schemes are environmentally destructive, economically exploitative, and culturally insensitive at its worst. They are also morally disconcerting because they mislead tourists and manipulate their concerns for the environment. The development and success of such large scale, energy intensive, and ecologically unsustainable schemes are a testament to the tremendous profits associated with being labeled as ecotourism.

Negative Impact of Tourism

Ecotourism has become one of the fastest-growing sectors of the tourism industry, growing annually by 10-15% worldwide (Miller, 2007). One definition of ecotourism is "the practice of low-impact, educational, ecologically and culturally sensitive travel that benefits local communities and host countries" (Honey, 1999). Many of the ecotourism projects are not meeting these standards. Even if some of the guidelines are being executed, the local communities are still facing other negative impacts. South Africa is one of the countries that are reaping significant economic benefits from ecotourism, but negative effects - including forcing people to leave their homes, gross violations of fundamental rights, and environmental hazards - far outweigh the medium-term economic benefits (Miller, 2007). A tremendous amount of money is being spent and human resources continue to be used for ecotourism despite unsuccessful outcomes, and even more money is put into public relation campaigns to dilute the effects of criticism. Ecotourism channels resources away from other projects that could contribute more sustainable and realistic solutions to pressing social and environmental problems. "The money tourism can generate often ties parks and managements to eco-tourism" (Walpole et al. 2001). But there is a tension in this relationship because eco-tourism often causes conflict and changes in land-use rights, fails to deliver promises of community-level benefits, damages environments, and has plenty of other social impacts. Indeed many argue repeatedly that eco-tourism is neither ecologically nor socially beneficial, yet it persists as a strategy for conservation and development (West, 2006). While several studies are being done on ways to improve the ecotourism structure, some argue that these examples provide rationale for stopping it altogether.

The ecotourism system exercises tremendous financial and political influence. The evidence above shows that a strong case exists for restraining such activities in certain locations. Funding could be used for field studies aimed at finding alternative solutions to tourism and the diverse problems Africa faces in result of urbanization, industrialization, and the over exploitation of agriculture (Kamuaro, 2007). At the local level, ecotourism has become a source of conflict over control of land, resources, and tourism profits. In this case, ecotourism has harmed the environment and local people, and has led to conflicts over profit distribution. In a perfect world more efforts would be made towards educating tourists of the environmental and social effects of their travels. Very few regulations or laws stand in place as boundaries for the investors in ecotourism. These should be implemented to prohibit the promotion of unsustainable ecotourism projects and materials which project false images of destinations, demeaning local and indigenous cultures.

Direct Environmental Impacts

Ecotourism operations occasionally fail to live up to conservation ideals. It is sometimes overlooked that ecotourism is a highly consumer-centered activity, and that environmental conservation is a means to further economic growth.

Although ecotourism is intended for small groups, even a modest increase in population, however temporary, puts extra pressure on the local environment and necessitates the development of additional infrastructure and amenities. The construction of water treatment plants, sanitation facilities, and lodges come with the exploitation of non-renewable energy sources and the utilization of already limited local resources. The conversion of natural land to such tourist infrastructure is implicated in deforestation and habitat deterioration of butterflies in Mexico and squirrel monkeys in Costa Rica. In other cases, the environment suffers because local communities are unable to meet the infrastructure demands of ecotourism. The lack of adequate sanitation facilities in many East African parks results in the disposal of campsite sewage in rivers, contaminating the wildlife, livestock, and people who draw drinking water from it.

Aside from environmental degradation with tourist infrastructure, population pressures from ecotourism also leaves behind garbage and pollution associated with the Western lifestyle. Although ecotourists claim to be educationally sophisticated and environmentally concerned, they rarely understand the ecological consequences of their visits and how their day-to-day activities append physical impacts on the environment. As one scientist observes, they "rarely acknowledge how the meals they eat, the toilets they flush, the water they drink, and so on, are all part of broader regional economic and ecological systems they are helping to reconfigure with their very activities." Nor do ecotourists recognize the great consumption of non-renewable energy required to arrive at their destination, which is typically more remote than conventional tourism destinations. For instance, an exotic journey to a place 10,000 kilometers away consumes about 700 liters of fuel per person.

Ecotourism activities are, in of itself, issues in environmental impact because they disturb fauna and flora. Ecotourists believe that because they are only taking pictures and leaving footprints, they keep ecotourism sites pristine, but even harmless sounding activities such as a nature hike can be ecologically destructive. In the Annapurna Circuit in Nepal, ecotourists have worn down the marked trails and created alternate routes, contributing to soil impaction, erosion, and plant damage. Where the ecotourism activity involves wildlife viewing, it can scare away animals, disrupt their feeding and nesting sites, or acclimate them to the presence of people. In Kenya, wildlife-observer disruption drives cheetahs off their reserves, increasing the risk of inbreeding and further endangering the species.

Environmental Hazards

The industrialization, urbanization, and unsustainable agriculture practices of human society are considered to be having a serious effect on the environment. Ecotourism is now also considered to be playing a role in this depletion. While the term ecotourism may sound relatively benign, one of its most serious impacts is its consumption of virgin territories (Kamuaro, 2007). These invasions often include deforestation, disruption of ecological life systems and various forms of pollution, all of which contribute to environmental degradation. The number of motor vehicles crossing the park increases as tour drivers search for rare species. The number of roads has disrupted the grass cover which has serious effects on plant and animal species. These areas also have a higher rate of disturbances and invasive species because of all the traffic moving off the beaten path into new undiscovered areas (Kamuaro, 2007). Ecotourism also has an effect on species through the value placed on them. "Certain species have gone from being little known or valued by local people to being highly valued commodities. The commodification of plants may erase their social value and lead to overproduction within protected areas. Local people and their images can also be turned into commodities" (West, 2006). Kamuaro brings up a relatively obvious contradiction, any commercial venture into unspoiled, pristine land with or without the "eco" prefix as a contradiction in terms. To generate revenue you have to have a high number of traffic, tourists, which inevitably means a higher pressure on the environment.

Local People

Most forms of ecotourism are owned by foreign investors and corporations that provide few benefits to local communities. An overwhelming majority of profits are put into the pockets of investors instead of reinvestment into the local economy or environmental protection. The limited numbers of local people who are employed in the economy enter at its lowest level, and are unable to live in tourist areas because of meager wages and a two market system.

In some cases, the resentment by local people results in environmental degradation. As a highly publicized case, the Masai nomads in Kenya killed wildlife in national parks to show aversion to unfair compensation terms and displacement from traditional lands. The lack of economic opportunities for local people also constrains them to degrade the environment as a means of sustenance. The presence of affluent ecotourists encourage the development of destructive markets in wildlife souvenirs, such as the sale of coral trinkets on tropical islands and animal products in Asia, contributing to illegal harvesting and poaching from the environment. In Suriname, sea turtle reserves use a very large portion of their budget to guard against these destructive activities.

Displacement of People

One of the most powerful examples of communities being moved in order to create a park is the story of the Masai. About

70% of national parks and game reserves in East Africa are on Masai land (Kamuaro, 2007). The first undesirable impact of tourism was that of the extent of land lost from the Masai culture. Local and national governments took advantage of the Masai's ignorance on the situation and robbed them of huge chunks of grazing land, putting to risk their only socio-economic livelihood. In Kenya the Masai also have not gained any economic benefits. Despite the loss of their land, employment favours better educated workers. Furthermore the investors in this area are not local and have not put profits back into local economy. In some cases game reserves can be created without informing or consulting local people, who come to find out about the situation when an eviction notice is delivered (Kamuaro, 2007). Another source of resentment is the manipulation of the local people by their government. "Eco-tourism works to create simplistic images of local people and their uses and understandings of their surroundings. Through the lens of these simplified images, officials direct policies and projects towards the local people and the local people are blamed if the projects fail" (West, 2006). Clearly tourism as a trade is not empowering the local people who make it rich and satisfying. Instead ecotourism exploits and depletes, particularly in African Masai tribes. It has to be reoriented if it is to be useful to local communities and to become sustainable (Kamuaro, 2007).

Threats to Indigenous Cultures

Ecotourism often claims that it preserves and "enhances" local cultures. However, evidence shows that with the establishment of protected areas local people have illegally lost their homes, and most often with no compensation (Kamuaro, 2007). Pushing people onto marginal lands with harsh climates, poor soils, lack of water, and infested with livestock and disease does little to enhance livelihoods even when a proportion of ecotourism profits are directed back into the community. The establishment of parks can create harsh survival realities and deprive the people of their traditional use of land and natural resources. Ethnic groups are increasingly being seen as a "backdrop" to the scenery and wildlife. The local people struggle for cultural survival and freedom of cultural expression while being "observed" by tourists. Local indigenous people also have strong resentment towards the change, "Tourism has been allowed to develop with virtually no controls. Too many lodges have been built, too much firewood is being used and no limits are being placed on tourism vehicles. They regularly drive off-track and harass the wildlife. Their vehicle tracks criss-cross the entire Masai Mara. Inevitably the bush is becoming eroded and degraded" (Kamuaro, 2007).

Mismanagement

While governments are typically entrusted with the administration and enforcement of environmental protection, they often lack the commitment or capability to manage ecotourism sites effectively. The regulations for environmental protection may be vaguely defined, costly to implement, hard to enforce, and uncertain in effectiveness. Government regulatory agencies, as political bodies, are susceptible to making decisions that spend budget on politically beneficial but environmentally unproductive projects. Because of prestige and conspicuousness, the construction of an attractive visitor's center at an ecotourism site may take precedence over more pressing environmental concerns like acquiring habitat, protecting endemic species, and removing invasive ones. Finally, influential groups can pressure and sway the interests of the government to their favor. The government and its regulators can become vested in the benefits of the ecotourism industry which they are supposed to regulate, causing restrictive environmental regulations and enforcement to become more lenient.

Management of ecotourism sites by private ecotourism companies offers an alternative to the cost of regulation and deficiency of government agencies. It is believed that these companies have a self interest in limited environmental degradation, because tourists will pay more for pristine environments, which translates to higher profit. However, theory indicates that this practice is not economically feasible and will fail to manage the environment.

The model of monopolistic competition states that distinctiveness will entail profits, but profits will promote imitation. A company that protects its ecotourism sites is able to charge a premium for the novel experience and pristine environment. But when other companies view the success of this approach, they also enter the market with similar practices, increasing competition and reducing demand. Eventually, the demand will be reduced until the economic profit is zero. A cost-benefit analysis shows that the company bears the cost of environmental protection without receiving the gains. Without economic incentive, the whole premise of self interest through environmental protection is quashed; instead, ecotourism companies will minimize environment related expenses and maximize tourism demand.

The tragedy of the commons offers another model for economic unsustainability from environmental protection, in ecotourism sites utilized by many companies. Although there is a communal incentive to protect the environment, maximizing the benefits in the long run, a company will conclude that it is in their best interest to utilize the ecotourism site beyond its sustainable level. By increasing the number of ecotourists, for instance, a company gains all the economic benefit while paying only a part of the environmental cost. In the same way, a company recognizes that there is no incentive to actively protect the environment; they bear all the costs, while the benefits are shared by all other companies. The result, again, is mismanagement.

Taken together, the mobility of foreign investment and lack of economic incentive for environmental protection means that ecotourism companies are disposed to establishing themselves in new sites once their existing one is sufficiently degraded.

Improving Sustainability

Regulation and Accreditation

Because the regulation of ecotourism is poorly implemented or nonexistent, ecologically destructive green washed operations like underwater hotels, helicopter tours, and wildlife theme parks are categorized as ecotourism along with canoeing, camping, photography, and wildlife observation. The failure to acknowledge responsible, low impact ecotourism puts these companies at a competitive disadvantage.

Many environmentalists have argued for a global standard of accreditation, differentiating ecotourism companies based on their level of environmental commitment. A national or international regulatory board would enforce accreditation procedures, with representation from various groups including governments, hotels, tour operators, travel agents, guides, airlines, local authorities, conservation organizations, and non-governmental organizations. The decisions of the board would be sanctioned by governments, so that non-compliant companies would be legally required to disassociate themselves from the use of the ecotourism brand.

Crinion suggests a Green Stars System, based on criteria including a management plan, benefit for the local community, small group interaction, education value and staff training. Ecotourists who consider their choices would be confident of a genuine ecotourism experience when they see the higher star rating.

In addition, environmental impact assessments could be used as a form of accreditation. Feasibility is evaluated from a scientific basis, and recommendations could be made to optimally plan infrastructure, set tourist capacity, and manage the ecology. This form of accreditation is more sensitive to site specific conditions.

Guidelines and Education

An environmental protection strategy must address the issue of ecotourists removed from the cause-and-effect of their actions on the environment. More initiatives should be carried out to improve their awareness, sensitize them to environmental issues, and care about the places they visit.

Tour guides are an obvious and direct medium to communicate awareness. With the confidence of ecotourists and intimate knowledge of the environment, they can actively discuss conservation issues. A tour guide training program in Costa Rica's Tortuguero National Park has helped mitigate negative environmental impacts by providing information and regulating tourists on the parks' beaches used by nesting endangered sea turtles.

Small Scale, Slow Growth and Local Control

The underdevelopment theory of tourism describes a new form of imperialism by multinational corporations that control ecotourism resources. These corporations finance and profit from the development of large scale ecotourism that causes excessive environmental degradation, loss of traditional culture and way of life, and exploitation of local labor. In Zimbabwe and Nepal's Annapurna region, where underdevelopment is taking place, more than 90 percent of ecotourism revenues are expatriated to the parent countries, and less than 5 percent go into local communities.

The lack of sustainability highlights the need for small scale, slow growth, and locally based ecotourism. Local peoples have a vested interest in the well being of their community, and are therefore more accountable to environmental protection than multinational corporations. The lack of control, westernization, adverse impacts to the environment, loss of culture and traditions outweigh the benefits of establishing large scale ecotourism.

The increased contributions of communities to locally managed ecotourism create viable economic opportunities, including high level management positions, and reduce environmental issues associated with poverty and unemployment. Because the ecotourism experience is marketed to a different lifestyle from large scale ecotourism, the development of facilities and infrastructure does not need to conform to corporate Western tourism standards, and can be much simpler and less expensive. There is a greater multiplier effect on the economy, because local products, materials, and labor are used. Profits accrue locally and import leakages are reduced. However, even this form of tourism may require foreign investment for promotion or start up. When such investments are required, it is crucial for communities for find a company or non-governmental organization that reflects the philosophy of ecotourism; sensitive to their concerns and willing to cooperate at the expense of profit. The basic assumption of the multiplier effect is that the economy starts off with unused resources, for example, that many workers are cyclically unemployed and much of industrial capacity is sitting idle or incompletely utilized. By increasing demand in the economy it is then possible to boost production. If the economy was already at full employment, with only structural, frictional, or other supply-side types of unemployment, any attempt to boost demand would only lead to inflation. For various laissez-faire schools of economics which embrace Say's Law and deny the possibility of Keynesian inefficiency and under-employment of resources, therefore, the multiplier concept is irrelevant or wrong-headed.

As an example, consider the government increasing its expenditure on roads by $1 million, without a corresponding increase in taxation. This sum would go to the road builders, who would hire more workers and distribute the money as wages and profits. The households receiving these incomes will save part of the money and spend the rest on consumer goods. These expenditures in turn will generate more jobs, wages, and profits, and so on with the income and spending circulating around the economy.

The multiplier effect arises because of the induced increases in consumer spending which occur due to the increased incomes - and because of the feedback into increasing business revenues, jobs, and income again. This process does not lead to an economic explosion not only because of the supply-side barriers at potential output (full employment) but because at each "round", the increase in consumer spending is less than the increase in consumer incomes. That is, the marginal propensity to consume (mpc) is less than one, so that each round some extra income goes into saving, leaking out of the cumulative process. Each increase in spending is thus smaller than that of the previous round, preventing an explosion.Ecotourism has to be implemented with care.

12

Moving Towards Medical Tourism

As more people around the world take an active interest in their health, a travel segment known as health tourism has evolved to fill customer needs. Not to be confused with medical tourism, which focuses more on surgical procedures, health tourism is a much broader concept centered mainly around resorts designed to pamper or improve the body and relax the mind.

Hundreds of health resorts and spas exist around the world, offering specialized beauty and fitness services, and extended programs to improve your health. These resorts are almost always located in stunning natural environments or in the trendiest city districts. Spas play a major role in health tourism, but this field also extends into areas like addiction treatment and weight loss.

Destination spas and health resorts are the most common and popular health travel venue. They offer a comprehensive range of services, from massage and Ayurvedic therapy to yoga and outdoor recreation facilities. The goal of these resorts is to send their guests home feeling happier, healthier, fitter and more relaxed. Everything is contained within the health spa resort, allowing guests to relax and focus on themselves.

Spa resorts often specialize in a particular health remedies. Mineral baths have been around for thousands of years, and countries like Bulgaria and New Zealand capitalize on these natural geothermal properties. Mud baths and other natural health cures are usually accompanied by a full menu of pampering services like massage and facials at these facilities. More holistic resorts offer treatments like acupuncture, colonic cleansing, hypnotherapy and meditation.

There are also specialized health centres for issues such as weight loss. These resorts place an emphasis on losing weight and improving eating habits. Guests typically follow a schedule lasting from a few days to a week or more. The meals are specially tailored to boost health and guests attend workshops to learn more about staying fit, eating right and keeping their weight down.

Another common specialized health destination is for addicts. Alcohol and drug addiction are the two most common problems dealt with at these facilities. They are set up like all-inclusive resort centers, except that there is more emphasis on monitoring the guests' behavior and keeping them on their rigid programs. These are not particularly relaxing resorts, but they can often break a person's addiction in a healthy manner.

Fitness holidays are gaining popularity with travelers who want to get some well-needed exercise while on vacation. This is the broadest category of health tourism, because the location is more important than the venue. Mountain resorts provide skiing in the winter and hiking and biking in the summer. Beach resorts are also popular for swimming and water sports. A fitness holiday places the impetus of action entirely on the traveller, and there are resorts at virtually every popular outdoor destination on the planet.

Origin and Development

The concept of medical tourism is not a new one. The first recorded instance of medical tourism dates back thousands of years to when Greek pilgrims traveled from all over the Mediterranean to the small territory in the Saronic Gulf called Epidauria. This territory was the sanctuary of the healing god

Asklepios. Epidauria became the original travel destination for medical tourism.

Spa towns and sanitariums may be considered an early form of medical tourism. In eighteenth century England, for example, patients visited spas because they were places with supposedly health-giving mineral waters, treating diseases from gout to liver disorders and bronchitis.

Process

The typical process is as follows: the person seeking medical treatment abroad contacts a medical tourism provider. The provider usually requires the patient to provide a medical report, including the nature of ailment, local doctor's opinion, medical history, and diagnosis, and may request additional information. Certified medical doctors or consultants then advise on the medical treatment. The approximate expenditure, choice of hospitals and tourist destinations, and duration of stay, etc., is discussed. After signing consent bonds and agreements, the patient is given recommendation letters for a medical visa, to be procured from the concerned embassy. The patient travels to the destination country, where the medical tourism provider assigns a case executive, who takes care of the patient's accommodation, treatment and any other form of care. Once the treatment is done, the patient can remain in the tourist destination or return home.

International Healthcare Accreditation

Because standards are important when it comes to health care, there are parallel issues around medical tourism, international healthcare accreditation, evidence-based medicine and quality assurance.

The oldest international accrediting body is Accreditation Canada, formerly known as the Canadian Council on Health Services Accreditation, which accredited the Bermuda Hospital

Board as soon as 1968. Since then, it has accredited hospitals and health service organizations in ten other countries.

In the United States, the best known accreditation group is the Joint Commission International (JCI). They have been inspecting and accrediting health care facilities and hospitals outside of the United States since 1999. Many international hospitals today see obtaining international accreditation as a way to attract American patients.

Joint Commission International is a relative of the Joint Commission in the United States. Both are independent private sector not-for-profit organizations that develop nationally and internationally recognized procedures and standards to help improve patient care and safety. They work with hospitals to help them meet Joint Commission standards for patient care and then accredit those hospitals meeting the standards.

QHA Trent Accreditation, based in the UK, is an active accreditation scheme. Prior to that, the Trent International Accreditation Scheme was a key player.

The different international healthcare accreditation schemes vary in quality, size, cost, intent and the skill and intensity of their marketing. They also vary in terms of cost to hospitals and healthcare institutions making use of them. A forecast by Deloitte Consulting regarding medical tourism published in August 2008 noted the value of accreditation in ensuring quality of healthcare and specifically mentioned JCI, ISQUA and Trent.

Increasingly, some hospitals are looking towards dual international accreditation, perhaps having both JCI to cover potential US clientele, Trent for potential British and European clientele and Accreditation Canada. As a result of competition between clinics for American medical tourists, there have been initiatives to rank hospitals based on patient-reported metrics.

Other organizations providing contributions to quality practices include:

- The United Kingdom Accreditation Forum (UKAF) is an established network of accreditation organisations with the intention of sharing experience good practice and new ideas around the methodology for accreditation programmes, covering issues such as developing healthcare quality standards, implementation of standards within healthcare organisations, assessment by peer review and exploration of the peer review techniques to include the recruitment, training, monitoring and evaluation of peer reviewers and the mechanisms for awards of accredited status to organisations.

Organizations and Association

Medical Tourism Association (MTA), the first for-profit trade association for medical tourism, is made up of international hospitals, healthcare providers, medical travel facilitators, insurance companies, and other affiliated companies and members with the common goal of promoting medical tourism in a global environment. The Association promotes the interests of its healthcare provider and medical travel facilitator members. The MTA has three tenets: Transparency, Communication and Education. The goal of these types of associations is often to raise awareness of medical tourism in the hopes of expanding the industry.

HealthCare Tourism International (HTI) is a 501(c) non-profit organization that is complementary to the Joint Commission International accreditation group. Health care organizations can apply for self-certification or accreditation on the HTI website.

Risks

Medical tourism carries some risks that locally-provided medical care does not. Some countries, such as India, Malaysia, or Thailand have very different infectious disease-related epidemiology to Europe and North America. Exposure to diseases without having built up natural immunity can be a hazard for weakened individuals, specifically with respect to gastrointestinal diseases (e.g. Hepatitis A, amoebic dysentery, paratyphoid) which could weaken progress, mosquito-transmitted diseases, influenza, and tuberculosis. However, because in poor tropical nations diseases run the gamut, doctors seem to be more open to the possibility of considering any infectious disease, including HIV, TB, and typhoid, while there are cases in the West where patients were consistently misdiagnosed for years because such diseases are perceived to be "rare" in the West.

The quality of post-operative care can also vary dramatically, depending on the hospital and country, and may be different from US or European standards. However, JCI and Trent fulfill the role of accreditation by assessing the standards in the healthcare in the countries like India, China and Thailand. Also, traveling long distances soon after surgery can increase the risk of complications. Long flights and decreased mobility in a cramped airline cabin are a known risk factor for developing blood clots in the legs such as venous thrombosis or pulmonary embolus economy class syndrome. Other vacation activities can be problematic as well - for example, scars may become darker and more noticeable if they sunburn while healing. To minimise these problems, medical tourism patients often combine their medical trips with vacation time set aside for rest and recovery in the destination country.

Also, health facilities treating medical tourists may lack an adequate complaints policy to deal appropriately and fairly with complaints made by dissatisfied patients.

Differences in healthcare provider standards around the world have been recognised by the World Health Organization, and in 2004 it launched the World Alliance for Patient Safety. This body assists hospitals and government around the world in setting patient safety policy and practices that can become particularly relevant when providing medical tourism services.

Legal Issues

Receiving medical care abroad may subject medical tourists to unfamiliar legal issues. The limited nature of litigation in various countries is one reason for the lower cost of care overseas. While some countries currently presenting themselves as attractive medical tourism destinations provide some form of legal remedies for medical malpractice, these legal avenues may be unappealing to the medical tourist. Should problems arise, patients might not be covered by adequate personal insurance or might be unable to seek compensation via malpractice lawsuits. Hospitals and/or doctors in some countries may be unable to pay the financial damages awarded by a court to a patient who has sued them, owing to the hospital and/or the doctor not possessing appropriate insurance cover and/or medical indemnity.

Ethical Issues

There can be major ethical issues around medical tourism. For example, the illegal purchase of organs and tissues for transplantation has been alleged in countries such as India and China prior to 2007. The Declaration of Istanbul distinguishes between ethically problematic "transplant tourism" and "travel for transplantation" .

Medical tourism may raise broader ethical issues for the countries in which it is promoted. For example in India, some argue that a "policy of 'medical tourism for the classes and health missions for the masses' will lead to a deepening of the inequities" already embedded in the health care system. In Thailand, in 2008 it was stated that, "Doctors in Thailand have become so busy with foreigners that Thai patients are having trouble getting care". Medical tourism centred on new technologies, such as stem cell treatments, is often criticized on grounds of fraud, blatant lack of scientific rationale and patient safety. However, when pioneering advanced technologies, such as providing 'unproven' therapies to patients outside of regular clinical trials, it is often challenging to differentiate between acceptable medical innovation and unacceptable patient exploitation.

World Medical Tourism

Africa and the Middle East

Countries in this region involved in medical tourism include Saudi Arabia, South Africa, and Tunisia.

Israel

Israel is emerging as a popular destination for medical tourists. In 2006, 15,000 foreigners travelled to the country for medical procedures, bringing in $40 million of revenue.

Medical tourists choose Israel for several reasons. Some come from European nations such as Romania where certain procedures are not available. Others come to Israel, perhaps most commonly from the US, because they can receive quality health care at a fraction of the cost it would be at home, for both surgeries and in-vitro fertilization treatments.

Other medical tourists come to Israel to visit the Dead Sea, a world-famous therapeutic resort. The Israel Ministry of Tourism and several professional medical services providers have set out to generate awareness of Israel's medical capabilities.

Jordan

Jordan is an emerging medical tourism destination, with related revenues exceeding one billion dollars in 2007. More than 250,000 patients from other countries sought treatment in Jordan that year. This included an estimated 45,000 Iraqis and approximately 25,000 patients each from Palestine and Sudan. An estimated 1,800 US citizens, 1,200 UK citizens, and 400 Canadians also sought treatment in Jordan that year. Treatment costs can be as low as 25 percent of costs in the US. The kingdom was rated as number one in the region and fifth in the world as a medical tourism hub in a study by the World Bank.

United Arab Emirates

Hospitals in Dubai and other emirates have expressed an intent to develop in medical tourism. Some have American-sourced international healthcare accreditation, while others are looking towards the UK, Australia and Canada for accreditation services.

The Americas

Countries in the Americas that are treating foreign patients include Argentina, Bolivia, Brazil, Colombia, Costa Rica, Cuba, Dominican Republic, Guatemala, Mexico, Panama, Peru and Uruguay.

Brazil

Brazil has long been known as a destination for cosmetic surgery. For non-cosmetic procedures, Brazil is only now entering the global market. However, Albert Einstein Jewish Hospital in São Paulo was the first JCI-accredited facility outside of the US, and more than a dozen Brazilian medical facilities have since been similarly accredited. Brazil requires visas for US citizens based on a reciprocal arrangement since Brazilians are required to obtain a visa to visit the US. Unlike in the U.S and other countries where medical procedures are simply done in an office, Plastic surgery in Brazil is done in specific plastic surgery only hospitals

Canada

Canada has entered the medical tourism field. In comparison to US health costs, medical tourism patients can save 30 to 60 percent on health costs in Canada.

Costa Rica

Costa Rica's popularity in the medical tourism industry has been growing steadily over the years. Currently there are 3 Joint Commission International accredited (JCI) Hospitals all of which are currently located in San Jose, Costa Rica. Recently announced by JCI accredited Clinica Biblica, is a $40 million dollar hospital in Guanacaste designed to target the influx of medical tourism arriving in the Liberia International airport every year. This will make for a total of over six major private hospitals and 22 public hospitals. When the World Health Organization (WHO) ranked the world's health systems in the year 2000, Costa Rica was ranked as no. 36, which was higher than the U.S., and together with Dominica it dominated the list amongst the Central American countries.

Costa Rica offers these levels of care ranging from Intermediate Life Saving capabilities, Complex Life Saving Treatment Capabilities, Advanced Life Savings Treatment Capabilities, and Life Style Treatment Services (Full range of dental work and cosmetic surgery).

Because of Costa Rica's close proximity to the USA, the country is able to attract over 20,000 US patients a year. It is also the prices of medical services that are quite attractive to consumers seeking quality care at an affordable price. The Deloitte Center for Health Solutions, in their 2009 report "Medical Tourism Consumers in Search of Value" reported cost savings average of between 30-70% of US prices.

Cuba

Cuba has been a popular medical tourism destination for more than 40 years. Thousands of patients travel to Cuba, particularly from Latin America and Europe, attracted by the "fine reputation of Cuban doctors, the low prices and nearby beaches on which to recuperate." In 2006, Cuba attracted nearly 20,000 medical tourists.

Medical treatments included joint replacement, cancer treatment, eye surgery, cosmetic surgery and addictions rehabilitation. Costs are about 60 to 80 percent less than US costs.

Cuba has hospitals for Cuban residents and others that focus on serving foreigners and diplomats. In the 2007 American documentary film, Sicko, which criticizes the US healthcare system, producer Michael Moore leads a group of uninsured American patients to Cuba to obtain more affordable medical treatment. Sicko has greatly increased foreigners' interest in Cuban healthcare. A recent Miami Herald story focused on the high quality of health care that Canadian and American medical tourism patients receive in Cuba.

The Cuban government has developed Cuban medical tourism to generate income for the country. Residents of Canada, the UK and most other countries can travel to Cuba without any difficulty, although a tourist visa is generally required. For Americans, however, because of the US trade policy towards Cuba, travelers must either obtain US government approval, or, more frequently, travel to Cuba from Canada, Mexico, the Bahamas, Jamaica or the Dominican Republic. Cuban immigration authorities do not stamp the passports of US visitors so that Americans can keep their travels a private matter. To date no Cuban facility has achieved JCI Accreditation.

Mexico

Americans, particularly those living near the Mexican border, now routinely cross to Mexico for medical care. Popular specialties include dentistry and plastic surgery. Mexican dentists often charge one-fifth to one-fourth of US prices, while other procedures typically cost a third what they would in the US.

In Texas, legislators explored the possibility of allowing health maintenance organizations to operate on both sides of the border. However, physicians in south Texas lobbied against the changes, arguing that local doctors could not compete with the lower costs in Mexico". US doctors point out that the Mexican legal system makes it almost impossible to sue Mexican doctors for malpractice.

However, many who travel to Mexico for care report that they are satisfied. According to a report commissioned by Families U.S.A., a Washington advocacy group for health-care issues, "About 90 percent [feel] the care they had received in Mexico had been good or excellent. About 80 percent rated the care they had received in the United States as good or excellent".

Indeed "some U.S. dentists ... have conceded to the competition and begun a 'reverse migration' opening offices in Mexico to take advantage of lower costs". More American insurers are providing coverage for travelers, as the out-of-pocket costs to them are much lower. "With healthcare costs in the United States continuing to rise, many employers in Southern California are turning to insurance plans that send their workers to Mexico for routine care, plans that are growing by nearly 3,000 people a year."

In addition to dental and plastic surgery, Mexican hospitals are popular for bariatric surgery for weight loss, considered an elective procedure that is not covered by some US insurers. A popular bariatric procedure, lap band surgery, which was approved by the FDA in the US in 2001, has been performed for longer by Mexican surgeons.

Panama

In Panama, health and medical tourism is growing rapidly. Factors drawing medical tourists include Panama's tourist appeal, position as a hub for international travel, and use of the American dollar as the official currency. Many of Panama's doctors are bilingual, board certified, and accustomed to working with the same medical equipment and technology used in the United States and Europe. On most procedures, Panama offers savings of more than 50% compared to the US and Europe. No Panamanian hospitals currently have international healthcare accreditation, whether through US, British, Australian or Canadian sources.

United States

Although much attention has been given to the growing trend of uninsured Americans traveling to foreign countries, a McKinsey and Co. report from 2008 found that a plurality of an estimated 60,000 to 85,000 medical tourists were traveling to the United States for the purpose of receiving in-patient medical care; the same McKinsey study estimated that 750,000 American medical tourists traveled from the United States to other countries in 2007 (up from 500,000 in 2006). The availability of advanced medical technology and sophisticated training of physicians are cited as driving motivators for growth in foreigners traveling to the U.S. for medical care, whereas the low costs for hospital stays and major/complex procedures at Western-accredited medical facilities abroad are cited as major motivators for American travelers. Also, it has been noted that the decline in value of the U.S. dollar is offering additional incentive for foreign travel to the U.S., although, costs differences between the US and many locations in Asia far outweigh any currency fluctuations.

Several major medical centers and teaching hospitals offer international patient centers that cater to patients from foreign countries who seek medical treatment in the U.S. Many of these organizations offer service coordinators to assist international patients with arrangements for medical care, accommodations, finances and transportation including air ambulance services.

Many locations in the US that offer medical care comparable in price to foreign medical facilities are not Joint Commission Accredited.

Uruguay

Uruguay recently entered the medical tourism market. A private medical tourism initiative, Uruhealth, has been created with support from the Ministries of Tourism and Public Health. The initiative involves the infrastructure, human resources and experience of two healthcare companies: MP Personalized Medicine (Montevideo) and SEMM-Mautone Hospital (Punta del Este).

Asia/Pacific

Many Asian Pacific countries are medical tourism destinations.

China

China is fast emerging as a desirable destination for individuals seeking medical care in a wide range of medical specialties, including cardiology, neurology, orthopedics and others. A number of private and government hospitals in major cities have established international departments. Many leading hospitals provide treatments integrating Traditional Chinese

Medicine with Western medical technology and techniques. China is home to leading stem cell research and treatment hospitals that offer Westerners who want to take advantage of stem cell treatments that are still considered experimental or have yet to be approved in their home country.

Hong Kong

As of 2006, Hong Kong had 12 private hospitals and 39 public hospitals, providing 3,124 and 27,755 beds respectively. A wide range of health care services are offered. All 12 of Hong Kong's private hospitals have been surveyed and accredited by the UK's Trent Accreditation Scheme since early 2001. This has been a major factor in the ascent of standards in Hong Kong's private hospitals. The Trent scheme works closely with the hospitals it assesses to generate standards appropriate to the locality (with respect to culture, geography, public health, primary care interfaces etc.), and always uses combinations of UK-sourced and Hong Kong-sourced surveyors. Some of Hong Kong's private hospitals have now gone on to obtain dual international accreditation, with both Trent and JCI (and have therefore attained a standard surpassing some of the best hospitals in Thailand and Singapore). Others are looking towards dual international accreditation with Trent and the Australian group. Hong Kong public hospitals have yet to commit to external accreditation.

India

India's medical tourism sector is expected to experience an annual growth rate of 30%, making it a Rs. 9,500-crore industry by 2015. Estimates of the value of medical tourism to India go as high as $2 billion a year by 2012. Advantages for medical tourists include reduced costs, the availability of latest medical technologies and a growing compliance on international quality standards, as well as the fact that foreigners are not likely to face a language barrier in India. The Indian government is taking steps to address infrastructure issues that hinder the country's growth in medical tourism.

Most estimates claim treatment costs in India start at around a tenth of the price of comparable treatment in America or Britain. The most popular treatments sought in India by medical tourists are alternative medicine, bone-marrow transplant, cardiac bypass surgery, eye surgery and orthopedic surgery. India is known in particular for heart surgery, hip resurfacing and other areas of advanced medicine.

Ministry of Tourism India(MoT) is planning to extend its Market Development Assistance (MDA) scheme to cover Joint Commission International (JCI) and National Accreditation Board of Hospitals (NABH) certified hospitals. A policy announcement of this effect is likely soon.

The South Indian city of Chennai is considered to be the healthcare capital of India as it is home to some of India's best medical centers.

South Korea

Listed on CNN.com as one of the "hot destinations" for medical tourism, South Korea is quickly establishing itself in the field of medical tourism.

However, The Korea Times reported in a series of articles that Korean hospitals have adopted a discriminatory pricing policy, charging foreigners two to three times more than the full-fee for locals.

The paper revealed that the price disparity in medical fees for foreign patients is extremely high, considering that the difference between the lowest and highest fees for the most-sought-after procedures exceeds more than 10 times on average.

It claims the government is overlooking soaring medical fees on foreign patients, who are unprotected from malpractice, discriminatory charging, overpricing and patient privacy rights under the Korean Medical Law.

In 2008, Korea had 27,480 foreign-based patients and the Korean health ministry expects that number to increase to 140,000 by 2015. Due to legislation passed in May 2009, state-licensed clinics and hospitals are now allowed to directly seek out foreign patients through various promotional activities.

Korean hospitals and clinics provide a variety of medical services for medical tourists including comprehensive health screening, cancer treatment, organ transplantation, joint/ rheumatism care, spinal treatment, ophthalmology, dental care, infertility treatment, otorhinolaryngology, and Korean traditional medicine. Currently, the most popular treatments for medical tourists are cosmetic procedures such as eyelid surgery, nose jobs, facelifts, and skin lightening.

Over 30 South Korean hospitals and clinics are member providers under the Council for Korea Medicine Overseas Promotion (CKMOP). Among these facilities are the "Big Four" - Seoul National University Hospital, Samsung Medical Center, Asan Medical Center, and Yonsei Severance Hospital.

Malaysia

Malaysia is well on its way to develop itself as a medical tourism hub. The country has excellent hospitals, English is widely spoken, and many staff have been trained to a high level in the UK or in the US. There is a highly active Association for Private Hospitals of Malaysia working to develop medical tourism. However, while Malaysia has a national accreditation healthcare scheme (MSQH) and many Malaysia's hospitals are currently firmly on the way to achieve international healthcare accreditation.

Malaysian hospitals such Gleneagles Hospital Kuala Lumpur , International Specialist Eye Centre, Penang Adventist Hospital are JCI accredited. The Ministry of Health has launched a medical tourism page.

New Zealand

New Zealand is a relatively new destination to medical travel. It has all the hallmarks of a very successful destination especially for North American based patients. This includes being a first world, developed economy with a sophisticated and comprehensive medical system. It is first and foremost

English speaking with a rich heritage of producing world class doctors and medical research.

Many of its private hospitals are internationally accredited, state of the art and offer an integrated package of care.

The cost of the surgical care in New Zealand is significantly cheaper. On average it is considered that New Zealand's surgical costs are around 15 to 20% the cost of the same surgical procedure in the USA. One patient who had his prosthetic hip replaced in New Zealand said the total cost including travel, lodging and the surgery at a private hospital was $20,000, as opposed to the $80,000 - $140,000 he was told the operation would have cost at home.

Added to this the personalized level of medical care, the world renown natural beauty and tranquility, the fact that New Zealand is one of the safest places in the world and only 12 hours direct flight from the west coast of North America, then New Zealand as a medical travel destination looks set to develop.

Pakistan

Pakistan has mentioned its keenness on working towards medical tourism and has considered it as a key element in its recent tourism policy. Despite suffering several blowbacks, due to insecurity and instability in the region, medical tourism in Pakistan has been arranging potential trips for many medical health and care procedures. A number of modern hospital facilities exist in Islamabad, Karachi and Lahore which are fully equipped and facilitated. Many doctors and surgeons in Pakistani hospitals tend to be foreign qualified. A number of patients from neighbouring countries have traveled to Pakistan for treatment.

Philippines

The Philippines has been growing as a destination for medical tourism. The US Medical Tourism Association magazine reported that this services sub-sector grew 8.0% in

2007. The number can be expected to grow as American health-care costs rise, or if pending legislation results in an increase in patient wait times for surgical procedures (as has been seen in other countries where care has been nationalized), due to the traditional political, economic and cultural connections between the United States and the Philippines.

The Philippines is one of a few countries that sends qualified nurses, physicians and dentists to the US, the thousands serving in American medical facilities being a testament to its quality of medical education. According to year 2000 WHO rankings of the world's health systems, the Philippines takes its position on no.60.

Singapore

Singapore has a dozen hospitals and health centers with JCI accreditation. In 1997 (published 2000), the World Health Organization ranked Singapore's health care system sixth best in the world and the highest ranked system in Asia.

Patients come from neighboring countries, such as Indonesia and Malaysia, and patient numbers from Indochina, South Asia, the Middle East and Greater China are growing. Patients from developed countries such as the United States and the UK are also beginning to choose Singapore as their medical travel destination for relatively affordable health care services in a clean cosmopolitan city.

Taiwan

The Taiwanese government has declared its determination for the country to become a medical tourism center. In 2007, the Department of Health launched a campaign to promote inbound medical tourism, focusing on integrating the resources of the government and academia to build Taiwan's brand as a medical tourism destination. Costs for procedures remain comparatively low. Taiwan is known for liver transplants, joint replacement surgery, bone marrow transplants, and reconstructive and plastic surgery.

Thailand

Medical tourism has been a growing segment of Thailand's tourism and health-care sectors. In 2005, one Bangkok hospital took in 150,000 treatment seekers from abroad. In 2006, medical tourism was projected to earn the country 36.4 billion baht.

Treatments for medical tourists in Thailand range from cosmetic, organ transplants, cardiac, and orthopaedic treatments to dental and cardiac surgeries. Treatments also include spa, physical and mental therapies, as well as procedures that are considered more along the lines of fringe medical practices. One patient who had coronary artery bypass surgery at Bumrungrad International hospital in Bangkok said the operation cost him US$12,000 (8,200 euros), as opposed to the $100,000 (68,000 euros) he estimated the operation would have cost him at home. Bumrungrad treated approximately 55,000 American patients in 2005 alone, a 30% increase from the previous year.

Hospitals in Thailand are a popular destination for other Asians. Bangkok Hospital, which caters to medical tourists, has a Japanese wing, and Phyathai Hospitals Group has interpreters for over 22 languages, besides the English-speaking medical staff. When Nepal Prime Minister Girija Prasad Koirala needed medical care in 2006, he went to Bangkok.

Many Thai physicians hold US or UK professional certification. Bumrungrad International hospital states that many of its doctors and staff are trained in the UK, Europe and the US. Bumrungrad International was accredited most recently in 2005 by the Joint Commission. Some of the country's major hospitals have also achieved certification by the International Organization for Standardization's ISO 9001:2000. However, ISO 2000 is not an accreditation scheme.

The World Health Organization's 2000 ranking put the Thai healthcare system at number 47, below the USA's ranking at 37 and the United Kingdom's ranking at 18.

Europe

Countries in Europe that have active medical tourism sectors include Turkey, Romania, Cyprus, Germany, Hungary, Estonia, Lithuania, Malta, Poland, Portugal, Czech Republic, Slovakia, Spain, and Ukraine.

Czech Republic

Czech Republic has built its medical tourism on spas and medical care equalling the world standards (for example Ostrava University Hospital).

Cyprus

Cyprus is actively developing its medical tourism industry. Currently very few hospitals have independent accreditation.

Estonia

Estonia is particularly popular among Scandinavians for medical tourism. The medical tourism industry achieves world standards and has to comply with EU regulation since it joined the EU in 2004. Estonia is known for its good medical care and scored particularly high in the Health Consumer Powerhouse report, produced on behalf of the European Union.

Germany

Germany is a destination for patients seeking advanced medical technology, high standards, safety, and quick treatment. All German citizens have health coverage, resulting in a high hospital density, with twice as many hospitals per capita as the United States. The high hospital density results in shorter waitlists for treatment. Costs for medical treatment compete well with other developed European countries and are commonly 50% of those in the USA.

Germany is an attractive destination for patients from the Middle East since traveling to the USA has become more difficult for them since the September 11 attacks. US citizens sometimes travel to Germany to seek treatments such as artificial cervical disc replacement that are not US Food and Drug Administration (FDA) approved.

Lithuania

Lithuania is one of several countries actively promoting medical tourism. Treatments involve cosmetic surgery, eye surgery, and other services.

Poland

Since 2004, when Poland joined the European Union, it has become another locale for people seeking cheaper medical treatments. The quality of care in Poland must comply with EU standards. The best hospitals and clinics in Poland are concentrated in the Polish Association of Medical Tourism (PAMT). The Association is responsible for the development of this sector of the economy in Poland.

Romania

Romania is a member state of the European Union. Medical tourism services in Romania varied but cover a large scope. The quality of services is implemented by both national and EU bodies of accreditation. Medical tourism in Romania is quality driven as outlined in the Medical Tourism Magazine, issue 18.

The private healthcare system in Romania is amongst the most dynamic in the country in terms of investments and growth. Market reports state that growth can still be expected in the private system in the years to come.

There are facilitators in Romania helping traveling patients access services, both medical and touristic services.

Turkey

Turkey attracts medical tourists from Europe and the Balkans, the United States, Eurasia and the Middle East, hosting about 40,000 annually,

The Turkish private healthcare system is striving to become a strategic global health service provider manufacturing center. Web site www.healthinturkey.org has been established by the DE?K-Foreign Economic Relations Board of Turkey Healthcare Committee and the Accredited Hospitals Association of Turkey. The site contains information on prices and hospital statistics, information about the healthcare, pharmaceutical and insurance environments as well as an international patient guide.

13

Moving Towards Agricultural Tourism

The concept of agrotourism is a direct expansion of ecotourism, which encourages visitors to experience agricultural life at first hand. Agrotourism is gathering strong support from small communities as rural people have realised the benefits of sustainable development brought about by similar forms of nature travel. Visitors have the opportunity to work in the fields alongside real farmers and wade knee-deep in the sea with fishermen hauling in their nets.

Agritourism, as it is defined most broadly, involves any agriculturally-based operation or activity that brings visitors to a farm or ranch. Agritourism has different definitions in different parts of the world, and sometimes refers specifically to farm stays, as in Italy. Elsewhere, agritourism includes a wide variety of activities, including buying produce direct from a farm stand, navigating a corn maze, picking fruit, feeding animals, or staying at a B&B on a farm.

Agritourism is a form of niche tourism that is considered a growth industry in many parts of the world, including Australia, Canada , the United States , and the Philippines . Agritourism overlaps with geotourism, ecotourism, and culinary tourism. Other terms associated with agritourism are "agritainment", "value added products," "farm direct marketing", and "sustainable agriculture".

Pick-Your-Own Projects

You provide for customers in your fruit orchards or vegetable fields, where your customers harvest the fruits or products.

Rent-a-Tree Operations

Here you rent/lease a tree or trees to your customer where all the fees on a particular tree belongs to them. The customer pays the farmer at the beginning of the season, the farmer takes care of the trees and either the farmer or the customer will do the harvesting.

Hospitality Provision

Where you offer bed and breakfast, room stays, overnight or longer visits, camping activities.

Short Term Visits

Where you offer your customers the opportunity to visit your farm for short periods of time where they enjoy many different activities

Tourism is the fastest growing business in the world. And since September 11, customers are seeking safer ways to have an enjoyable experience. Agricultural tourism can bridge the gap between farm and city dwellers, to the benefit of both. At one time most city people had relatives in the countryside, they no longer have them available since so few people live on farms. Many city people want farm vacations, to get away, but they don't have relatives or friends who are farmers. They also want to eat locally grown food, particularly organic food.

Agricultural tourism provides enjoyment and education for the public, promotes products from the farm, and increases income for the farm. Already in many areas, there are pumpkin festivals, fruit festivals, flower festivals, bird watching trips, hikes, hay-wagon rides. You can create mountain bike trails, horseback riding trails. Most of all, they want to see how a real farm works and to be a part of that cycle of life for a time.

Roadside stands have been used by farmers for years. U Pick your own have become more and more common all over the farming countryside. A new concept that of farm stay with bed and breakfast is rapidly growing. The fact is, that it is up to farmers to promote the knowhow about the importance of farming in our country. Your project must have strict rules for customers and teach your customer about farming and how the presence is allowing them to preserve their farms.

If you want to develop a successful agricultural tourism you will need to really be interested in developing such a project and have the kind of personality that loves to meet new people and share fun and learning with them. Your land or farm must have enough acreage, good ambience, land and water or scenery, and be able to develop accommodations for them. You need to be close enough for the kind of clients you are seeking. And a source for needed startup and seed capital.

In addition, you must set up a library of information, reach every website on agricultural and other tourism available print off copy, develop your own idea book.

You've got to really want to do this. That means a sincere interest, a personality that is outgoing and patient, land and water resources sufficient to accommodate the chosen venture, capital for start-up and conversion costs, and an accessible location.

You need to want to become an expert in people interaction and the kinds of activities you will be offering. You will need a business plan and create relationships with other farmers in the area that you can use for diversification of long term visitors to your farm. And you need to want to teach, to be a place of fun ways and enjoy meeting and talking with people who know absolutely nothing about farming. Can you be genteel with those who are totally in the dark, and be willing to explain over and over again the same activity or operation.

Remember customers need community. They need to feel they belong, to have a home. People want to experience nature, to see what its like to live on the land, and want to know people who live the natural life. They need to regenerate, they need a hayride, animals to pet, sack races. You can create cooking classes, pickling classes, canning and drying seminars. You can show them how to pick flowers and dry them. You need to understand how to make them pack into two weeks the experience of a whole year. Your place can become their place of renewal, of connection to the natural life.

There is a downside such as traffic, noise, water use. But when you develop a business, there are going to be problems and issues. It's up to you to decide if the potential profits is worth the problems and efforts.

A key to a successful agricultural tourism project is to expand it into a multiple profit Enviroadventure project. By doing that you can develop multiple attractions. For example bird watching can also be combined with wildlife watching. Restoring streamside habitat, protecting wetlands, and creating favorable conditions for bird feeding, birding trails, natural trails, are all options you can pursue.

Make your guests want to stay longer than overnight by creating a community/family feeling. Let them experience farm life with a farm family. Have them experience eating together and actually talking about the days events together. Set up a community with membership cards, newsletter and website where members can enroll and communicate with others who visit your place. You have many options such as short trips and daylong trips with lunch.

New Tends of Agrocultural Tourism

Agriculture is backbone of Indian Economy. 85 percent of the population is directly or indirectly dependent on Agriculture where as 26 percent of GDP comes from Agriculture. 110 million farmers are dwelling in 6.25 lakh villages producing more than 200 MT of food grains feeding the country. More than profession, business, agriculture is culture. Hence, adding additional income generating activities to existing Agriculture would certainly increase contribution of Agriculture to national GDP. Serious efforts need to be made in this direction. Agri-Tourism is one such activity.

Tourism is termed as instrument for employment generation, poverty alleviation and sustainable human development. During 1999-2000, direct employment created by tourism is 15.5 millions. Besides, tourism also promotes national integration, international understanding and supports local handicrafts and cultural activities. During 2000, number of foreign tourists visited India is 26.41 lakhs. India share in world tour market is just 0.38 percent. With this meager share, foreign exchange earned is Rs.14,475 crores. Turnover in domestic tourism is much more than this. To promote domestic tourism, thrust areas identified by Government of India are development of infrastructure, product development and diversification, development of eco-adventure sports, cultural presentations, providing inexpensive accommodation, streamlining facilitation procedures at airports, human resource development, creating awareness and public participation and facilitation of private sector participation. In this process, important stakeholders are state and central department of tourism, Indian Institute of Tourism and Travel Management, Tourism Development Corporations, foreign embassies, Travel Agents Association of India (TAAI), Indian Association of Tour Operators (IATO), Tourists, Transport Operators Association, Indian convention promotion bureau and Pacific Asia Travel Association (PATA).

Promotion of Agri-tourism involves some more important stakeholders namely Ministry of Agriculture and line departments at state and central governments and farmers. Promotion of Agri-Tourism needs conceptual convergence with Rural Tourism, Eco-Tourism, Health Tourism, Adventure Tourism and culinary adventures. Greatest advantage of Agri-Tourism are:

1. It brings major primary sector Agriculture closer to major service sector tourism. This convergence is expected to create win-win situation for both the sectors.
2. Tourism sector has potential to enlarge.
3. Agriculture sector has the capacity to absorb expansion in Tourism Sector.

Scope for Agri-Tourism:- Agri-Tourism has great scope in the present context for the following reasons.

An inexpensive gateway:- The cost of food, accommodation, recreation and travel is minimum in Agri-Tourism. This widens the tourist base. Present concept of travel and tourism is limited to urban and rich class which constitute only small portion of the population. However, the concept of Agri-tourism takes travel and tourism to the larger population, widening the scope of tourism due to its cost effectiveness.

Curiosity about the farming industry and life style:- The urban population basically which has roots in villages always has curiosity about sources of food, plants, animals, raw materials like wood, handicrafts, languages, culture, tradition, dresses and lifestyle. Agri-tourism which revolves around the farmers, villages and agriculture has the capacity to satisfy the curiosity of this segment of population. Agri-tourism provides scope for re-discoursing the rural life which is rich in diversity.

Strong demand for wholesome family oriented recreational activities villages provide recreational opportunities to all age groups i.e. children young, middle and old age, male, female, in total to the whole family at cheaper cost. Rural games, festivals, food, dress and the nature provides variety of entertainment to the whole family.

Health consciousness of urban population and finding solace with nature friendly means Modern lifestyle has made the life stressful and average life span has comedown. Hence, people are in constant search of pro-nature means to make life more peaceful. Ayerveda which is pro-nature medical approach has roots in villages. Indigenous medical knowledge of villagers is respected. Organic foods are in greater demand in urban areas and foreign countries. In total, health conscious urban population is looking towards pro-nature villages for solutions.

Desire for peace and tranquility:- Modern life is the product of diversified thinking and diversified activities. Every individual attempts to work more, in different directions to earn more money to enjoy modern comforts.

Hence, peace is always out of his system. Tourism is the means for searching peaceful location. Peace and tranquility are inbuilt in Agri-tourism as it is away from urban areas and close to nature.

Interest in natural environment - Busy urban population is leaning towards nature. Because, natural environment is always away from busy life. Birds, animals, crops, mountains, water bodies, villages provide totally different atmosphere to urban population in which they can forget their busy urban life.

Disillusionment with over crowded resorts and cities - In resorts and cities, over crowded peace seekers disturb each others peace. Hence, peace is beyond cities and resorts. Even though efforts are made to create village atmosphere in the sub urban areas through resorts, farm houses, it looks like a donkey painted with tiger colour. Artificiality is highlighted and not satisfying.

Nostalgia for their roots on the farm Cities are growing at the cost of villages. Villagers are migrating to cities in search of jobs and seeking comforts of modern life. Hence, yesterday villagers are today urbanites. Deep in the heart of urbanites lies the love and respect for their ancestors and villages. Hence, visit to villages satisfies their desire. This is also expressed through the hatredness of urbanites to flat culture and love for farmhouses located in the outskirts of cities. Any opportunity to visit villages and spend time with family is dream of any urbanite. But, minimum decent facilities are always problem. Agri-tourism attempts to overcome this problem.

Rural recreation Villages provide varieties of recreation to urbanites through festivals and handicrafts. Villagers (farmers) lifestyle, dress, languages, culture / traditions which always add value to the entertainment. Agriculture environment around farmers and the entire production process could create curiosity among urban taught. Places of agriculture importance like highest crop yielding farm, highest animal yielding farm, processing units, farms where innovations tried add attraction to the tourists. Agriculture products like farm gate fresh market, processed foods, organic food could lure the urban tourists. As result of this Agri-atmosphere in the villages, there is scope to develop Agri-tourism products like Agri-shopping, culinary tourism, pick and own your tree / plot, bed and breakfast, pick and pay, bullock cart riding, camel riding, boating, fishing, herbal walk, rural games and health (Ayurvedic) tourism.

Educational value of Agri-Tourism:- Agri-tourism could create awareness about rural life and knowledge about agriculture science among urban school childrens. It provides a best alternative for school picnics which are urban based. It provides opportunity for hands on experience for urban college students in Agriculture. It is a means for providing training to future farmers. It would be effectively used as educational and training tool to train agriculture and line department officers. This provides unique opportunity for education through recreation where learning is fun effective and easy. Seeing is believing, doing is learning and most importantly experiences are USP of Agri-tourism.

Basic principles of Agri-Tourism : Agri-tourism should ensure the following three basic principles.

1. *Have something for visitors to see*:- Animals, birds, farms and nature are the few things which Agri-tourism could offer to the tourist to see. Apart from these, culture, dress, festivals and rural games could create enough interest among forest in Agri-tourism.
2. *Have something for visitors to do*:- Participating in agricultural operations and swimming, bullock cart riding, camel riding, buffalo riding, cooking and participating in the rural games are the few activities to quote in which tourist can take part and enjoy.
3. *Have something for visitors to buy*:- Rural crafts, dress materials, farm gate fresh agriculture products, processed foods are the few items which tourist can buy as memento for remembrance.

Three important factors which contribute to the success of Agri-Tourism

1. *Farmer*: Majority of the cases, farmer is less educated, less exposed and innocent. For farmer, any outsider is a guest and treated wholeheartedly without any commercial motive. Treating guest is pleasure for them than pain. He entertains the guest while entertaining himself in the process. He is not like an exploitative natured businessman which itself facilitate a clean tourism atmosphere
2. *Village* : Village, which is located far from the city lacks urban facilities, but blessed with natural resources. The investment is made by nature in the form of water bodies, fields, forest, mountains, deserts and islands. Community is more homogenous and treating a guest is part of their culture rather than a profession leading to natural environment required for urban tourist.
3. *Agriculture* : Rich resources in agriculture namely land, water and plants are unique from place to place bringing diversity and creating curiosity. Each field is unique which adds to the attraction of tourists. The way of cultivation and the products are great attraction to the urban population. Indigenous knowledge of rural people is a wealth, which adds to novelty and curiosity of urban population.

Combination of farmer, village and agriculture create a wonderful situation which provides unlimited satisfaction to the tourist specially from urban areas.

AgroTourism Limited

AgroTourism Limited has been serving the European community since 2005. We specialize in high-end investments for selected clients in real estate under the guidance of a Licensed Real Estate Broker (Licensed since 1987) with many years experience in commercial real estate, and our staff offers quality and reliable investment services based on real estate especially land, large estates, farms which are unlikely to depreciate during an economic downturn. Investments are made through Switzerland and Liechtenstein using specially created companies. The investment package includes bank accounts and management services. This is a personal and confidential service. All funds must be proved legal and of non-criminal origin to our satisfaction and of our bankers. This is not a tax avoidance scheme and taxes will be paid where appropriate. Our accountants and lawyers will work with you to minimise taxes. There are non-refundable upfront costs to establish bank accounts and corporations and our fee for undertaking this work. Investments are secured by the property. In addition, our friendly and professional staff is here to answer any questions you may have about our company or our services.

Whether you need a total services package that includes property management services, or an specific service, we have what you need at a reasonable price. At AgroTourism Limited, our goal is to provide you with courteous, expedient, professional service of the highest calibre.

Agritourism in the United States

Agritourism is widespread in America Agritourists can choose from a wide range of activities that include picking fruits and vegetables, riding horses, tasting honey, learning about wine and cheesemaking, or shopping in farm gift shops and farm stands for local and regional produce or hand-crafted gifts.

According the USDA, Cooperative State, Education and Extension Service, "Tourism is becoming increasingly important to the U.S. economy. A conservative estimate from the Federal Reserve Board in Kansas, based on 2000 data, shows that basic travel and tourism industries accounted for 3.6 percent of all U.S. employment. Even more telling, data from the Travel Industry Association of America indicate that 1 out of every 18 people in the U.S. has a job directly resulting from travel expenditures."

Through the Small Farm Center at the University of California, "Agricultural tourism or agritourism, is one alternative for improving the incomes and potential economic viability of small farms and rural communities. Some forms of agritourism enterprises are well developed in California, including fairs and festivals. Other possibilities still offer potential for development." The UC Small Farm Center has developed a California Agritourism Database that "provides visitors and potential entrepreneurs with information about existing agritourism locations throughout the state."

In Western North Carolina, the organization HandMade in America is using agritourism to develop their local economy and craft trades, and to educate visitors about agriculture practices. On the web site, Hand Made in America, they look at agritourism as a "... niche market [that] not only assists communities with solutions to help diversify their economic base, but it also helps our regional urban centers and increasingly suburban populations to understand the important role that farming and rural life plays in our history, by highlighting the need for it in our contemporary society. Agri-tourism projects reinforce the need to support local growers and sources and allow the visitor to experience what it is to be part of the land..."

The publication Promoting Tourism in Rural America explains the need for planning and marketing your rural community and weighing the pros and cons of tourism. According to the publication, local citizen participation is helpful and should be included in starting any kind of a tourism program. Citizen participation in planning tourism can contribute to building a successful program that enhances the community.

Additional websites that promote and publicize agritourism in the United States include Rural Bounty, founded by agritourism consultant Jane Eckert, Sleep in the Hay, a nationwide directory of farm stays, and Farm Stay USA, a blog that profiles farm stays and tracks agritourism news.

Agro Tourism in Bulgaria

Agro tourism in Bulgaria Bulgaria is one of the most visited tourist destination in Europe. In 2006 the country attracted 5 million foreign visitors. To date in 2007, Bulgaria has attracted

4 million visitors. Bulgaria contains historical cities and towns, summer resorts, and high-developed mountain ski resorts. is presented by the cottages on the Bulgarian Black Sea resorts, farm houses in the vicinity of Veliko Tyrnovo, villas at the foot of the Pirin, Rila and Rodopi mountain peaks. Agro tourism in Bulgaria means staying next to the picturesque sights of the country, learning the culture, lifestyle and cuisine of Bulgaria Bulgarian cuisine is a representative of the cuisine of Southeastern Europe. , proper recreation in the many orchards.

The number of agro tourist farms in Bulgaria since 2000 has constantly been increasing. Today their number is over 100. These include both traditional rural coaching inns in Bulgaria, as well as family hotels, cottages, houses and campsites, including the territory of the national parks of Bulgaria. Due to the variety of territories, agro tourism in Bulgaria remains popular all year-round. In summer mansions and villas welcome guests on the beaches of Varna and Albena, in autumn Bulgarian farms invite tourists for the holidays and the new wine festivals to small villages on the banks of the Danube and other rivers, in winter - to the mountainous areas of winter recreation not far from such resorts as Bansko and Pamporovo, in spring a to the famous Festival of Roses in the valley at the top of Stara Planina. Portal cottages-for-holidays.com has dozens and even hundreds of accommodation options in rural Bulgaria. Search of suitable housing is automated. Just select the time and place of arrival and send your request.

Agro tourism in Bulgaria is developed everywhere. Among the places that now offer rent of traditional Bulgarian houses are Balchik, Ribarica, Elena, as well as famous seaside resorts of Sozopol and Nesebr. Wine-making regions, where in addition to Bulgarian coloring, traditions and folklore tourist will be offered also excellent Bulgarian wine Grape growing and wine production have a long history in Bulgaria, dating back to the times of the Thracians. Wine is, together with beer and grape rakia, one of the most popular alcoholic beverages in the country. are such towns as Lovech, Pleven, Assenovgrad and Suhindol.

Bulgarian national cuisine and products - for agro tourism cooking in this country remains one of the most exciting and delicious ways to get acquainted with the Bulgarian everyday culture. Dobrugia, Koprivshtica, Bozency - these and other villages and towns in Bulagria offer to taste flavored homemade bread made from wheat.

Architectural traditions and unique character of the Bulgarian village life can be seen in such places as Tryavna, Batak, Chiflika and Aprilci.

The cost of living in agro tourist estates in Bulgaria ranges from 60 to 100 euros per week. However, the number of officially licensed agro tourist farms here is still low. Many owners offer recreation Bulgarian villages without a license.

Agro-tourism in Syangja

People in Syangja district have been promoting agriculture as a tourism product. Agro-tourism has been launched in Jagat Bhanjyang, Sirsekot, Majhkot and Jagatradevi village development committees (VDCs) of the district which are famous for commercial agricultural production. Govinda Gurung, chief of the Pitlek Rural Agriculture Tourism Development Committee, said that they were giving importance to agriculture research, observation spots and display of farm products to promote agro-tourism. There is also a home stay scheme for five persons per house, he added. Tourist inflow has increased in all the four VDCs in recent days. According to Chet Nath Adhikari, senior officer of District Agriculture Development, representatives from more than 25 districts including Kathmandu have visited Jagat Bhanjyang and they were impressed by the ongoing development here.

There is a rotating house and view point in Jagat Bhanjyang from where views of 16 districts can be observed. Antique household goods are displayed in the rotating house constructed at Sirsekot. Ananta Shrestha, vice chairman of the District Tourism Development Committee, said these VDCs could be models of agro-tourism as they were famous for agricultural products. In addition, Pitlek of Jagat Bhanjyang

VDC is rich in art and culture. The farmers here have been using solar panels for commercial vegetable and coffee farming. A trainer Ramesh Gurung said 40 villagers have received training in kitchen management, service management and home stay management involving a family member from each household.

Agrotourism in Chania

Agricultural activities are an integral part of culture and history of the place and its people. The island's economy was based for centuries, the fertile plains and the hilly areas, growing up today old olive trees, vineyards, citrus, vegetables and fruits. In recent decades no longer cultivated cereals, as before, and the industrialization of agriculture has made it uneconomic traditional production methods.

Alongside new species, such as avocado, made their appearance, the cultivation of which proved very profitable for our climate. In the mountains of Chania, wild rock has extensive agricultural land for cultivation, beyond the plateaus Plateau and Plateau. Residents of those areas dealing with livestock, breeding large numbers of sheep under field conditions. In addition, several traditional cheese dairies producing high the site in herbs and spices give a unique quality honey, which is famous since ancient times.

Let us examine in detail the rural life and production methods in the Cretan countryside.

Harvest of vines and wine. Minoan varieties still grown in the same soil and many times with almost the same house has its own wine. The cultivation of vines, beginning after harvest with a basic pruning. The main pruning is, depending on the location and altitude, in January or February, followed by milling, korfologima shoots, sulfuration, and perhaps thinning the grapes. The maturation and harvesting take place depending on the variety and the altitude of the region from the first ten days of August until early October. Until then the vine requires constant supervision and work on prevention of various diseases.

The social dimension of the vintage gives us a typical picture of rural life in Crete. From the dawn friends and relatives tartaric and carry the grapes. When harvesting is finished, the grapes are pressed in the wine press or motor, or sometimes even on foot and grape produced. The large sunny Crete gives the grape sugars and often enough so we have several high-ranking wines.

This is the time when the housewife gets grape from the wine press, will "cut off" the boiling with ash and cook the moustalevria adding walnuts almonds, sesame and cinnamon. When finished pressing, the must enters or remains in barrels for the wine press a few hours to get color and tannins. Then comes the celebration. All sit in ample table with the best wines of the house and hope the landlord. The no of days becomes available for a song and dance.

Wines are put in barrels and the boiling is complete, the fall has been put on the good and the smoke stoves in villages. The wet earth smell everywhere. This is the time when the chestnuts to accompany raki. Slowly begin preparations for the picking of olives. Marc (strafyla), the remnants of grapes after pressing that have been sealed in barrels and on completion of fermentation is ready for distillation.

The raki, in accordance with applicable law, we have 37.5% and the maximum alcohol content of methanol should not exceed 8 grams. per liter. The distillation of all Greece is allowed only with permission. In every village there are stills known boilers that put the marc and the liquid drums, sealed tightly and then boil to reach the temperature in the appropriate grades to start the distillation. The lid of a cauldron begins tube usually cooled externally with liquid water to the steam that comes out then as raki. The "protoraki is the first spirit that runs from the boat and are very senior. In Crete, several villages still distilled and produced the berries mournoraki. Formerly made by distillation and arbutus on koumaroraki.

Anyone who distills usually invites friends and autumnal landscape with charcoal grills from the heat of the cauldron and makeshift tables Cretan dishes: very wild mushrooms, chestnuts, kalitsounia, and greens, all typical products of this period of time. Even today the tradition continues showing through agricultural activities how important is the commingling of people on Cretan society.

The olive is the main crop in Crete. Endless slopes in the sun shine when it illuminates the silver-green foliage them. This produced the best olive oil in the world. Rich in aroma and flavor and low acidity is the main source of fat of the Cretan diet. The collection of olives and elaiopoiisi activity is almost all Cretan. Chania grown mainly two kinds of olives. The first is Lianos, trees whose fruit is relatively small but numerous and which producers cane and pick their fruit into nets, which stretch out below. The trees are pruned low umbrella-shaped. The harvest season begins in November and continues until February, according to altitude, which is mainly indicative of the degree of ripeness. If you have "oiling" the olives produce more and better oil.

In other areas, such as Selino primarily because of topography, the Tsounati grown olives, large trees covered with nets fixed layer and harvested every 15-20 days from the nets. Thus, the harvest often lasts until May or June. The olives are then transported to mills where the grinding and extraction of oil. Various are the ways in which they operate factories are still some millstones presses like the old days and make so cold pressing, centrifugation and other work with other acupuncture. The oil produced here, unique in flavor and nutrients, is famous worldwide. Is excellent and table olives are produced in the region. The seliniotikes alatsolies, black salted, the neratzolies, sharp and cracked in vinegar or lemon juice, all have the flavor of Crete and accompany any meal. Sometimes a component and the component as the cuttlefish with fennel or tsigariasta greens. Also accompanying the krasaki or raki.

The mountain of Chania, which is rich in herbs and spices kept thousands of sheep. Livestock production has always been the main occupation of the inhabitants of mountain regions Selino, mountainous and natural Apokoronas of Sfakia. The cultural tradition of Crete would be impoverished without the mountain, the songs tell of life most of these people. A difficult but life and freedom. A method and a philosophy of life simple, proud and welcoming.

Real Crete continues to find ways of expression in the saddle and the peaks in Sfentoni and Koumas not even reach the roads and "convenience" culture. Of course it is impossible to produce traditional cheese products without the knowledge of thousands of years now in conjunction with modern methods to ensure quality.

In modern dairies first pasteurized milk and then adding culture, heated at specified temperatures to become the famous Cretan gruyere which will mature for several months before it is ready for consumption. Other cheeses that are famous, is the cheese, and athotyros, white cheese and two. Great is the yogurt which is made from sheep's milk.

Another product that is characteristic of the region of Chania is the honey. Previously the melissokipoi were permanent and there was the possibility of their transfer. Today, beekeepers move their hives as the flowering in a different place each time. Thus, in early spring to go to orange and generally at low altitudes to collect the bees juice from flowering plants and later elevate to higher altitudes, where blooming aromatic plants and herbs and thyme particularly given the unique characteristics of the Cretan honey. The "harvesting" takes place during July August and September. Citrus♦fruit is a key area of agricultural production in Crete. Especially in the area of the Plain of Chania climate and abundant water from the White Mountains encourage the cultivation of oranges, mandarins, lemons, etc.

In portokalochoria of the oven, the Skine and up the beaches near Platanias and Tavronitis the green portakalaionon, the blooming trees generously spread the scent of spring and the vibrant colors of fruits in winter are a feature of the Cretan topiou.Anaptyxi shows return to mild forms of cultivation and increasing demand and production of certified organic citrus Cretan.

BIBLIOGRAPHY

- "Agritourism." Davis, California: University of California, Small Farm Center.

- "AJ Hackett Bungy". Bungy.co.nz.

- "California Agritourism Database." Davis, California: University of California, Small Farm Center.

- "Can you Hackett?". Unlimited - Inspiring Business. 23 August 2004.

- "Economic Research: Economic Impact of Travel and Tourism." (2004). Travel Industry Association of America.

- "Ernest Hemingway FAQ part 5".

- "Extreme Sports - Encarta". Microsoft Encarta Online Encyclopedia. 2008. Archived from the original on 2009-10-31.

- "'Generation Y' Drives Increasingly Popular...". AmericanSportsData.com. August 1, 2002.

- "Guinness World Record - the Highest Commercial Decelerator Descent". Macautower.com.mo. 2005-08-17. http://www.macautower.com.mo/eng/press/award02.asp.

- "Rural Tourism." (February 2008). USDA Cooperative State, Education and Extension Service. Retrieved December 30, 2008.

- "Tourism and Travel: Agri-tourism." Asheville, NC: HandMade in America.

- [http://dictionary.reference.com/browse/lake a body of fresh or salt water of considerable size, surrounded by land. "Dictionary.com definition"]. http://dictionary.reference.com/browse/lake a body of fresh or salt water of considerable size, surrounded by land.
- Adams, C.E. (1994). "The fish community of Loch Lomond, Scotland : its history and rapidly changing status". Hydrobiologia 290 (1-3): 91-102. doi:10.1007/BF00008956. http://cat.inist.fr/?aModele=afficheN&cpsidt=3302548.
- Aerial Extreme Sports (2008). History of Bungee.
- AJ Hackett (2008). History. Retrieved on 17 October 2008.
- Bailey, Robert G. (April 2004). "Identifying Ecoregion Boundaries" (PDF). Environmental Management 34 (Supplement 1): S14. doi:10.1007/s00267-003-0163-6. PMID 15883869. http://www.fs.fed.us/institute/news_info/Identifying_ecoregion_boundaries.pdf.
- Brittanica online. "Lake (physical feature)". http://www.britannica.com/EBchecked/topic/328083/lake.
- Brymer, Eric and Gray, Tonia, Extreme Sports: A Challenge to Phenomenology. University of Wollongong, Australia, 2004.
- Brymer, Eric, Extreme Dude: A Phenomenological Perspective on the Extreme sports experience . University of Wollongong, Australia, 2005
- Cox, Steven M. and Kris Fulsaas, ed., ed (2003-09). Mountaineering: The Freedom of the Hills (7 ed.). Seattle: The Mountaineers. ISBN 0898868289.
- CRUZ FILHO, F. Murillo, Bartolomeu Lourenço de Gusmão: Sua Obra e o Significado Fáustico de Sua Vida, Rio de Janeiro, Biblioteca Reprográfica Xerox, 1985
- Cymerman, A; Rock, PB. Medical Problems in High Mountain Environments. A Handbook for Medical Officers. USARIEM-TN94-2. US Army Research Inst. of Environmental

Medicine Thermal and Mountain Medicine Division Technical Report.

- Eadington, W.R., and V.L. Smith (1992). The emergence of alternative forms of tourism, in Tourism Alternatives: Potentials and Problems in the Development of Tourism. Pennsylvania, USA: University of Pennsylvania Press.

- Eric Larson, 2003 p135, The Devil in the White City; Murder, Magic, and Madness at the Fair that Changed America. Citing Chicago Tribune, Nov. 9, 1889.

- Hamilton, AJ. Biomedical Aspects of Military Operations at High Altitude. USARIEM-M-30/88. US Army Research Inst. of Environmental Medicine Thermal and Mountain Medicine Division Technical Report.

- http://ga.water.usgs.gov/edu/hydrology.html/

- John, Patricia LaCaille (2008). Promoting Tourism in Rural America. National Agricultural Library, Rural Information Center. Retrieved December 30, 2008.

- Jungmin Lee,(2004)Extreme Sports Evaluation: Evidence from Judging Figure Skating,Econometric Society

- Odum, EP (1971) Fundamentals of ecology, third edition, Saunders New York

- Pidwirny, Michael (2006). "Introduction to the Biosphere: Introduction to the Ecosystem Concept". Fundamentals of Physical Geography (2nd Edition). http://www.physicalgeography.net/fundamentals/9j.html.

- Pidwirny, Michael (2006). "Introduction to the Biosphere: Organization of Life". Fundamentals of Physical Geography (2nd Edition). http://www.physicalgeography.net/fundamentals/9d.html.

- River {definition} from Merriam-Webster. Accessed February 2010.

- Roach, James M. and Schoene, Robert B. (2002). "25". High-Altitude Pulmonary Edema. In: Medical Aspects of Harsh Environments. 2. Washington, DC.

• Roach, Robert; Stepanek, Jan; and Hackett, Peter. (2002). "24". Acute Mountain Sickness and High-Altitude Cerebral Edema. In: Medical Aspects of Harsh Environments.

• SILVA, Inocencio da, ARANHA, Brito, Diccionario Bibliographico Portuguez, Lisboa, Imprensa Nacional, T. I, pp. 332-334

• Spilhaus, Athelstan F. 1942 (Jul.). "Maps of the whole world ocean." Geographical Review (American Geographical Society). Vol. 32 (3): pp. 431-5.

• TAUNAY, Affonso d'Escragnolle, Bartolomeu de Gusmão: inventor do aerostato: a vida e a obra do primeiro inventor americano, S. Paulo, Leia, 1942

• The Development of Social Network Analysis Vancouver: Empirical Press.

• Tomlinson, Joe (2004). Extreme Sports: In Search of the Ultimate Thrill. Hove: Firefly Books Ltd. ISBN 1-55297-992-X.

• USGS - U.S. Geological Survey - faqs, #17 What is the difference between mountain, hill, and peak; lake and pond; or river and creek?

• Wilkerson, Chad (2003). "Travel and Tourism: An Overlooked Industry in the U.S. and Tenth District." Economic Review, Third Quarter 2003. Federal Reserve Board in Kansas.

INDEX

P

Q

R

S

T

U

V

W